1

An Unprecedented Literary Event: *Anunnaki Creation of a New Human Race for the 21st Century*

A direct contact with a high cast, full Anunnaki leader? Doesn't it sound like wishful thinking, a fantasy? And yet, this is exactly what our readers can expect in the near future.

Normally, the highly esteemed Sinhar Marduchk would not be likely to contact mere humans. But two factors made him give us a facsimile of one his notebooks, full of explosive information regarding the horrific cleansing of the earth that is about to happen in 2022, and the creation of a new human race to fill it with decent people, free of Grays' contamination, once again. First, Sinhar Marduchk was one of the original creators of the human race, eons ago. As a result, he had maintained an interest and had taken up a few missions on earth after the Anunnaki left it in disgust, realizing how contaminated the humans became due to contact with the Grays. Second, he is the husband of Victoria (Sinhar Ambar Anati to her people on Nibiru), and because of her and her son, the human senator whom Sinhar Marduchk had mentored, he has a strong concern for the fate of humanity once again.

The notebook was sent to the authors just after Victoria had destroyed the contaminated part of an air base, and returned to Nibiru, risking death in the process. Written in Anakh, the Anunnaki's ancient language, it is not easy to understand, but fortunately, Sinhar Marduchk thoughtfully provided the authors with a lexicon. The authors plan to study and decipher the notes carefully, and then, with Sinhar Marduchk's permission, publish them as a book that may change the fate of many. Stay tuned!

3

Anunnaki Ultimatum: End of Time

Autobiography and Explosive Revelations of a Human Anunnaki Hybrid

Second Edition

By Ilil Arbel
and
Maximillien de Lafayette

*** *** ***

LIBRARY OF CONGRESS
CATALOGING-IN-PUBLICATION DATA

Title. Anunnaki Ultimatum: End of Time
Author. Ilil Arbel.
ISBN: 978-1-4477-5567-8
Date of Publication: 2011
Printed in the United State of America

Books by Ilil Arbel

- The Ecology of Nature Spirits (2010)
- The New Chronicles of Barset (2010)
- On the Road to Ultimate Knowledge (With Maximillien de Lafayette, 2008)
- Miss Glamora Tudor! (2007)
- The Lemon Tree (2005)
- The Cinnabar Box (2003)
- Maimonides: A Spiritual Biography (2001)
- Witchcraft (1997)

Books by Maximillien de Lafayette in this series

- **1**-From Zeta Reticuli to Earth: Time, Space and the UFO Technology. (400 Pages)
- **2**-The Biggest Controversies, Conspiracies, Theories and Coverups of our Time: From the Secret Files of Science, Politics, The Occult and Religion. (400 Pages)
- **3**-Inside A UFO: Alien Abduction, Hypnosis, Psychiatry, Quantum Physics and Religions Face to Face. (400 Pages)
- **4**-UFOs and the Alien Agenda. The Complete Book of UFOs, Encounters, Abduction And Aliens Bases On Earth. (400 Pages)
- **5**-Extraterrestrials Agenda: Aliens' Origin, Species, Societies, Intentions and Plan for Humanity. (400 Pages)
- **6**-The Anunnaki's Genetic Creation of the Human Race: UFOs, Aliens and Gods, Then and Now. (400 Pages)
- **7**-Extraterrestrials-US Government Treaty and Agreements: Alien Technology, Abduction, and Military Alliance. (400 Pages)
- **8**-Biographical Encyclopedia of People in Ufology and Scientific Extraterrestrial Research: People Who Matter. (740 Pages)
- **9**-Zeta Reticuli and Anunnaki Descendants Among Us: Who Are They? (400 Pages)
- **10**-UFO-USO and Extraterrestrials of the Sea: Flying Saucers and Aliens Civilizations, Life and Bases Underwater (400 Pages)
- **11**-What Extraterrestrials and Anunnaki Want You To Know: Their True Identities, Origins, Nibiru, Zeta Reticuli, Plans, Abductions and Humanity's Future (300 Pages)
- **12**-UFOs and Extraterrestrials Day By Day From 1900 To The Present: Flying Saucers and Aliens Civilizations, Life and Bases Underwater (400 Pages)
- **13**-Hybrid Humans and Abductions: Aliens-Government Experiments (400 Pages)

- **14**-UFOs, Aliens Impregnated Women, Extraterrestrials And God: Sex with Reptilians, Alien Motherhood, The Bible, Abductions and Hybrids (300 Pages)
- **15**-460,000 Years of UFO-Extraterrestrials Biggest Events and Secrets from Phoenicia to The White House: From Nibiru, Zetas, Anunnaki, Sumer To Eisenhower, MJ12, CIA, Military Abductees, Mind Control (400 Pages)
- **16**-Extraterrestrials, UFO, NASA-CIA-Aliens Mind Boggling Theories, Stories And Reports: Anunnaki, Zeta Reticuli, Area 51, Abductees, Whistleblowers, Conspirators. The Real & The Fake (400 Pages)
- **17**-Anunnaki Encyclopedia: History, Nibiru life, world, families, secret powers, how they created us, UFO, extraterrestrials. Volume I (400 Pages)
- **18**-Anunnaki Encyclopedia: History, Nibiru life, world, families, secret powers, how they created us, UFO, extraterrestrials. Volume II (400 Pages)
- **19**-Anunnaki Encyclopedia: History, Nibiru life, world, families, secret powers, how they created us, UFO, extraterrestrials. (Condensed Edition, 740 Pages)
- **20**-Revelation of an Anunnaki's Wife: Christianity, The White House, and Victoria's Hybrid Congressman Son (310 Pages) co-authored with Ilil Arbel.
- **21**-2022 Anunnaki Code: End of The World Or Their Return To Earth? Ulema Book of Parallel Dimensions, Extraterrestrials and Akashic Records (400 Pages)
- **23**-Anunnaki Greatest Secrets Revealed By The Phoenicians And Ulema. Are We Worshiping A Fake God? Extraterrestrials Who Created Us. The Anunnaki who became the God of Jews, Christians and Muslims (310 Pages)
- **24**-2022 The Return of the Anunnaki; The Day the Earth Will Not Stand Still (350 Pages)

*** *** ***

Also by Maximillien de Lafayette in other fields

- 1-Washington Does Not Believe in Tears: Play Their Game Or Eat The Blame!
- 2-What Foreigners Should Know About Liberal American Women
- 3-The Nine Language Universal Dictionary. (New Edition: The Ten Language Universal Dictionary
- 4-Anthologie De La Literature Française (Anthology & History of French Literature)
- 5-The Dating Phenomenon In The United States: Great Expectations or Justified Deceptions
- 6-Marmara the Gypsy: Biography of Baroness Myriam de Roszka (The script of the original play at the John F. Kennedy Center for the Performing Arts.)
- 7-One Hundred Reasons Why You Should And Should Not Marry An American Woman: Take Him to the Cleaners, Madame!
- 8-The United States Today: People, Society, Life from A to Z
- 9-Causes Celebres from 2,000 BC to Modern Times
- 10-The World's Best and Worst People
- 11-How Psychologists, Therapists and Psychiatrists Can Ruin Your Life in Court of Law in America
- 12-International Encyclopedia of Comparative Slang and Folkloric Expressions
- 13-Encyclopedia of Science of Mind: Religion, Science, and Parapsychology
- 14-Essay on Psychocosmoly of Man, Universe and Metalogics
- 15-The Social Register of the Most Prominent and Influential People in the United States
- 16-How to Use Easy, Fancy French & Latin to Your Advantage and Impress Others
- 17-How People Rule People with Words: From speechwriters and tele-evangelists to lawmakers and politicians
- 18-How to Protect Yourself from Your Ex-Wife Lawsuits
- 19-Divorces for the Highest Bidders

- 20-The International Book of World Etiquette, Protocol and Refined Manners
- 21-Bona Fide Fide Divas & Femmes Fatales: The 700 Official Divas of the World
- 22-How Not To Fail In America: Are You Looking For Happiness Or Financial Success?
- 23-How to Understand People's Personality and Character Just by Looking at Them
- 24-The Art and Science of Understanding and Discovering Friends and Enemies
- 25-New Concise Dictionary of Law for Beginners
- 26-Comparative Study of Penal Codes As Applied In France and Great Britain
- 27-How to Understand International Law
- 28-La Pensee Arabe Face Au Continent Europeen
- 29-Beyond Mind & Body: The Passive Indo-Chinese School of Philosophy & Way of Life
- 30-New Approach to the Metaphysical Concept of Human Salvation in the Anthropological Psychology of Indian Religions
- 31-Worldwide Encyclopedia of Study and Learning Opportunities Abroad.
- 32-World Who's Who In Contemporary Art
- 33-World Who's Who in Jazz, Cabaret, Music and Entertainment
- 34-Thematic Encyclopedia of Cabaret Jazz
- 35-United States and the World Face to Face
- 36-Music, Showbiz and Entertainment
- 37-Entertainment: Divas, Cabaret, Jazz Then and Now
- 38-Showbiz, Pioneers, Best Singers, Entertainers & Musicians from 1606 to the Present
- 39-Best Musicians, Singers, Albums, and Entertainment Personalities of the 19th, 20th and 21st Centuries
- 40-Entertainment Greats From the 1800's to the Present: Cinema, Music, Divas, Legends
- 41-You, the World, and Everything Around You
- 42-World of Contemporary Jazz: Biographies of the Legends, the Pioneers, the Divas
- 43-Living Legends and Ultimate Singers, Musicians and Entertainers

11

- 44-People Who Shaped Our World
- 45-International Register of Events and People Who Shaped Our World
- 46-United States Cultural and Social Impact on Foreign Intelligentsia
- 47-Directory of United States Adult and Continuing Postsecondary Education
- 48-Comprehensive Guide to the Best Colleges and Universities in the United States
- 49-The Best of Washington: Its People, Society, and Establishments
- 50-Credentials Academic Equivalency and New Trends in Higher Education Worldwide
- 51-How Foreign Students Can Earn an American University Degree Without Leaving Their Country
- 52-Comprehensive Guide to the Best Academic Programs and Best Buys In College Education In The United States
- 53-How to Learn Seven Thousand French Words in Less Than Thirty Minutes
- 54-Comprehensive Guide to the Best Colleges and Universities in the U.S.
- 55-World's Best and Worst Countries: A comparative Study of Communities, Societies, Lifestyles and Their People
- 56-World Encyclopedia of Learning and Higher Education
- 57-How Much Your Degree Is Worth Today In America?

- 58-Worldwide Comparative Study and Evaluation of Postsecondary Education
- 59-Thematic Encyclopedia of Hospitality and Culinary Arts
- 60-Five Stars Hospitality: La Crème de la Crème in Hotel Guest Service, Food and Beverage
- 61-Hospitality Best & Worst: How to Succeed in the Food and Hotel Business
- 62-Encyclopedia of American Contemporary Art
- 63-Encyclopedia of Jazz: Life & Times of the 3.000 Most Prominent Singers & Musicians

- 64-Encyclopedia of Jazz: Life and Times of the 3.000 Most Prominent Singers and Musicians (V.2)
- 65-Concise Encyclopedia of American Music and Showbiz
- 66-The World Today: Headliners, Leaders, Lifestyles and Relationships
- 67-Evaluation of Personal and Professional Experiences: How to convert your knowledge and life experiences into academic degrees.
- 68-Contemporary Art, Culture, Politics and Modern Thought
- 69- Maximillien de La Croix « Mistral », Life and Times of Maximillien de La Croix de Lafayette
- 70-International Rating Of Countries in Higher Education And Comparative Study of Curricula, Degrees And Qualifications Worldwide
- 71-Alternative Higher Education
- 72-Dictionary of Academic Terminology Worldwide
- 73-Fake Titles Fake People
- 74-How to Use Greek, Latin and Hieroglyphic Expressions and Quotations to Your Advantage and Impress Others.
- 75-The Best and Worst Non-Traditional and Alternative Colleges and Universities in the United States
- 76-Directory of United States Traditional and Alternative Colleges and Universities
- 77-The Non Traditional Postsecondary Education in the United States: Its Merits, Advantages and Disastrous Consequences
- 78-Lafayette's Encyclopedic Dictionary of Higher Education Worldwide
- 79-Academic Degrees, Titles and Credentials
- 80-Independent Study Programs
- 81-America's Best Education at a Low Cost
- 82-Fictitious Credentials on Your Resume
- 83-Distance Learning
- 84-New Trends in American Higher Education
- 85-Directory of United States Postsecondary Education
- 86-Directory of United States Traditional and Alternative Colleges and Universities

- 87-National Register of Social Prestige and Academic Ratings of American Colleges and Universities
- 88-The Book of Nations
- 89-The World's Lists of Best and Worst
- 90-The Ultimate Book of World's Lists, Volume I
- 91-The Ultimate Book of World's Lists, Volume 2
- 92-Biographical Encyclopedia of the Greatest Minds, Talents and Personalities of our Time
- 93-Encyclopedia of the 21st Century. Biographies and Profile of the First Decade
- 94-Hospitality and Food Best and Worst: How to Succeed in the Food and Hotel Business
- 95-The Biggest Controversies, Conspiracies, Theories & Coverups of our Time, Vol. I
- 96-The Biggest Controversies, Conspiracies, Theories, & Coverups of our Time, Vol. II
- 97-Ulema: Code and Language of the World Beyond
- 98-The 1,000 Divas and Femmes Fatales of the World
- 99-140 Years of Cinema
- 100-Ulema: Code and Language of the World Beyond
- 101-Anunnaki Map of the After Life: Where And How You Continue Your Life After Death

Encyclopedias:

- 1-International Encyclopedia of Comparative Slang and Folkloric Expressions
- 2-Encyclopedia of Science of Mind: Religion, Science, and Parapsychology
- 3-World Encyclopedia of Learning and Higher Education
- 4-Worldwide Comparative Study and Evaluation of Postsecondary Education
- 5-Thematic Encyclopedia of Hospitality and Culinary Arts
- 6-Encyclopedia of American Contemporary Art
- 7-Encyclopedia of Jazz: Life & Times of 3.000 Most Prominent Singers and Musicians
- 8-Concise Encyclopedia of American Music and Showbiz (2 Volumes)

- 9-Encyclopedia of the 21st Century. Biographies and Profile of the First Decade
- 10-Biographical Encyclopedia of the Greatest Minds, Talents and Personalities of our time
- 11-Biographical Encyclopedia of People in Ufology and Scientific Extraterrestrial Research: People Who Matter and Most Important Figures
- 12-Thematic Encyclopedia of Ufology and Extraterrestrial Sciences (En route)
- 13-Anunnaki Encyclopedia (A set of 2 Volumes)
- 14-Maximillien de Lafayette Anunnaki Encyclopedia (1 Volume. Condensed Edition)

*** *** ***

Dictionaries:

- 1-The Nine Language Universal Dictionary: How to Write It and Say It in Arabic, English, French, German, Italian, Japanese, Portuguese, Russian, Spanish (4 Volumes)
- 2-How to Learn 7,000 French Words in Less than Thirty Minutes
- 3-Lafayette's Encyclopedic Dictionary of Higher Education Worldwide
- 4-Dictionary of Academic Terminology Worldwide
- 5-How to Use Easy, Fancy French & Latin to Your Advantage and Impress Others

*** *** ***

15

TABLE OF CONTENTS

Chapter Eight: Honeymoon at the Domain of the Dead......149
About how a charming wedding trip to Paris can end up in one of the most frightening underground places on earth, about experiencing alien spirit possession, and learning something new and unexpected about my husband.

Chapter Nine: At the Anunnaki Academy......161
I am given an orientation at the Academy in preparation for discussing my mission, and I undergo the purification and the creation of the all-important mental Conduit.

Chapter Ten: Surprises and Decisions......173
A startling revelation about the Grays, my future mission is considered, and a personal decision of great moment is made.

Chapter Eleven: Visiting the Hybrids......185
My first encounter with the hybrid children, and my first glimmer of understanding of what eternity is like.

Chapter Twelve: Reporting to the Council......207
My return to Nibiru at the end of my mission, the Akashic Library, and my report to the Council. I am now waiting for my daughter's arrival, and planning an astounding time-travel trip to meet one of the most important persons in human history.

Chapter Thirteen: Jesus and Mary Magdalene......223
My first shape-shifting and time travel; how I met Jesus and Mary Magdalene – who turned out very differently than expected.

Chapter Fourteen: Envoy to Earth......249
How my daughter, Sinhar Ninlil, persuaded me to take up my new mission. How the Council sent me to negotiate with high echelon government military personnel on earth. Rosewell's legacy, Eisenhower's historic first meeting with the Grays, Dulce Base, and more information about the treaties between our governments and the Grays.

INTRODUCTION

For the first time in history, the wife of a high-ranking Anunnaki, an earth woman who is a direct descendant of the Phoenician/Anunnaki race, has come forward to reveal new and astounding information about many subjects that have, until now, been top secret. The woman, who is known only by her first name, Victoria, was born on earth and adopted by a prominent family. A brilliant woman, Victoria attended one of the best universities in the Northeast and became a successful business woman, but through unforeseen events had been approached by a high ranking Anunnaki with the request to bear a child, who is now a prominent U.S. senator, and instrumental to the future of the human race. Eventually, Victoria became the envoy of the planet Nibiru, the home of the Anunnaki, to various governments on earth, was involved with top security missions, and at a certain time in her career, hunted by the CIA.

At age sixty, when Victoria was ready to return to Nibiru to be rejuvenated and prepared for a lifespan of hundreds of thousands of years, she decided to give the benefit of her experience to humanity. Victoria approached two authors with her request to publish her story, choosing them carefully. Maximillien de Lafayette is a well-known authority on UFOs, extraterrestrial issues, and particularly the Anunnaki.

His latest book, The Anunnaki Encyclopedia, has just been published. But Mr. de Lafayette is not a Ufologist – he is a historian, an academic, and the author of over a hundred books and encyclopedias on many other subjects. He has made it a point to let the public know that he is not affiliated with any Ufology group, and maintains his objectivity and independence. Ilil Arbel is also far from being an Ufologist. She has published biographies and memoirs, and is a contributor to a noted online Encyclopedia, and to a literary society. After pursuing the work of many authors, Victoria found them most appropriate for her publication plan.

The book is highly newsworthy not only for these reasons, but for the subject matter and the revelations. It includes such explosive subjects as earth governments cooperating with alien abductions for their own gain; high-ranking officials adopting hybrids and allowing them to merge with society, thus contaminating our genetic material; the current acceleration of alien atrocities; the Anunnaki's creation of the human race – in their image – starting with the first woman; the truth about Jesus and Mary Magdalene, and some mistaken beliefs of Christians, Jews, and Muslims; alien technology; immortality and life after death; and much, much more. The reader follows Victoria for forty years, as she gives birth to her Anunnaki son, studies at the Nibiru Academy, views the horrors of alien experiments, works on an earth base of aliens as part of her mission, learns to use telepathy, attends the Akashic library, marries a most attractive, high-ranking Anunnaki, and escapes those who wish to kill her, be it government officials or ancient, evil spirits. The book combines high suspense with scholarly explanations, and will appeal to a variety of readers – historians, Ufologists, readers of biographies and memoirs, and anyone else who loves a good adventure.

HOW THE AUTHORS MET VICTORIA

A note from Maximillien de Lafayette:

This story was recently sent to me in a letter. As soon as I opened it and read the first few lines, I knew this was extraordinary, and as I kept reading I realized it was explosive. I feel it is my duty to bring the knowledge it gives to everyone, and indeed the writer gave me permission to publish her story, as long as her privacy is maintained. Since I only know her as Victoria, which is not her real name, nor do I know her address, keeping this condition would not be difficult. Some of the readers may be shocked, others may feel elated, but no one who will read it will be able to ignore the facts and their interpretation. I am printing the letter as it was sent – no editing, no comment. Let Victoria speak for herself.

Victoria's letter:

Dear Mr. de Lafayette:

After much soul-searching, I have decided to write to you. Because of my unique experience, I have read many books about the Anunnaki, but your book, *The Anunnaki's Genetic Creation of the Human Race* was the one nearest the truth, and I appreciated its spirit of investigation and non-judgmental attitude. However, there is much in there which is incorrect. The wrong material was based on articles and statements of American Ufologists, and unfortunately, they lack the necessary knowledge. Allow me to give you an example.

23

Most of the people who claim to have met the aliens describe them as three to four feet tall, gray, and possessing big, dark, bug eyes. This is not the case. Some of the aliens do, indeed, answer to this description, but generally they do not, and often they look just like us since they are shape changers. When the alien appears to you, the first thing you notice is dusty light with tiny particles in it. Soon the particles begin to coagulate, to form a center, and suddenly you see the form of small baby. Then, an explosion-like phenomenon occurs, and the shape changes to a grown human, but it is deformed, as if still adjusting itself. For example, his back may overlap his neck, or part of his hips extends far from his body. That lasts a few minutes, and then the shape rearranges itself into a perfectly normal human.

You may wonder how I know, maybe even think I am being arrogant and unreasonable. But this is not so. My certainty is based upon my personal relationship with the Anunnaki, and particularly, with the one who is, to all intents and purposes, my husband, even if our marriage ceremony was non-traditional. I would also like to note that my alien husband does not object to my revelations. In fact, since the year 2022 is almost upon us (and I don't have to tell you the significance of this year) he feels the time has come to be more open about the relationship between humans and extraterrestrials.

The first time the alien appeared to me, many years ago, his eyes looked like glittering light. I could not take my own eyes off them, and could not move, as if I were hypnotized. Then, his eyes calmed down, became normal, and immediately I felt I could move again.

Another claim which I did not find to be true is that the aliens speak to us telepathically. It was nothing of the sort with me. The alien spoke, but that was even stranger than telepathy, because at first he sounded like an old record that was played at the wrong speed – fast, squeaky, scratching. Then the sound adjusted, and the voice became a normal human voice. A very pleasant human voice.

What really upsets me, though, is the idea that all aliens are out to rape, mutilate, and generally harm their abductees. This was not the case with me – exactly the opposite. I have never met such respect, such gentleness, such willingness to accommodate the other person, in any human being. Nor was I abducted in the sense that anything was done against my wishes. True, I was asleep in my bed, and I woke up in a strange place, but as soon as I got out of my strange inability to move, and Sinhar Marduchk adjusted his voice, he immediately reassured me I was a guest, that I could go home any minute I chose to, and that all he wanted was to tell me certain things he felt I should know. I could see no reason to object, seeing here was an opportunity to learn so much, and that no harm would come to me. Besides, Sinhar Marduchk was so incredibly handsome and charming, I rather enjoyed his companionship and did not see any reason to cut my visit short. Therefore, I expressed my gratitude for the invitation, and was ready to listen.

The first thing Sinhar Marduchk told me, after introducing himself, was indeed a shock. He informed me that I am a descendant of the Phoenician-Anunnaki! That I am really and truly one of them. While shocking, it made a strange sort of sense. You see, Mr. de Lafayette, I did not really know my birth parents. I was adopted in infancy by a wonderful couple who made excellent parents and loved me very much. I would have known I was adopted even if they had not told me, because here I was with olive skin, black hair, and dark brown eyes, while my parents, who came from England, were both blond. When I expressed a

25

wish, as a teenager, to find out who my birth parents were, they tried to help, but we did not have much luck, so I gave up. All the information was locked up and unavailable.

Therefore, when my new alien friend informed me that my ancestry went back to the relationship between the early Anunnaki and the "daughters of men," I was shocked, but not for long. Apparently, I was born in Iraq, and my birth parents were Ashurians, who are Middle Eastern Christians, related to the Syriac, who still speak Aramaic among themselves. "Would you like to speak your own language?" asked Sinhar Marduchk, smiling, his large, black, Anunnaki eyes full of humor.

"Of course," I said. "But it would probably take years to learn, right?"

"Wrong," said Sinhar Marduchk. He looked into my eyes, and his own eyes started acting as before, with the hypnotic glittering light. I felt paralyzed again, but only for a few seconds. Then it stopped, I shook myself, and to my utter disbelief found myself talking and understanding a language that I have never heard before.

"Will I forget it as soon as I go home?" I asked.

"No, it is my gift to you. You can now read it, too." I was thrilled. From then on we always speak Aramaic between us.

Anyway, I have so much to tell you, Mr. de Lafayette, so possibly my own story is of less importance than the revelations and knowledge I acquired from my new friends and family. The Anunnaki live for thousands of years, and their understanding of history is very deep. We, who live such short lives, make many historical mistakes, even when written records are available. Take, for instance, the issue of Jesus and the crucifixion. I was raised a Presbyterian, and my parents took me quite often to church. It had become a habit and I never questioned or even thought about the Crucifixion. Well, imagine my surprise when Sinhar Marduchk told me that Jesus did not die on the cross! I hope I am not upsetting anyone, but the real story involves the existence of two tombs. Apparently, two disciples planned it all out with Jesus' mother and with his wife, Mary Magdalene. One of them gave Jesus a rag soaked in something that made him sleep. Later in the day he was indeed stabbed with a spear, but not fatally, and at sunset the soldiers assumed he was dead and took him down. The two disciples that had arranged the matter wrapped him with a shroud, and took him to a faraway cave to hide him and help him recover, but then they took the bloody shroud and left it in the tomb everyone expected him to be in. He was never there, and in the morning, the other disciples, or anyone else interested in him, assumed he left the tomb and left the shroud there, thus giving rise to the story of the resurrection.

They took Jesus secretly to Phoenicia, where he fully recovered, then put him and his wife on a Phoenician boat that went to Cyprus. Eventually, they fled to Marseille, where they settled permanently and had children. Jesus worked in his profession, a handyman (he never really was a carpenter, this is a translation mistake), lived peacefully, and avoided all matters of religion for the rest of his life. His descendants lived in France, and perhaps some of them still exist, I really don't know.

"Does that story bother you?" asked Sinhar Marduchk. "Not at all," I said. "I am no longer a religious person, and I would much rather know the truth than live in ignorance." Sinhar Marduchk smiled with appreciation. Apparently he liked to see that I kept an open mind. I must tell how I was later rewarded by being taught how to time travel, and thus be able to meet Mary Magdalene and Jesus in person.

Also, another major revelation about other great religions such as Islam, Sinhar Marduchk told me that the Koran, the holy book I really admire and respect, did not descend on Muhammad from Heaven, but he learned it from a Christian ascetic monk in the desert. This monk was known in the area as "Raheb Bouhayrah" meaning, priest, or monk, of the lake. After all, Muhammad could not read and write, as is well known. He had to remember by heart what the priest told him on a weekly basis.

Probably you are not very religious, and will not pay attention to these details, but would you be interested to learn about very influential politicians from different countries, and belonging to different faiths, who manipulate the fate of humanity, and even very ordinary people, through an international organization headquartered in Europe? I am willing to give you their names, and a detailed description of their political and economical agenda. Please believe me, that you see them almost every day on television, where they fight each other verbally, when competing for a public office or an election. But as soon as this public charade, or masquerade, is over, they go to their secret meetings to decide the fate of nations.

"I have to tell you something personal," he said gently. "I think you are ready for it. Twelve years ago, we met for the first time. We fell in love." This did not exactly surprise me, since I found him extremely attractive, but I was at a loss to understand why I did not remember our previous meeting, and asked him about it.

"You would have remembered, but you have asked me to wipe out the memory – for a while, at least. You see, you were a very young girl, not yet in college. We were together for a while, and you became pregnant – by the Anunnaki way, which is very different from human sexuality. You told me that you cannot as yet handle the

28

burden, would rather, if possible, get on with your life, but you could not abandon the baby if you remembered him. I explained to you that this was, really, a very good decision. I had important plans for your son."

Well, the plans were astounding. Sinhar Marduchk had a family in mind, a wonderful couple that he wished would adopt our son, belonging to a very powerful Washington dynasty. He wanted our son to be raised as a politician, to learn the ropes, and eventually become an important member of government. The couple he had in mind was also descendants of the Anunnaki, decent, intelligent, and longing for a child. To make a long story short, he manipulated their minds to believe that the woman had given birth to this infant, and rearranged the paperwork so that the birth certificate would say so. The lady actually came out of a hospital carrying the infant, accompanied by her proud husband, and the whole hospital crew also had their minds manipulated to believe the events. He took care to do the same with the couple's friends and relatives. Manipulating minds and events is something the Anunnaki can do very well.

"So where is the child now?" I asked Sinhar Marduchk.

"He is going to school in Washington, doing very well. Your son will grow up to be a credit to us."

Now I understood my life so much better. This must be why I never married, why I even disliked dating. Deep in my brain I knew I was married to this wonderful, spiritual, kind individual, and anyone else would never do. I do not want to weary you with personal details, but of course Sinhar Marduchk and I acknowledged our married state. We could not live together on a regular basis, since he had to spend much of his time on his home planet, Nibiru, and I could not stay there more than a few years at a time because my body would not withstand it without many changes. My husband promised me a very long life, and most important, that as the years go by I will develop the necessary physical attributes that would allow me to stay permanently on Nibiru. We had a daughter, which is very different in her interests from my son, who is now a senator on earth. She is a linguist, and the number of languages she speaks is astounding. I am very proud of her.

I am now sixty years old, but of course age mean nothing to anyone who is married to an Anunnaki. I look considerably younger, and my husband, who knows so much, promises me that not only I shall live a very long life, but that death itself does not exist. When we die we move on to another dimension, giving up our physical bodies, and where we go is very much influenced by our thoughts and desires. As my husband promised me, I shall live until he is ready to move on, and then we can spend eternity together. So there is nothing to be afraid of, ever.

There is so much more to tell, but this letter is so long already, I am afraid you will put it aside and refuse to read more. I do hope I have given you something to think about, and perhaps, if you like, we can correspond. It is up to you – I will be happy to be the conduit through which the Anunnaki speaks with humanity.

Mr. de Lafayette, I know you are a very scientific person, and because you have practiced law, as I have found out, you want facts, not fiction. Don't ever believe or let your readers believe that communication with extraterrestrials can be done through channeling, as many people pretend. This is impossible, because they are in different worlds and your thoughts and state of trance could not reach them through certain frequencies. The human thoughts, even though they emanate frequencies and vibes like electrical and radio emissions, they do stop at the end of the solar system, and the mind transmission cannot go beyond that limit. Extraterrestrial have not and would not communicate telepathically. If you show interest in my letter, I will show you step by step, detail by detail, how communication can be done with an extraterrestrial, as my Anunnaki husband taught me. I can stay in constant contact with you to tell you where the Anunnaki descendants live, in what countries, in what cities, and how to recognize them. Also, I might mention that they do come not only from Nibiru, but from several other planets, as the United Stated government and scientists from Europe will discover before 2022.

Sincerely,
Victoria

From Maximillien de Lafayette:

Naturally, I agreed to correspond with Victoria. She is, as you can see from this letter, an extraordinary woman with much to tell us. I shall never meet her – her desire for anonymity is too strong – but I have persuaded her to collaborate on a book, based on our correspondence and telephone calls. The book will include so much more information, of course, and will touch on subjects that I believe will be of interest to anyone with an open mind. I can promise you more revelations about Christianity, politics, government conspiracies, the afterlife, spirituality, and history that may seem revised – but is really the truth. And this is just the tip of the iceberg – the book will change your life.

Victoria's Explosive Revelations (The Second Letter)

The following material is the second letter I received from Victoria. Again, it is in her own words and I will not attempt to change, edit, or even form judgment.

Dear Mr. de Lafayette:

Since you have so kindly shown an interest in my story, I am writing to you again, and this time I plan to give you much more elaborate information. Therefore, I think it may be advisable to separate the material under explanatory titles. This way we will avoid confusion, and present the information in manageable sizes.

The first creators of the human race: The Igigi

The Anunnaki were not the first to experiment with and on humans. Some 145,000 years ago, a different race called the Igigihl or Igigi, were the first extraterrestrials to create quasi-human specimens. At the very beginning of their genetic experiments, the results were catastrophic. Their creations looked awful – bestial, very ugly, even frightening. This may have happened because the Igigi were more terrestrial explorers than geneticists, and therefore more interested in certain molecules found in terrestrial water, and in various minerals, than in creating a perfectly shaped human race.

The Igigi did co-exist with the Anunnaki, and shared some traits with them, but they were totally dissimilar in their physical shape, and had different intentions as far as the human race was concerned. The Igigi were 245 million years older than the Anunnaki.

At one point in time, they were ferocious toward the early quasi-human beings, treating them very badly, since they considered the early version of human beings on earth as a lower working class without intelligence. Incidentally, the earth was extremely cold and the Igigi had to cover the human bodies with lots of hair to protect them from the elements. It took the quasi-human race thousands of years to evolve into an early human form, and even then not totally human, but looking like apes. Some of them had bizarre skulls and facial bones. My husband told me that the history and theories of human creation and evolution are distorted by both theologians and scientists.

The Igigi were great mineralogists

The Igigi were highly advanced in mineralogy and minerals transmutation. The Anunnaki were geneticists and engineers with a strong appreciation for esthetics. Therefore, the Igigi created a very primitive form of living beings on earth, exactly as we, the humans, created very unappealing early forms and shapes of robots and related mechanical devices at the dawn of robotics. These robots were functional but not pretty to look at, and the early quasi-humans were not much more than machines with limited mental faculties.

The early thirteen faculties of the quasi-human race

In the genes, molecules and DNA of the early quasi-human race, the Igigi programmed thirteen faculties, or functions. The most important abilities were as follows:
1. move
2. sense danger
3. understand by association

4. memorize
5. see forms and shapes in four colors. These colors were bright yellow, representing gold; grey, representing minerals and rocks; blue, representing the atmosphere, air, and water; and a very strong red, representing heat and blood. Other colors such as green, purple, lilac, etc, were not visible or known to the early and primitive form of quasi-humans.

The Anunnaki taught humans how to speak and how to write

The first genetically created race could not speak, and the concept of Language was completely unknown to them. Thousands of years later, the Anunnaki taught the newly race of humans how to speak, read, and write. The Anunnaki's first genetically created human race was the seed of humanity as we know it; they were the ancestors of modern humans, beginning to populate the earth 25,000 years before the construction of the great pyramids. I am only citing the pyramids as a landmark in human history to give you a chronological perspective. Greater, taller and bigger monuments were erected centuries before the construction of the pyramids, and some ruins can still be found in Phoenicia (Modern Lebanon today) particularly in Baalbeck, and in Mesopotamia (Modern Iraq today).

"Women of the Light": The early female-form on earth

Contrary to all beliefs, including what Judaism, Christianity and Islam teach us, Eve was not created from the rib of Adam. Men were created from an early female form that was "fertilized" by the leaders and the elite of the

Anunnaki. They lived in quarantined cities, and had both sons and daughters fathered by the Anunnaki.

Some of the most puzzling sites of these cities, due to their size and functionality, were in Ur, Amrit, Ougarit, Petra (Batra), Tyre and Sidon. Early humans who lived during that era called the quarantined city of these women "The City of Mirage", and "The City of Beautiful Illusion," since the most attractive women from earth lived there. And the quasi-humans who were made out of earth were *not* allowed to interact with these women.

Thousands of years later, the inhabitants of what is today the Arab Peninsula and the lands bordering Persia, the United Arab Emirates, and India, called these women "The Women of Light", and those who were allowed to "mix with them" were called "The Sons of Light". From this early human race, all humans came to life. God had nothing to do with us. In other words, the God we know, revere, and fear today did not create us. Even the word or term "God" did not exist in the early stages of the existence of the human race on earth. Instead "Gods" or "Heavenly Masters" were used. And thousands of years later, those terms were changed to "Giants," "Elohim," "Nephilim," "Anakim," "Fallen Angels," you name it...

46 different races of humans and quasi-humans populated the earth.

Some 300,000 years before the creation of the cities of "The Women of Lights," forty-six different races of humans and quasi-humans populated the earth. The greatest numbers were found in Africa, Madagascar, Indonesia, Brazil, and Australia. These races died out not because of famine, ecological catastrophes, or acts of war, but because of the disintegration of the very molecules and composition of their cells. The Anunnaki created the "final form" of human beings, and we, all the ordinary and normal people, are their descendents.

Sumerians, Ashurians, Hyskos, and Phoenicians are the direct descendants of the Anunnaki

Eusebius, the Bishop of Cæsarea, Palestine, had genealogical records of the descendants of the Anunnaki who became Syriac. At the Council of Antioch in 363 A.D., Bishop Eusebius intended to bring this subject in his "Theophania" to the attention of the members of the Council. But for obvious reasons, no additional information or manuscripts about what happened at the Council were provided. In the Syriac manuscripts of Zachariah of Mitylene, who frequently corresponded with Eupraxius, two references were made to the Anunnaki as the ancestors of the Ashurian-Syriac. Another bishop by the name of Proterius tried to destroy these letters. Fortunately, two hand-written copies were made, as the tradition of this era dictated, and were saved in the vault of a scribe. Those letters resurfaced in 1957 in a personal acquisition of Cardinal Maouchi, the Patriarch of the Maronite Church in Lebanon. After of Maouchi's death, those files were kept in the secret vaults of Al-Kaslik Monastery in Lebanon.

The original language of the Anunnaki is still intact and is currently being used by top American scientists and researchers who work in secret American-Aliens military bases in the United States and Mexico. In 1947, the first attempt was made by American linguists, who previously worked at the OSS (Precursor to the CIA), to decipher it. They tried to compare it with the Sumerian, Hebrew, Armenian and Phoenician Alphabet, languages which are directly derived from the Anunnaki's written language. The problem they faced and could not resolve were the geometrical symbols included in the written Anunnaki's texts. But in 1956, they cracked down the puzzle. Those mathematical figures hold great secrets regarding an alien advanced technology used for peaceful and constructive purposes. The American military intelligence and what's left from Dr. Fermi's group at Los Alamos wanted to use this alien technology for military purposes.

Early remnants of the Anunnaki.

The earliest among the final terrestrial human race were the Phoenicians, the Hyskos, the Philistines, the very early Etruscans, the earliest Druids, Minoan, people of Mu, and the first inhabitants of Sumeria. Later on, the Ashurians resided among the last remnants of the Anunnaki who visited earth and lived there for 600 more years. After that, the Anunnaki left earth for good, never to return again, except as visitors. One of the reasons for their departure was the discovery of the "tree of life", also known as "The Tree of Knowledge" by humans – a metaphor for the acquisition of knowledge and understanding by the human race, on its own. The acquisition of this supreme knowledge caused the humans to rebel against the Anunnaki.

The secret written language of the Anunnaki

The Anunnaki have two kinds or styles of languages; one is spoken and the other one is written. The spoken language is the easiest one to learn, and it is used by the Anunnaki's population. The written one is exclusively used in books and consists of twenty-six letters. Seven of these letters represent the planets that surround their star.

Many of the Anunnaki's letters cannot be pronounced by Westerners because of the limitation of their vocal chords. There are seven additional letters that are complete words, and these words represent the attributes of their "Grand Leader." Translated into terrestrial language, the grand leader becomes the creator of energy, in other words, "God." However, the Anunnaki do not believe in a God in the same sense we do, even though they were the ones who created and originated the early forms of religions on earth. The god they brought to earth is a vengeful and terrifying god, something that the Gnostics and early scholars of the Coptic Church in Egypt were fully aware of. Their doctrines show their disdain for such a god, and consequently, they called him the "Creator of Evil and Darkness." Later on in history, the early Gnostics began to spread the word that this earth was not created by the God of the Church, but rather by an evil demigod. The early human beings who interacted with the Anunnaki shared similar beliefs. But they were mistaken, and were intentionally mislead by a lower class of the Anunnaki who hated other extraterrestrials who visited the earth, and particularly by the Igigi who treated humans like slaves and robotic machines.

The differences between Anunnaki, Nephilim, Elohim, Anakim, Zeta Reticulians and other extraterrestrials.

Scholars like Sitchin and Gardner have equated the Anunnaki with the Nephilim. This is not totally correct. The lower class of the Anunnaki are the Nephilim, although many historians call them sometimes Anakim or Elohim. The higher class of the Anunnaki is ruled by Baalshalimroot, and his followers or subjects are called the "Shtaroout-Hxall Ain", meaning the inhabitants of the house of knowledge, or "those who see clearly." The word "Ain" was later adopted by the early inhabitants of the Arab Peninsula. "Ain" in Arabic means "eye". In the secret teachings of Sufism, visions of Al Hallaj, and of the greatest poetess of Sufism, Rabiha' Al Adawi Yah, known as "Ha Chi katou Al Houbb Al Ilahi" (The mistress of the divine love), and in the banned book *Shams Al Maa'Ref Al Kubrah* (Book of the Sun of the Great Knowledge), the word "eye" meant the ultimate knowledge, or wisdom from above. "Above" clearly indicates the heavens. Later on, it was used to symbolize the justice of God or "God watching over us." And much later in history, several societies and cultures adopted the "eye" as an institutional symbol and caused it to appear on many temples' pillars, bank notes, money bills, and religious texts.

Freemasons, Illuminati, Trilateral Commission, military uniforms in secret underground bases, UFOs, and the Anunnaki-Nibiru symbol/insignia

The Freemasons' and Illuminati's favorite symbol is the Anunnaki's eye. And as everything changes in life and takes on different forms and meanings, the "eye" became a "triangle," a very secretive and powerful symbol. George Washington carried this triangle with him wherever he went, and wore it during official ceremonies. If you double and reverse the triangle, you get the Star of David. This very triangle is visible on many extraterrestrial spacecrafts and on uniforms of military personnel in secret American military bases underground, working on alien technology and propulsion systems.

The powerful Trilateral Commission was founded by David Rockefeller, the Chairman of the Chase Manhattan Bank of New York, in July 1973. It is recorded that in their first board meeting, Rockefeller proposed to adopt the Anunnaki's triangle as the official symbol/logo of this world organization.

According to an official statement issued by the Commission, the principal and official aim of the Trilateral Commission is "to harmonize the political, economic, social, and cultural relations between the three major economic regions in the world." The Commission divided the world into a triangle joining three regions consisting of the Far East, Europe, and North America, all within the perimeter of a triangle. Basically, the Trilateral Commission aims at controlling the world under the auspices of a centralized American power-group consisting of bankers, financiers, selected political leaders, top military echelon and members of the cabinet from each administration. On February 17, 1953, an American millionaire by the name of Paul Warburg shouted before the Senate of the United States of America: "We shall have world government whether or not you like it, by conquest or consent."

Many members of the Trilateral Commission are descendants of a lower class of an extraterrestrial race. Some passed away, but many of them still live among us. It is impossible for ordinary people to recognize them. But the good and decent descendants of our extraterrestrial teachers can identify them very easily. In future letters, I will give you their names and explain their plans.

The "Triangle" is also a negative force

When integrated without balance and cosmic harmony (spatial equilibrium) in architectural design and lining up territories, the triangle becomes a negative force on the map. My husband told me that if the three sides of the triangle are separated, such separation can cause serious health problems. The triangle becomes three lines of negative energy. This energy is not easily detected; nevertheless it runs strong and deep underground. People who live above these lines suffer enormously. In many instances, this negative power or current can negatively affect the present and future of many human beings. Similar to some Ufologists who can identify UFOs' hot spots on earth, usually above ground; descendants of the extraterrestrials can identify and locate the negative currents underground. Each country has these negative currents or circuits underground. I do not wish to scare you, but I must inform you that some American states are located above these lines; for example, Mississippi, Alabama, the northern part of Washington, DC, and two areas in Brooklyn, New York share this misfortune.

Our Human ancestors borrowed many words from extraterrestrial languages, and learned the secret 7 powerful names of God

Many of the Phoenician linguists and early creators of their Alphabet borrowed numerous words and expressions from the higher class of the Anunnaki. Ancient Phoenician texts and poems, recorded on tablets found in Tyre and Sidon, included reference to symbols and words taken from the written language of the upper class of the Anunnaki. Members of an early Anunnaki expedition to Phoenicia taught the Phoenicians how to create their language, and revealed to them the secret powerful names and attributes of Baalshalimroot. They instructed them not to use these words for ill purposes. Particularly, the word "Baalazamhour-Il" is never to be said, spelled, or written. Later on in history, the Hebrews religiously observed this

41

instruction, and pronouncing the word of name of God became forbidden. However, the Anunnaki revealed to the Phoenicians and Sumerians seven positive and powerful names/attributes of the Grand Leader. If well used, these words can bring prosperity, good health, and salvation in moments of difficulty. The prophet Mohammad learned these seven words from an early Christian ascetic, a Sahara hermit called Raheb Bouhayra. Today, Muslims all over the world are aware of these seven words or names. They call them in written Arabic "Asma' Al Lah Al Sabha' Al Housna," meaning the seven lovely names of God. Those names do not have numerical value or secret meanings as many scholars claim, simply because they were not originally written in a geometrical form. None of these words appeared in the so-called hieroglyphic measuring tape that the Americans found at the crash site in Roswell. The symbols and geometrical signs Americans found in Roswell were biochemical symbols.

Extraterrestrial lexicon in use by military personnel in secret bases in the United States

The American top military scientists who work in secret military bases and aliens' laboratories on earth have an extraterrestrial lexicon, and use it constantly. In that lexicon, or dictionary, you will find variations of Phoenician and Sumerian symbols. Some letters represent maritime and celestial symbols and measurements. The fact that the Americans are still using this extraterrestrial language should be enough to convince you that extraterrestrials, Anunnaki and Nibiru descendants, live among us, otherwise why would anyone learn a language that cannot used to communicate with people who speak it and write it?

On some of the manifestos of military parts used in anti-gravity secret laboratories underground in the United States, several letters were borrowed from the "Enuma Elish" of Sumeria and regularly appeared on the top right corner of each document. In the eighties, those Sumerian numbers were replaced by an Americanized version.

Early names of the Hebrew God were of an extraterrestrial origin

It is true that the Sumerian ancient texts and records mentioned names of some of the Anunnaki leaders such as Utu, Ningishzida, Ninki, Marduk, Enki, Enlil, Inanna, but the greatest name of all remains Baalshalimroot, also referred to as "Baalshalimroot-An'kgh." Terah, the father of Abraham, mistakenly worshiped Baalshalimroot-An'kgh. Early Semites made the same mistake when they worshiped the leaders of the Anunnaki as gods who later became Bene Ha-Elohim, meaning the children of gods. The Anunnaki never introduced themselves as gods. The words: El Elyon and Yahweh or Jehovah were taken directly from the Anunnaki's written language. The original word was "Yah'weh-El' Ankh" and El Elyon was "Il Ilayon-imroot."

Extraterrestrial families are the origin of the hybrids and/or extraterrestrial human beings living among us today

The Early Anunnaki who visited earth were extremely tall. Some reached the height of 9 feet, and lived as long as 400,000 years. These Anunnaki did not leave descendants on earth. Those who came to earth much later, before the regional deluge, and right after that huge

43

Tsunami, left families behind them when they returned home. By home, I mean Nibiru, Zeta Reticuli and Ashartartun-ra. These families are the origin of the hybrids and/or extraterrestrial human beings living today among us. It is very important to learn and remember this.

Another important detail, contrary to what many believe that only Grays or reptilians live on Nibiru, the Anunnaki had also occupied vast territories on Nibiru, and by now you know that they are not the Grays or reptilians, as wrongly described in Ufology literature.

Mr. de Lafayette, even though I have given you quite a bit of scientific and historical data, I don't want you to think that this is all I have to say. My relationship with the Anunnaki is personal, loving, and involving family and friends. This book is really about the fact that we must seek similarities and affiliations between sentient beings, rather than always harp on the differences. I want to tell you so much more – I want the world to know about my dear sister-in-law, Sinhar Marduchk's twin sister, who came all the way to earth to help me choose a dress for my wedding, and became my closest friend. I want to tell you all about the guests who came to our wedding – and what a list that was… I want you to know about my nieces and nephews and the other lovely Anunnaki children I met on my own trips to Nibiru. We had hours of fun as the children demonstrated their shape-changing talents to me, assuming what they thought would be such frightening or amusing personalities. So I would like to hope that this is the beginning of a profitable and pleasant correspondence, even friendship, even though we can never meet in person.

All the best,
Victoria

CHAPTER ONE
Meeting with the Extraterrestrials

My first meeting with the extraterrestrials, and the bizarre plan they made me follow. My trip to Nibiru and its disturbing aftermath.

February 1965, Maine

At this time of year darkness fell early, and the roads were not busy on that extremely cold night. I was enjoying the drive despite the snowy and slippery conditions because I was so young, and just having a car was a novelty and an adventure. I was going home after an afternoon's study at a good friend's house. We planned to prepare for our high school finals, but we were so excited about the prospect of college, that we could barely concentrate. Both of us applied to the archaeology-anthropology department of a well-known New York university, and were thrilled with the fact that our parents would allow us to spend four years on our own in the huge and exciting city. As I cautiously wound my way, I was dreaming about myself in New York, wearing sophisticated clothes and drinking coffee at some marvelous little places, when I noticed that a large vehicle, possibly a lorry, was blocking the road at a little distance. I could not make it out clearly, so I drove carefully until I was about fifteen feet or so behind it. I was considering going to the vehicle to see if the driver needed help, when I suddenly noticed a bright, yellow shaft of light moving from the vehicle toward me. It was a dusty sort of light, with particles moving in it at a random motion, much like a sunbeam through a window on a summer afternoon, but brighter and highly visible against the dark evening. I stared at the light, trying to figure out what it could possibly be, until it stopped just in front of my car. The little particles stopped moving in their crazy random way, and instead, started to coagulate, moving toward the center in a rather orderly way. I was mesmerized by the movement, and I cannot tell how long it took, but I think only a few minutes. The particles at the center formed a globe, while the rest of the shaft of light was clean and empty of particles. Then, a sudden visual but silent explosion took place in the center – there is really no other way to describe the phenomenon – as if the center burst into fireworks. Then, the fireworks rearranged themselves into the shape of a baby!

Suddenly I was horribly afraid. Before I saw the baby form, it could have been a natural phenomenon of some sort, but when this shape took place, no reasonable explanation existed. I looked at it, not knowing what to do and feeling trapped, since I could not drive away and escape with the vehicle in front of me on the narrow road, nor could I turn the car. Leaving the car and running would be insane. I sat, trembling, and the baby form started growing. It expanded, changed, filled out the shaft, and seemed to become a grown-up man. But the man was deformed. Part of his back overlapped his neck, his hips jutted away from his body, and the face was blurred. My heart was beating so quickly that I felt it would explode, too. The fear almost paralyzed me, and then everything became even worse. The man rearranged himself and became normal, and stepped out of the shaft of light. The shaft remained where it was, waving gently and illuminating the man. He waved at me, in a friendly and normal fashion, and moved toward my car, but I still could not see his face since the light was behind him. All I saw was something really horrifying. The man's eyes were glowing in the relative darkness, like the eyes of a wolf. Like two little lantern, they shown at me as he approached. I think I screamed, because the man, suddenly realizing my terror, waved his hand in a circular motion, the shaft of light moved to his side, illuminating the most handsome face I had ever seen.

The striking face was matched by the rest of his physique. I am tall, five feet eleven inches in my bare feet, but this man seemed to be almost seven feet tall, like some of the basketball players I used to watch. And the broad shoulders and perfect proportions, clearly visible in the uncanny illumination, added to his movie-star attraction. He seemed to be in his mid twenties.

The glow in his eyes subsided, but the eyes in that perfect face were still not normal. They seemed to glitter, so brightly that I was not able to make out their color. I could not take my own eyes off them, as if hypnotized, and was not able to move at all; my limbs felt as if they were made of iron. I have no idea if my paralysis happened because of the fear, or because it does occur every so often when humans meet aliens, though not in every case. Then the glitter died down, and I could see that his eyes were very dark, almost black in the golden light, and very large, much like my own. As a matter of fact, the man's olive skin and black hair were exactly like mine. My paralysis completely disappeared.

"I hope I have not frightened you, Victoria," he said. Kind words, but I did not even notice that he knew my name, because his voice was so startling. It sounded like one of those old records you played on an old-fashioned turntable – if you put it on the wrong speed, it became fast, squeaky, and scratchy, very unpleasant. He stopped, made some elaborate movements with his hands, and spoke again, this time with a very pleasant, normal human voice. "I am sorry. I am a bit out of practice, and these changes and adaptations of my traveling form into regular shape and sound can be tricky."

I found my voice. "Regular shape and sound? Who are you? What are you? And what do you want of me? Yes, you scared me a lot – I should think you could have changed before I came and then stopped me in a simpler way, rather than do this dramatic appearance, like a grade B horror movie?" I was infuriated, but astonishingly, no longer terrified. At the time, I could not understand why I was not paralyzed with terror. Now, of course, I know that part of my mind was willing to accept it, which makes sense in the light of the events that followed, and the secrets that were told. But also, let's face it, perhaps I was also influenced by the mysterious stranger's great looks... teenage girls *can* be silly about very handsome men.

The stranger laughed at my defiant words, but rather kindly, not at all in a mocking way. Later, he confessed that he was quite relieved that I was exasperated rather than horrified to a point of fainting or shrieking helplessly. "You are right. I should have thought about a nicer way to meet you. I apologize... Anyway, to answer your very reasonable questions, my name is Sinhar Marduchk and I am an Anunnaki. I come from Nibiru."

Anunnaki. I have heard this word before, in school, something from ancient history. I did not remember too well. Nibiru could have been in China for all I knew. Never heard of it.

"Well, I am pleased to meet you, Mr. Sin... Mard... Sorry, I can't say your name too well."

"No wonder. It's quite a name, I suspect. But some of my human friends call me Marduchk at first," said the

48

apparition, his teeth gleaming by the light of the shaft. "Eventually, they get used to the long name."

"My name is Victoria… wait, you just called me by my name. I was too confused to notice. You know me?"

"Of course I know you. I came specifically to meet you. We have a small job for you to do, if you agree to cooperate with us."

"What sort of job?" I asked suspiciously.

"I wonder if I can tell you without some preparation," he said. "It has something to do with who you really are."

"I see," I said. "So you know I am adopted. You know a lot about me, Marduchk. It's a little disconcerting."

"I know more than you think, to be honest, but no, you should not worry about it. Naturally, when you want someone to perform a very important task, you try to learn something about them, right?" said Marduchk. "And yes, of course I know you were adopted. That is the whole point."

Indeed, I was adopted in infancy by a wonderful couple who made excellent parents, and loved me very much. I would have known I was adopted even if they had not told me, because I had olive skin, black hair, and eyes that were so dark as to be almost black, as I mentioned before. My parents, whose ancestors came from England, were both blond. A couple of years ago I expressed a wish to find who were my birth parents, and my adoptive parents tried their very best to help, but we did not have any luck. Wherever we turned, all the information was blocked, deleted, or carefully hidden away. We finally gave up, and I was not too troubled about it after all. I had such a good life at home, I knew I did my best to find out the truth, and not succeeding, I decided to just forget about the whole issue and get on with my life. I must say my parents were much relieved, they were afraid I would mope about it.

"So do tell," I said.

"You were born in Lebanon," said Marduchk. "Your birth parents were Ashurians, who are Middle Eastern Christians, related to the Syriacs, who still speak Aramaic among themselves."

"Wow, Lebanon, of all places. No wonder we could not fine out anything about my birth parents, it's a different country, even a different continent..." I said.

"I have something to tell you about them, too," he said. "The reason why I was sent to meet you was that your DNA, which of course you inherited from both of your birth parents, is very rich in Anunnaki genes. All modern humans have Anunnaki genes, since the original human race, as you know it, was the product of the Anunnaki and what was the human race in ancient times, but some people, in certain areas of the world, maintained a stronger pool. Many live in Iraq, of course, since it exists on top of the Sumerian and Babylonian civilizations."

"I am an Anunnaki? Like you, then?" I have to admit that while this may be shocking to some, to me it sounded like a wonderful fairy tale. Besides, having common ground with this gorgeous guy was not so bad...

"Well, yes, you are, to a large extent. Not totally an Anunnaki, and physically changed by your life on earth, but close enough."

"And you chose me specifically for some splendid job?"

"I don't know if you will find it splendid. Well, maybe you will, since it involves some courage and some sacrifice."

"Maybe you want me to be a spy? Or an agent? Hunt bad aliens that fight good aliens like you? Will I be carrying a space weapon?"

"Nothing like it. Sorry. It's totally different."

"Am I the first one to be chosen?"

"Oh, no. We have to employ many people. We always contact many women, since women are paramount in our experiments, much more important than men, I am afraid. But you were personally selected for this particular task, that is, if you agree to do it." I rather liked hearing how important women were in the Anunnaki's plans. Usually, I felt women had to always fight for their rights.

"Why are you employing humans, anyway? What are the connections between the Anunnaki and us?"

"We are your creators. The Anunnaki's first genetically created human race was the seed of humanity as you know it, the ancestors of modern humans, beginning to populate the earth 25,000 years before the construction of the great pyramids. Contrary to all of your beliefs, including what Judaism, Christianity and Islam teach you, Eve was not created from the rib of Adam. Men were created from an early female form that was 'fertilized' by the leaders and the elite of the Anunnaki. The women lived in quarantined cities, and had both sons and daughters fathered by the Anunnaki. Thousands of years later, the inhabitants of what is today the Arab Peninsula and the lands bordering Persia, the United Arab Emirates, and India, called these women 'The Women of Light', and those men who were allowed to mix with them, including their sons, were called 'The Sons of Light.' From this early human race, all humans came to life."

"What about God and his creation?" I asked.

"God had nothing to do with us," said Marduchk. "In other words, the God you know, revere, and fear today did not create you. Even the word or term 'God' did not exist in the early stages of the existence of the human race on earth. Instead 'Gods' or 'Heavenly Masters' were used. And thousands of years later, those terms were changed to

51

'Giants,' 'Elohim,' 'Nephilim,' 'Anakim,' 'Fallen Angels,' you name it…"

"So the Bible was not entirely right," I said, reflecting on my Sunday School lessons.

"Some is right, some is myth, some is fable," said Marduchk. "But it has great stories. I personally like it very much."

"This is fantastic," I said. "Scary, though."

"As a matter of fact, it should not be scary. Some day I will tell you how much there is nothing to fear, how much we are all the children of the universe and of eternity, and how we can look forward to eons of joy and peace. But we can't go into it now. We must concentrate on our task."

"So you still take an interest in our affairs?"

"Yes, even though at some point you rebelled against us… but then again, don't all children rebel against their parents, and the parents still love them? We do love you, Victoria."

"What do I have to do?" I was not going to refuse, even though I was a bit scared of what was to come. I knew that if I refused, he would go away and contact another girl, and I did not want to lose him. I was already beginning to fall in love, even though of course I did not know it.

"Have a baby," he said simply.

"WHAT?" I screamed. "I am not yet eighteen years old! I can't get married and have babies! I am going to college next year!"

"You don't have to get married. You don't have to raise the baby. We have plans for this baby. We just want your genetic material, always with your permission."

"Plans? For my baby? Doesn't a baby need a mother? Are you people as cruel and as mad as to deprive a child of his mother?"

52

"This baby has to grow to be a pivotal figure in the government of this country. He is important for world peace, for recovery from hunger and want, for freedom. He has a great task ahead of him, which I can already tell you he will fulfil admirably, since I am able to see a great deal of the future, though not all, not the part which requires free will. Therefore, we have a couple in mind who will adopt this child. Both belong to very powerful Washington dynasties, they are longing for a child, and they are decent and intelligent. They will be extremely kind and loving to their child. What's more, I am going to manipulate their minds. They will believe that the baby is their birth child, that the woman has actually given birth to this child. I will change all the records, rearrange the paperwork and the birth certificate, and at the right moment the woman will come out of the hospital, carrying the infant and accompanied by her proud husband. The whole hospital crew will have their minds manipulated to believe all these events."

I was quiet, thinking. Marduchk was quiet, letting me mull over it. Finally I said, "My goodness, the things you can do... Anyway, if I agree, I have a condition."

"Which is?"

"You said you can manipulate minds. If I agree, I want you to make me forget the whole incident, until I am ready to face the situation. I cannot bring myself knowingly, consciously, to give away my baby; I simply cannot perform such an act. But I can see that it is needed, and in addition, for some reason I simply can't bring myself to refuse. Can you do that?"

"It will be very easy," said Marduchk. "And I can revive your memory when you have accomplished everything you want to do, and we can meet again and take up our lives from there. We can even decide at what age

53

you would want to do it. Would you feel more comfortable if we got married first?"

"You want to marry me?" I felt elated, in my teenage way, but thoroughly confused.

"Yes, I do," said Marduchk in the most matter of fact way. "I am, after all, going to be in charge of this baby. And I know we will be very happy together, if you accept."

He was going to be involved with my baby. One way or another, Marduchk was to remain a permanent factor in my life, if I accept. If I don't accept, Marduchk will disappear from my life, and make me forget this has ever happened. Why did he matter so much to me? And why did I trust him so implicitly? He was almost a hallucination, and yet I did trust him, completely. But marriage? That was the issue.

"No," I said decisively. "I am too young to marry. When we meet again, if we feel we want to do that, then we shall. I suspect I will want to marry you very much, but let's wait on that. However, I will take up the task. I accept it."

"That is wonderful," said Marduchk. "As for the marriage, I promise you I will not change my mind; an Anunnaki never does. And you will know your own mind then."

"But how can I disappear for the nine months of pregnancy? I can't let my parents know, they will be horrified."

"You don't have to," said Marduchk. "For us, past, present, and future are all one and the same. I will take you away on my machine to Nibiru, where you shall spend the time quite happily with my sister and me, and when I have the baby safely in my arms, and you are well and on your feet, I will return you to this car, one second after our current conversation. You will know nothing, forget it ever

54

happened, drive home safely, and get on with your life. And ten, twelve years from now, you will have a little surprise. We will then see how good I was in my brain manipulation..."

"I hope I really do forget," I said. "If I have bits and pieces of memory intruding on me it would be so confusing. And yet, I have to give everything up for so long. This is all so confusing."

"I have an idea that might cheer you up," said Marduchk. "How would you like to speak your own language, Aramaic?" His smiling, large, black Anunnaki eyes were full of humor.

"Of course, I would love to, it would be wonderful," I said. "But it probably will take years to learn, right?"

"Wrong," said Marduchk. He looked into my eyes and his own eyes started acting as before, with the hypnotic glittering light. I felt paralyzed again, but only for a few seconds. Then it stopped, I shook myself, and to my utter disbelief found myself speaking and understanding a language that I have never heard before.

"Will I forget it as soon as we part?" I asked, enjoying speaking in Aramaic.

"No, it is my gift to you. You can now read and write it, too. It will be great for your college studies, considering the subject you have chosen. You will believe, and tell your teachers, that you have learned it on your own when you were in high school, in preparation for your archaeology and history college career, from various books. These books are now on your shelf, at home, I just placed them there. They look well used, and your parents are going to believe it, too." By now, I was not even surprised that Marduchk knew what subject I was about to major in. Incidentally, Marduchk and I always speak to each other in

Aramaic, and such a pleasure it is to be able to share something that is so close to our emotional core.

"Very well, let's get on with it" I said, rather bravely getting out of the car. We walked toward his vehicle. I must admit I felt very important... again, girls can be so silly sometimes. I did not really grasp then that so many women have been approached, over the centuries, for such important tasks; significant motherhood is a universal pattern. Still, looking back, I am so happy I followed my instincts, trusted Marduchk, and helped shape humanity in my own little way. And how rewarding it turned out for my own life as well, I can't even begin to tell.

April 1977, New York

I took the subway from fifty-third street to my home in Greenwich Village. Dinner with Marge was pleasant, she is a good friend, but why do women always have to concentrate on what is wrong? Why do we complain so much to each other? Life has been pretty good until this point, after all.

When I graduated from college, I decided not to continue with a graduate program, for two reasons. First, I always felt that the classes lacked something, that history, anthropology, and archaeology missed something very important and was always inaccurate. Second, I was not sure I was the right fit for academia. So I took a job in retail, since New York had so many of these positions in the myriad clothing and accessories lines, and I love fashion. I did well and was quickly advancing in my position, when tragedy struck. In 1973, my parents were killed in an automobile accident, hit by a drunk driver, who was killed as well. I was lost for a while, sunk into depression and felt I was all alone in the world. However, after a few months I decided to pull myself together since I knew my parents would not have wanted me to destroy myself by protracted mourning. I looked into my financial situation, realized that the money they left me could help toward buying my own business, and bought a small store that sold accessories and costume jewelry. I suppose I am a natural business woman, because even though I was so young, the store, which was failing with the previous owners, recovered and began to do very well.

As for Marge, she was an opera singer. She sang at the Met, and while not the star that she would have wanted to be, she was quite successful and always employed. But her personal life is sad. Marge longed to be married and have a family, and as we sat at dinner, she told me about all the men she had dated in the past year, all of them turning out to be no good.

"Maybe that is why I don't date at all," I said.

"I don't know how you can stand it," said Marge. "Don't you even want to try to marry, have a family?"

"I don't know, Marge," I said. "I have tried a few times. No one was good enough, I was bored to death with every one of them, so ordinary…"

"But what about sex?" she asked. "Don't you miss it?"

"I think sex is overrated," I said. We both laughed, but perhaps this is true for me; I was not particularly interested in sex. At any rate, I really never loved anyone, and I did not think this would change; I accepted that and did not seek a change. And yet I went home feeling slightly sad. I showered, went to bed, and started reading a new detective book by P.D. James. I like her style and her understanding of true evil; I think she has a better grasp of human psychology than most professional therapists. Sad to say, though, I fell asleep just as the murderer was about to be caught.

Suddenly I woke up. It was almost pitch black, since I prefer sleeping in the dark and never keep a nightlight. I usually sleep well and do not wake up at night, and if I do, I go right back to sleep. This time, after the large dinner Marge and I ate, I was very thirsty, and decided to go to the kitchen for a glass of water. I tried to turn on the lamp beside me, and to my amazement it just wasn't there. I thought I might have upset it somehow during the night, so I just stayed there for a few minutes to allow my eyes to adjust to the dark before getting up. Something was wrong. As I was beginning to make out the shapes of the furniture, it was clear to me that I did not wake up in my own apartment. Was I in a hospital? Perhaps I had an accident. Often, people who have a serious accident do not remember it right away. I tried to move, to see if I was hurt, and I felt just fine. So what in the world happened? I sat on the bed, trying to decide what to do, and a dim light turned itself on. I saw I was in a small bedroom, simply but nicely furnished, and certainly not in a hospital.

"Please do not be alarmed, Victoria," said a very calm and pleasant female voice through an intercom. Ah, the nurse, I thought, still clinging to my idea of a mishap. Perhaps I had a stroke? I was a bit too young for that at age thirty, but one never knows, things like that do happen, and after all, I had no idea of my birth parents' medical history.

"Where am I?" I asked. "Am I ill? Or hurt?"

"Not at all," said the voice. "You are quite well, you just happen to be our guest. I will be with you in a few moments. There is a robe hanging on the chair, and a glass of water on the little table next to your bed. The bathroom is behind the door on the right side of your bed. Would you like me to bring you a cup of tea, or perhaps coffee?"

"Coffee will be wonderful," I said, my alarm subsiding. This was mysterious, but I was sure the nurse, or attendant, or whoever she was, would explain. I put on the robe, drank my water, went to the bathroom to wash my face and see if my hair needed fixing, and then sat waiting for the nurse to come. A light knock on the door, and a most attractive woman came in, carrying a tray. She wore a black outfit, which immediately settled that she was not a nurse. She was tall and elegant. Her eyes were large and black, much like mine, and her hair, which was also black and softly curly, had a beautiful reddish sheen, making it glow under the dim lights.

"I am so happy to make your acquaintance, Victoria," she said. "My name is Miriam. At least, this is the closest I can get to my real name, which is Sinhar Semiramicsh, which I imagine would be a little difficult for you to pronounce, at present." She poured out a cup of coffee for me. "Milk and sugar?" she asked.

"Just milk, please," I said. "What an interesting name. I can't make out from where it comes. Where were you from?"

"It is an Anunnaki name," said Miriam casually. "You may have heard of us before." She looked at me in a curious way, as if she expected something from me, but I could not imagine what it was, and so I sipped my excellent coffee. "I have heard the name Anunnaki, many years before, in school," I said. "I recall they are a vanished race that have lived in the Middle East, but obviously I am wrong, since you are an Anunnaki. Or do you just bear an ancient name, and the people did vanish?"

"No, we have not vanished," said Miriam. "Western archaeology and history do make some mistakes."

"Tell me about it," I said somewhat bitterly. "That is what made me leave the field, in which I majored;

nothing was taught right, or so I thought at the time. So where are the Anunnaki to be found these days?"

"There are many of them in Iraq," said Miriam. "But my brother and I are from a place called Nibiru." That did not ring a bell at all. "My brother will be here in a minute," she continued. "You have met him before. I wonder if you will remember him." Another knock on the door and a man walked in, looking vaguely familiar. He was tall and unusually handsome, and greatly resembled his sister. In a flash of thought I felt it was strange that I could have forgotten having met such an amazing, arresting face, but he shook my hand in a friendly manner, and said "Sinhar Semiramicsh, I think our guest is entitled to some explanations."

"Indeed, I would like to know where I am. I imagine something happened to me and you have rescued me? But what? I strongly remember having gone to sleep after having dinner with my friend Marge. All the details, even the conversation we had, are clear in my head."

"I think I will go back to my post and let you do the explanation, Sinhar Marduchk," said Miriam. "I shall see you soon, Victoria."

Sinhar Marduchk. I knew I have heard this name before. Something in my brain shifted, moved, trembled, as if shaken by a sudden memory. This was a bizarre sensation I have never felt before. The man smiled. "It is beginning to work," he said. "I am returning your memory of our first meeting, and everything that followed. I have started when you were asleep."

I stared at him, suddenly alarmed. Maybe all this was not as benign as I thought? Maybe these two people, beautiful and charming as they seemed, actually kidnapped me? Perhaps they had the most horrible plans for me? Where the hell was I? Sinhar Marduchk must have noticed my sudden change of mood, because he said, "I am sorry. I seem to have a knack of alarming you, for some reason... just like I have done the time we met. I must lack judgement, and perhaps I should have let Sinhar Semiramicsh do all that, but I was so anxious to see you again. Anyway, you are not kidnapped, you are not a prisoner. You can leave any time you wish; you are merely a guest. But I do beg you, stay just where you are for a few more minutes. You will know everything as soon as the memory takes effect." Like I had a choice, I thought bitterly. I have no idea where I am, where to go, what's going on. "Where am I?" I said. "Do tell me right now, I am getting very nervous."

"You are on our machine, our vehicle," he said. "We are traveling around while we talk to you, and my sister is minding it."

"So I can't get out even if I wanted to," I said, angrily. "Suppose I asked you to stop and let me out? Would you do that?" I tried to sound strong, but I lacked conviction. That something that was working in my brain was growing stronger, and I felt dizzy and confused. I could not have gone anywhere on my own. I could not even get up.

"Yes, I would let you go," said Sinhar Marduchk. "Of course I would, but I would have to watch over you while you walk, since right now you must be dizzy." He might have given me a drug, I thought dizzily. Oh my God, he is drugging me... what are they going to do to me... I felt very faint, the room was spinning around me. Suddenly it all stopped. I opened my eyes and screamed, "Marduchk! It's you!" and I fainted.

When I came to, I remembered everything. Marduchk was sitting right next to my bed, holding my hand, a very concerned look on his face. Yes, I remembered everything… not only our first meeting, twelve years ago on the deserted road in Maine, but our time on Nibiru. "How is he?" I asked anxiously. "How is my baby?"

"He is very well," said Marduchk. "He has a wonderful family, his parents had two more boys, in the normal way, and he is the best big brother imaginable. He is doing extremely well in school, has lots of friends, and already told his parents that he is determined to go into politics when he grows up… they were not surprised, exactly, since they let him see and learn a lot about what is going on in Washington, and they do have all the necessary resources. What a nice couple. I got to know them well over the years. They love their children dearly. Would you like to see him?"

"Why yes, of course," I said, trembling. I have not seen my son since I let him go, all these years ago, and at the time could not stop crying until Marduchk did as he promised and took away the memory, returning me to my car, one second after our trip to Nibiru. I had no memory left at all. I drove straight home, not even recalling why I stopped in the first place, and resumed my life.

Marduchk took out a small object from his pocket, looking like an ordinary flashlight. He touched something on it and a circle of light, about the size of a basketball, was created on the wall. It stretched into a square, looking like a television screen, and something like a movie began to enfold. I saw a little boy in a beautiful, sunny garden, stretched on the grass and reading a very large book for someone his age. His hair was black and what I could see from his face was very beautiful. Then two smaller boys came running to him, obviously calling him to do something, and he got up, smiling, and ran away with them, carrying his book. All three looked healthy and happy. I felt good, though I realized I was crying. My baby was okay, and that was the most important thing. I smiled at Marduchk, and he turned the device off.

"What is his name?" I asked.

"Joseph," he said. "He will have quite a life, Victoria. And so will you. Don't be unhappy."

"I am not unhappy. At this time I can handle it, like I thought I would," I said. "I can live with the results of my actions, really I can, Marduchk. Don't be distressed for me."

"Do you remember your first day on Nibiru?" he asked, smiling.

"Oh, yes. How strange it was, landing and not being able to see anything, neither plants, nor buildings, nor people, with this heavy, strange atmosphere that would block my vision. And I was so afraid when you told me I can only see everything if I take the cure that would make my eyes adjust…"

"But you were brave enough to try, Victoria. And wasn't Nibiru beautiful?"

"I loved it. What a happy time it was with you and Sinhar Semiramicsh. I learned so much and had such fun."

"And now you can come back to us."

"But I cannot live there, Marduchk. You know that. Not until many years pass and with the Anunnaki help, my body will grow and adjust to the Nibiru conditions."

"What of it? You will live for hundreds of years, there is all the time in the world. Do you remember that part of your learning? You will live for centuries, and then we will pass together into eternity."

"I still don't quite understand eternity, I confess," I said.

"Eternity is not an easy concept," said Marduchk. "But you will, I promise you. There is no such thing as death, life is eternal. The Anunnaki know that, scientifically, not on faith alone, like you do on earth."

"How joyful to really know that you will never have to lose your loved ones," I said.

"And as time goes by, I will come to Earth often, and work with you on what is needed, and so will Sinhar Semiramicsh. And you will come to Nibiru for longer and longer periods. And you must remember what you have learned there – that you will never have to age, you can choose the physical age you wish to be at any time, and you can devote your time to anything you like to do."

"Do you remember, you taught me how to navigate time and space, at least the rudimentary principles? I would like to work on that, and then study historical periods by going there. Of course I will keep the store, the world must think I am leading a normal life on earth and making a living, but I could have such fun going to these places and times."

"Of course, and we will develop your gifts and abilities much further. Besides, we will enhance your language skills. Remember how you learned Aramaic instantly? We can have you develop this talent so you can learn any language, past or present, in the same way."

"This will help my studies tremendously, Marduchk. But we will always speak our own language, Aramaic, between us, won't we?"

"For ever and ever," said Marduchk. "It's still my favorite language. And you will love speaking Anunnaki, too."

At that moment, a knock was heard on the door, and Sinhar Semiramicsh came in. "So, Victoria, should we prepare for the wedding, Anunnaki style?" she asked, smiling. "Many friends are waiting for us on Nibiru. You should see the wedding dresses I got for you to choose from…" I had to laugh.

*** *** ***

CHAPTER TWO
My First Months on Nibiru

My trip on the spaceship, my difficulties of adjusting to Nibiru, and the lifestyle of the Anunnaki on their home planet.

February 1965, Maine

Marduchk and I approached the spaceship. In the dim light, it looked seamless, rounded, and silvery, as if made from aluminum or stainless steel, though of course it could have been any other metal, as far as I knew. A door glided silently and we entered a room. At the time, I was not aware of the distinct levels that contained the scientific apparatus and the machinery that was used to guide the craft. I was not thinking about such matters, anyway, being too absorbed with my own concerns, and with the fact that I was actually boarding a space ship, like something out of a science fiction movie. I had an insane desire to say "Take me to your leader," but thankfully I avoided the bad joke and tried to not be stupidly hysterical. Marduchk settled me in a small room on the middle level, attached to the control room and used for sitting when the craft was on automatic. It was stark, containing only a small table and few simple but comfortable chairs, all made of metal. Everything was surrounded by a kind of archways that met in the center. Marduchk went into the control room to activate the spaceship, and while he was away, the archways became transparent, and showed some writing in a language I could not understand. Then, he returned to the little room and sat down.

"I put the ship on an automatic," he said. "It won't be a long trip, we are using all the tricks of the trade, that is, in time and space. In the meantime, would you like a cup of normal, ordinary earth coffee?"

"Don't you drink some exotic and strange things that would probably kill me?"

"Yes, sometimes, but to tell you the truth, after my numerous trips to earth and many stays there, I became rather fond of coffee and I make a very good cappuccino. We poor travelers have to adapt…"

I laughed and accepted the offer. Marduchk stood up, waved his hands above the little table, and two big white cups of cappuccino, complete with perfect foam, appeared out of thin air. "No, it's not magic," he said when my mouth dropped without any class or style. "Merely a form of technology; I called some vibrations in. Would you like some sugar?" He produced a beautiful cut crystal bowl. I said nothing, put some sugar in my cup, and sipped the cappuccino. It was superb, and the warmth of the cup helped me relax as I watched Marduchk bring, out of thin air, a bunch of really nice cookies and paper napkins. I nibbled on one of the cookies, my fear and nervousness returning. A baby, I was thinking. What did I get myself into. I am too young, I don't want any man to touch me, not even this glorious specimen who can produce cookies from nothing. I am just not ready. My heroic and patriotic decision gave way to sheer terror, and my eyes filled with tears I could not control. For heaven's sake, I thought. I am alone in a spaceship with an alien being, going God knows where… have I gone mad? Why didn't I run away into the woods?"

My fears must have shown very clearly, because Marduchk said, "I think it would be fair to tell you what you will have to do right now, rather than wait for the briefing on Nibiru. I can see you are getting very nervous even though you are very bravely trying to hide it. Listen to me and stop being so scared. It is not at all ominous, Victoria. I promise you."

"Not ominous?" I burst out loud. "Even if we don't think of the baby quite as yet, I am supposed to mate with a total stranger – whoever he is – and even if it turns out to be you who would father the child, you are still a stranger. I am calling it mating because it is not love making when you don't know each other and only do it for procreation, like cattle! And you say it is not ominous?"

"You will not need to mate with anyone," said Marduchk calmly. "We could never ask a child like you to face such a frightening thing. No, in Nibiru we have our babies very differently."

"Whatever do you mean?" I asked, bewildered. "How do I get pregnant if I don't have intercourse?"

"The Anunnaki have long ago separated love from procreation. We do marry, and we marry strictly for love. Our unions are permanent. Once we make our choice for a life partner, we have no wish to stray and remain paired forever, like some birds do in your world. Certainly nothing like the marriage of humans, of which fifty percent end in divorce, or worse."

"So you don't have sex at all?"

"Not the way you do. Our way of expressing love is through light. When Union, as we call it, occurs, each partner starts to emit golden light. The lights grow strong, mingle, and this mingling causes intense physical, mental, and spiritual joy. It is much better than anything humans experience though sex, since the sensations go directly to the brain. It is also much more beautiful, aesthetically, than any physical sex could be. What humans do, to put it

69

plainly, may be pleasurable, but certainly not aesthetically pleasing..."

"Wow, that sounds nice, mingling lights, "I said. "Not at all frightening. I would actually like to try it."

For once, Marduchk seemed extremely startled at my blunt statement, and looked at me in a rather horrified way. But then suddenly he laughed. "How human of you to say that," he said. "You don't understand how serious the blending of lights is for an Anunnaki. It's sacred, really. You don't just try it with anyone, ever. You must be married first."

I felt a little subdued, as if I said something terribly inappropriate. "So what will happen to me?" I said.

"You will go into a very nice hospital-like place," said Marduchk, obviously relieved to get away from the previous subject that seemed to embarrass him. "They will help you lie down on a table, much like one of the examination tables in any doctor's office on earth. The attending physicians will be all females, very gentle and extremely skilled. Using a special machine, they will beam a light right through your body; the light will search for your ovaries. You will feel nothing at all, it's just light, nothing will probe, or hurt, or even annoy you. Once the light reaches the ovaries, it will activate one of the eggs, fertilize it, and have it move very smoothly into the uterus. You will then become pregnant, of course, and the fetus will begin to grow. Anunnaki women have the egg removed by the light, placed in a special tube, and grow the baby in a machine. They don't have birth in the same sense humans do, but take the baby home after he or she is ready in the advanced incubator. However, in your case, since you are human, we thought it would be best not to tamper with your nature and allow you the full term, protecting the baby inside your body."

"Wow," I said. "That is not very scary at all… are you sure that is the way it goes? I heard such stories about alien abductions, and how they torment people with these probing machines."

"The other aliens, maybe. The grays, the reptilians, they are not too gentle and they don't particularly care how the humans feel. Still, many of the stories you hear might be a bit exaggerated. As for being sure about our procedures, why, yes, I have gone through that before, many times. I am perfectly sure. And my sister will be with you all the way."

"Did you ask any of the women to marry you?"

"No, I did not," said Marduchk.

"How come someone who looks like you never married?"

"I was married in another universe," said Marduchk, ignoring my remark about his looks in a gentlemanly manner. "My other self is still married to his choice, of course, very happily so; they have three children, and I still watch them once in a while through the viewer. But I had to branch out, thirty thousand years ago, and now I am not married. Thirty thousand years is a very short time for an Anunnaki, you know. One needs time to make a decision about a life partner." I gave up. I did not believe I will ever understand anything on Nibiru, and I was not going to question, at that moment, the issues of other selves and branching out to new universes… it made my head spin, so instead I ate another cookie. I was pleased he was not married in this universe, nonetheless.

After a short trip, lasting perhaps an hour, we landed on Nibiru. Before we went out, Marduchk said, "Don't be upset if you see nothing except swirling gray air. This is what happens to humans when they land here, and we can fix that in a couple of days. It is daylight now on Nibiru, the sun is shining. If necessary, just close your eyes."

It all sounded a little ominous, but I found it was an understatement. The reality was much worse. I stepped out into a world which looked like a sand storm on a completely gray planet. It was horrible and it made me dizzy. I swayed and grasped Marduchk's arm. "It's all right," he said reassuringly. "I will take you indoors right away." We entered a building which I could not see, but inside, with a dim light, everything was clear and nice. A lady came toward me, smiling, her hand extended to shake mine. She was gorgeous, tall, elegant, and looking remarkably like Marduchk, except that her hair was long and curly and glowed with a reddish sheen. She wore a beautiful long dress of deep sea green silk, and a long necklace of baroque pearls that glowed softly in myriad colors. "Welcome," said the lady. "I am Sinhar Semiramicsh, Sinhar Marduchk's sister. Thank you for coming to Nibiru."

"Sinhar... Semi? I can't say it." I said weakly. Why are they both Sinhar, I was wondering. Later I found out that "Sinhar" is at the beginning of each name of an Anunnaki of high caste. It is similar to the habit of the Irish to precede names with "O'" and the Armenian habit of ending each name with "ian."

"Yes, I know," the lady smiled. "My human friends call me Miriam. Please do so, it will be easier."

"Yes, Miriam will be nice... But what is happening?" I asked, still dizzy. "Why can't I see anything outside?"

"It's the atmosphere. There is no pollution, no smoke, no oil fuels, since pure electromagnetic energy is all we use. It is so bright, so clear, that it creates a strange effect on your retina, which is used to different conditions. We are going to take care of it tomorrow morning. I would like you to rest, eat, and then sleep the night. Let me take her to her room, Sinhar Marduchk. The child is very tired from all this excitement."

"Of course," said Sinhar Marduchk. "Go with Miriam, Victoria, she will take good care of you, and I will see you in three days or so."

I looked around me. The house was incredibly beautiful. The living room had very high ceiling, and there were platforms, or levels that ran smoothly into each other, each decorated with plants, little ponds, and flower basins. All the windows were covered with curtains, presumably for my sake, but it was clear that the windows were very large and normally admitted an enormous amount of light and air. I followed Miriam obediently to a smaller, very cozy room, which contained the most comfortable bed I have ever slept on and had sky blue ceiling and what seemed like hundreds of plants and flower vases. She gave me a beautiful nightgown and robe to put on, and served me a light supper of a delicious fruit salad and something that tasted like yogurt. I was tremendously excited, but to my amazement my eyes were literally closing with fatigue. Then, Miriam tucked me in bed like a mother, told me to have a good nap, and I slept instantly.

When I woke up, my treatment began. Miriam took me to a little room where she showed me a basin filled with aquamarine-tinted fluid. She asked me to go in, relax, and think only about colors, nothing else, preferably about one specific color. She would come back in an hour or so, she said, and the water will keep their gentle warmth as long as I was in. I climbed into the bath which felt wonderful and was fragrant with some floral scent I did not recognize. I closed my eyes and thought about the color lavender,

73

beautiful, gentle soft kind of lavender. For a while nothing happened, but after a few minutes, all of a sudden a stream of lavender light filled the basin and then lifted and surrounded me like a beautiful web. To my surprise, at the same moment, a joint pain I developed on earth disappeared. It was in my ankle, which I have hurt a year ago while running, and it did not heel properly, giving me occasional pain. I twisted it when I left the spaceship and stumbled, and it hurt when I woke up from my nap. Now it was perfectly well. Later they explained that as they adjust the vision, they must cure all the weaknesses of the human body, my genes, and all the possible disease and sicknesses that I might have in the future. Even at my young age I could feel the difference between the human condition and perfect health.

On the second day, Miriam led me through a connecting corridor to a surgical room in another building. They have these corridors, connecting houses and buildings to each other, and they never lock any doors. Such a trusting, simple lifestyle, such a pleasure. She introduced me to a nurse, or physician, who asked me to lie down on a table. I did, and a machine came from the ceiling, shining a laser-like beam. Apparently, they scanned my brain, and the nurse told me to look at the screen on my right side and see how the cells in my brain would create new visual faculties. This was utterly amazing. I could actually see how the human brain worked! The nurse explained that many cells, millions of particles of the brains, are never used by humans, and now many of them would become mine to use. After a short time, the nurse put a bandage around my eyes and a metallic band around my forehead. This was needed for readjusting the energy and reactivating part of the cells. They told me that this will not only adjust my vision, but will develop a telepathic power in due time.

Indeed, to my great delight and astonishment, at a later day I was able to communicate telepathically with the Anunnaki, at will. When the treatment was completed, my vision was perfect, and Miriam told me that I could go out and see Nibiru for the first time.

Marduchk was waiting for us outside the door of the surgical room, and together the three of us went outside. I gasped. The air was pure, light, and full of rainbows of colors. I have never seen such colors, they were not known on earth. Some of the colors of the sky blended with the colors of the landscape, giving me the feeling that the ground united with the sky. Then, I realized that something very strange was happening. My vision was not limited to straight lines. I could see, magically, to the left and right, like surrounding vision. Gorgeous buildings glimmered under the brilliant sky, the trees, bushes, and flowers filled every available space, and beautifully dressed, smiling people walked in the streets. How different from what I thought was a gray planet with swirling sand in its atmosphere! Later, I could very well understand when Marduchk told me that the colors blend with the psyche of the Anunnaki. They teach colors to children from a very early age, and it is so very important because understanding colors is essential for traveling through worlds and dimensions.

It was daytime, so the sun was shining. The whole celestial system is different on Nibiru, naturally. The day is not composed of twenty-four hours. It's made up of forty-eight hours. The sun rises around four o'clock in the morning, and the glorious sunrise takes about two hours; the colors at that time are beyond description. The sun shines for eighteen hours, then takes two hours for sunsets that seem to burn the sky with their intensity. Then, they have four moons. All rise harmoniously one after the other,

75

and line up in four different directions. They stay for about ten hours. When they fade, it's again one after the other in the same synchronized manner, and the moonset is like molten silver filling the sky. Then comes the night, but it is never one hundred percent dark. It's like deep dusk. The Anunnaki don't need full darkness because their eyes do not have the usual retina, but another structure. Even so, the stars are highly visible in the clear, clean atmosphere.

And now I was ready to enjoy myself. Everyone I met was extremely friendly and charming, people treated me as if I was a hero of some sort, following a mission of great importance, and I liked being lionized. I did not have to worry about my parents, since I knew Marduchk will take me to earth one second after my car stopped, so I felt free, mature, and sophisticated, except that I was falling for Marduchk like a star-struck child. But I suppose that was to be expected by someone my age. Miriam gave me the most beautiful clothes to wear, and I would try them all before the mirror and be amazed at what they could do for my looks. My nieces, Miriam's daughters, were of course much older than me but still children, according to Anunnaki life, so they were still very much interested in creating endless forms of things – flowers, plants, jewels, clothes – and we had the greatest fun. Only later, once they hit the age of seventy-one, Anunnaki become adults, and they lose their passion for creating endless forms and concentrate on the intellectual pursuits of their race, things like philosophy, poetry, and so on. Not that they stop producing art, but it's done differently by the adults. They like frescoes, huge paintings. Nothing is miniature, all art is big, except jewelry, very well developed. For every color, they have four hundred different shades. And they have lots of huge sculptures. Artists work on them in their studios, and students work on them in schools, and when they are done, they teleport it to public places for exhibitions. Physical labor is not part of the psyche of the Anunnaki. All is mental.

They took me to the beautiful parks and gardens The Anunnaki are great gardeners, and constantly create new species of wonderful plants, both for food and for beauty. Children spend many years studying plants. The children are extremely creative, appealing, and kind. They don't like or create weapons or not even sharp instruments. The idea of hurting or even annoying anyone does not even cross their minds, so they are capable of creating great beauty. The plants, by the way, don't follow the four seasons. The trees and flowers bloom constantly and never die. Also, the color of the leaves changes according to the moods, feelings and thoughts of the person who planted it. But there are no seeds, since the reproduction is so different on the Anunnaki world. Many of them look like the ones we have on earth, but their structure has major differences. No one waters them on Nibiru; there is no need. They get nourishment and water directly from the air. Come to think of it, there is a similarity between the plants and the Anunnaki. Both find their energy in the air they breathe. The roses have no thorns. The trees don't have bark, they are soft on the outside because many of them are used as a source of nourishment. Plants produce milk, oil, and Anbar, which is a delightful perfume. To me it seemed that the nature of the world itself is friendly, working with the needs of the people who live on it.

I was thrilled with their houses, too. They are never high-rise, since the Anunnaki discovered that when the body is far away from the earth, it loses some of its energy. Nor do they like square rooms; everything is rounded, soft, flowing, and the houses have high ceilings. Usually they contain several floors, but not in the usual boxed way, but

77

divided into levels. They don't use stairs, the levels merge smoothly with each other. At every level, you see indoor pools and plants. As I saw with the surgical room that Miriam took me to, one part of the house is always connected to the neighboring house though a corridor. This is done for the sense of unity, and they never have locks. The ceilings, by the way, change color with the seasons, to match the temperature outside. In winter, the ceiling is dark gray, and brings warmth. In summer, it becomes white, or the color of champagne. All is smooth and meant for comfort. For example, doors don't swing back and front, and never bang, rather they go up, sliding. Materials used are natural stone, like marble or granite, and some trees that are grown especially for the purpose of building. One interesting stone is called ourjan, and its color is saffron. Parts of it can be ground to make a good die to color clothes. To my amazement, they told me that on earth, the Phoenicians found it in the Mediterranean and called it ourjawan, also known as "the color of royalty," since on earth, absorbed by the murex shell in the Mediterranean and corrupted by salt, it is no longer saffron, but purple.

What I really found strange, more than anything else, was the issue of animals. The Anunnaki believe that the animals on earth were created by evil spirits, since animals are treated so badly by humans. The Anunnaki did not want to create animals. They were working in their genetic laboratories on creating new life forms for the human or quasi humans. Working often by trial and error, one formula produced cats. They called them Bessa. Strangely, in Coptic, Arabic, and other Semitic language, the cat is called Bess. Strange similarity for two separate civilizations that are apart by million light years! Somehow, only female cats were created, and the Anunnaki, who never hurt anyone or anything, let them live and actually started to like them very much. They noticed that the cats responded to music and to the pleasant sound of falling water, something they always taught children to enjoy in school. But the cats, without training, appreciated what the educated and trained children do. And so the cats became great companions for the Anunnaki, and they live in most houses as part of the family. One of the gifts that the Anunnaki gave the early friendly monarchs of the earth was a set of cats, trusting that these people will treat the cats well. You can see that in the history and mythology of Egypt, where the cats were downright sacred, and that shows another connection between the lineage of the early pharaoh and the Anunnaki. The cats of the Anunnaki have psychic powers, and although they don't sense fear and danger like earth cats, they predict weather. And another unique characteristic – they can talk. They talk to the Anunnaki in a language derived from the Anunnaki language. It's simple, and uses only nouns, not adjectives or verbs. These conversations may be simple, but they are perfectly clear. The cats look a bit like our Siamese, but with pure white fur, and a rainbow of blue and gray around the neck. They are about double the size of earth cats, and the color of their eyes is very light blue.

The only other animals created by the Anunnaki, and that was done deliberately, are birds. Infinity of types and colors were created, and they all sing. Many of them give excellent eggs. There are no insects, only butterflies, because they blend well with the beauty of the landscape and they were also created by genetic formulas. The genetic formulas are not carried on by advanced scientists, as on earth. The children create life forms. It's part of their curriculum, but also it is a second nature for an Anunnaki to create. This extends to other materials – such as metal transmutation and solid matter vibes and frequencies.

According to their needs, they can change gold to iron, iron to silver, etc., depending entirely on necessity. On earth, we value diamonds and gold. On Nibiru, they are meaningless and without value, except for their prettiness and use as decorative materials. The Anunnaki have other elements, minerals, and metals that are more important, because they are needed to create energy for spaceships, and for levitating and teleporting heavy weight blocks and materials.

Another thing I truly enjoyed were the libraries. Marduchk took me to one of them, a marvelous marble building, always opened for everyone to visit. The books, which seemed to be numbered in the millions, were not square like ours, but conical. They were placed on shelves. You would go to the shelf, select your cone, and touch it with one finger. The cone would spin, throw out silvery light, and instantly you will absorb all its contents. I could see spending eternity in such a place, who needed a university… but they had those as well, and I was going to visit them too, eventually. And the museums! So many museums. Mostly, they displayed tools and apparatus that help the Anunnaki navigate different galaxies, past and present. Those I did not understand at all. But I loved some other objects – they have instruments that produce musical sound never heard on earth. One note can be very high and very low at the same time, but the human ear cannot absorb it until some adjustments are made. Fortunately, my cure worked in this direction too, and I could enjoy the music. The high sound goes to right ear, and the low sound goes to the left ear. You have your own symphony. Many of these instruments do not even need playing, you just touch them and they give sounds. I spent hours experimenting with them.

But business was business, and although I was allowed to have fun, after about a week Miriam told me that everything was prepared for my fertilization. I was to visit the hospital early in the morning, go through the procedure, rest the day, and then just have a good time on Nibiru until the birth. I thought I was emotionally prepared, but the evening before the operation I was scared again. The fear struck me when Marduchk and I were strolling in one of the gardens, and suddenly I could not talk.

"Victoria, I can see you are not in the best of moods. Do you have second thoughts? Tell me and I will immediately cancel everything and take you to earth. It's never too late to withdraw. This has to be entirely voluntary or not at all."

"I am scared, but it's not that I want to cancel. I am suddenly worried about having a baby, just like that, without being married... we don't do that easily. If my parents knew, they would be so horrified. On the other hand, if it were not for my parents, I would have maybe asked you to stay here with you and raise the baby, perhaps... I am so confused."

"First, the whole point is that the baby must be raised on earth, Victoria. By these particular parents. You were happy with your adoptive parents, right? Surely you trust that I would choose the perfect parents?"

"Yes, but..."

"And more important, you are not ready for such a decision, anyway. I would not want you to choose a certain life because you were dazzled by the new conditions, or because you imagine that you are emotionally involved. I would want you to choose such a life only when your feelings are real, concrete, finalized. Yes, I did ask you if you would feel better being married before you gave birth.

But it was a mistake on my part, based on my compassion for your stress when we met."

"So you have changed your mind about marrying me?"

"I have not changed my mind. One never does. I will come back for you when you are thirty, and then I shall ask you to marry me. I have already made that choice. But my choice was not made lightly. Remember, I have known you for a very long time, since I watched over you for years, ever since they told me about your genetic makeup and your mission. In addition, I looked at what is available of your future self – the kind of woman you will become – though of course you don't understand as yet what I mean… So yes, I do know you very well, and I will ask you to marry me. But you cannot accept or reject me now – because your decision will not be based on true self knowledge."

· "But that is mean, Marduchk. Thirty? That is twelve years from now! What if I get run over by a car and die at twenty-five?"

"Then I will make a skip in time, and come and get you five seconds before the car hits you," said Marduchk, laughing.

"Deal," I said, feeling better.

"And stop worrying about the operation. You will feel nothing."

I did not believe him and I stayed up all night, fretting. But he was right. The operation took thirty minutes, at most, the light found its way into my body with no trouble at all, did its thing, and I left the surgical table feeling as good as ever. Miriam came to get me, and we walked home for lunch, and that was that!

"So, now I have nine months vacation, right? What shall I do, other than romp with the children, dress up, and annoy you and Marduchk?" I asked as we were eating.

"You will go to plays, to concerts, and to combination orchestra/dancing events, with musicians that are dancers, too, and carry on illustrative movements that extend the message of the music. I adore this form of entertainment and I think you will like it too. You will get to know many charming people who will become dear friends and would welcome you if you decide to return to us. Marduchk will teach you as many ancient languages as you feel would help you in your studies on earth, and get you all the books you want to read. And we will all take the children to picnics and row on the canals, under the flowering trees."

"I love the canals. You have so much water on your planet."

"About fifty/fifty to the land, the ratio is, but we also have some wonderful water underground. I will show you the underground lakes, they are as blue as a sapphire, contained in glittering grottos. And how about swimming? Do you know that our oceans are sweet, not salty? Swimming is very nice."

"I will look like a whale, Miriam. I am pregnant, remember?"

"Not in the kind of bathing suit my daughter already designed for you. You will look like a mermaid."

"A very fat mermaid. Did you ever see a manatee, those sea cows, Miriam? Our sailors used to think they are mermaids. They are very fat..."

*** *** ***

CHAPTER THREE
A Visit with Sinhar Inannaschamra

> The history of the creation of the human race, and its
> relationship to the extraterrestrial races.

I was now in my fourth month of pregnancy. I felt
remarkably well, due to the incredible diet I was given. I
really should not call it a diet, it was more like a
sophisticated, gourmet vegetarian cuisine, since on Nibiru
they do not eat any meat, fish, or seafood. They do have
wonderful milk and cheese-like foodstuffs that are
produced from a fruit that is much like a coconut, and
excellent eggs from the variety of birds that flourish on
Nibiru, but more on that later, since I plan to devote an
entire chapter to telling about the diet and lifestyle of the
Anunnaki, which has so much to do with their longevity
and perfect health, and it has done wonders for me. These
days, at age sixty, I look like a woman half my age, and I
had not as yet needed to resort to any advanced Anunnaki
technology to achieve that; after all, the Anunnaki can live
up to 500,000 years, so I have no idea when I will need cell
rejuvenation. Come to think of it, while it is rare that the
Anunnaki come to earth, sometimes, when they do, they
may give the youth formula to someone and he or she can
live to be over two hundred years old. Human scientists
have recently begun to say that earth people have the
genetic capacity to live for a hundred and fifty years – truth
is, they can live up to five hundred, if they choose the right
formula... Incidentally, speaking of birds and cats, they are
so unusual and have such astonishing traits that perhaps the

flora and fauna of the planet Nibiru deserve their own chapter, too.

On that particular day, I went for an afternoon visit with Sinhar Marduchk's and Sinhar Semiramicsh's great grandmother. I call her great grandmother for lack of a better term, but she was quite a few generations further from being just the mother of their grandmother. Sinhar Inannaschamra was immeasurably old, 400,000 years to be exact.

Sinhar Inannaschamra sat under a shady tree, and she rose as she saw me and came to greet me. A strikingly beautiful lady, she had masses of glossy black hair, piled up high on her head. Her skin was creamy and smooth, and her black eyes shown with wisdom and the joy of living. She was tall and elegant and always beautifully dressed, this time wearing a crimson robe with a silver belt and heavy silver necklace and earrings, all bearing deep carving and symbols representing the secret powerful names of the Anunnaki first Creator – Aal-Khal Leck-Malkshrink-Nar. I liked her very much from the moment we met, since she and I shared an interest. She was an expert in human history, archaeology, mythology and folklore, subjects she taught at one of the great Nibiru academies. Her knowledge was acquired at first hand – she traveled over time and space, learning, observing, writing. Her books were masterpieces. I never stopped asking questions, and she delighted in imparting information, so we got along extremely well.

We settled ourselves under the beautiful tree that was looked very much like a willow, but in the curious way of Nibiru trees, was connected to two other trees of the same species; the trees there seem to nourish and feed each other. Perhaps that is one of the reasons the trees constantly bloom and fruit. She served me some gorgeous fruit, Wer-

Dah Nour-Mar. The name is quite poetic, it means "the flower or fruit of the light." She also handed me a delicate, almost transparent goblet made of onyx marble and filled with fragrant a rose water drink I found utterly delicious, named Ma-Ah Wer-Dah Anbar. We ate and discussed our favorite subject. I already knew that the Anunnaki were not the first to experiment with and on humans, that about 145,000 years ago, the Igigihl, or Igigi, were the first extraterrestrials to create quasi-human specimens. But I wanted to know more about what I was told were grotesque experiments.

"Yes," said Sinhar Inannaschamra. "At the very beginning of their genetic experiments, the results were catastrophic. Their creations looked awful – bestial, very ugly, even frightening. This may have happened because the Igigi were more terrestrial explorers than geneticists, and therefore more interested in certain molecules found in terrestrial water, and in various minerals, than in creating a perfectly shaped human race."

"What were the Igigi like?" I asked. "Did they look like you?"

"Oh, no," said Sinhar Inannaschamra. "The Igigi did co-exist with the Anunnaki, and shared some traits with them, but they were totally dissimilar in their physical shape. They were huge, bigger even than the Anunnaki, but not graceful like them. They had strong facial features and lots of hair. And believe me, their appearance was not enhanced by their outlandish clothes. Nothing elegant or pleasant, everything was made out of metal shields. They liked to adorn themselves with many iron bracelets and necklaces that sported some strange insignia that to anyone but an Igigi would be quite ominous... not a very attractive species. The Igigi were 245 million years older than the Anunnaki. But you must hand it to them, they were highly

87

advanced in mineralogy and minerals transmutation. The Anunnaki were geneticists and engineers with a strong appreciation for aesthetics. Therefore, the Igigi created a very primitive form of living beings on earth, exactly as you, the humans, created unappealing early forms and shapes of robots, and related mechanical devices, at the dawn of robotics. These robots were functional but not pretty to look at, and the Igigi considered the early quasi-humans to be not much more than machines with limited mental faculties."

"So what did the early humans look like?"

"Apes, really. You see, the earth was extremely cold at the time, and the Igigi had to cover the human bodies with lots of hair to protect them from the elements. It took the quasi-human race thousands of years to evolve into an early human form, and even then not totally human, still looking like apes. Some of them had bizarre skulls and facial bones. I will show you pictures if you come to the Academy. They actually experimented a bit with the early human-forms. First, they created the 'Nafar Jinmarkah' meaning 'individual on three legs.' They consisted of a very strong physical body but lacked agility. Those bodies were created to carry heavy weight. The three legs' purpose was to support heavy loads they could lift and carry. Later on, the Igigi worked on a new human form that consisted of a body with two legs, to bring speed and better agility. Yet, early humans remained terrifying, nothing like the Biblical descriptions. The Igigi tried four times. I mean, they experimented in four different ways. Each time, they faced a problem in designing the human skull. Early Igigi creators did not want to put brains in the skull so human-forms-bodies would not think... it was horrible. Yes, you could consider these early human-forms as the world's first robots. The Anunnaki were the ones who created the brains for the humans. These early brains contained two million cells. But the Anunnaki too worked several times on the prototypes of humans. In their final genetic experiments, the Anunnaki programmed humans with the thirteen original faculties."

"Did the Igigi treat the humans well?"

"Not really. They were pretty vicious toward the early quasi-human beings, treating them very badly."

"This is so different from what science and religion argue about on earth, Sinhar Inannaschamra," I said wistfully. "We don't seem to know much…"

"Well, the history and theories of human creation and evolution are distorted by both of you theologians and scientists," said Sinhar Inannaschamra. "But you can't blame them. Much of the evidence has been lost. Anyway, to understand the quasi-human race, one must know about the thirteen faculties."

"The quasi-humans' faculties?" I asked, a little confused.

"Yes. In the genes, molecules and DNA of the early quasi-human race, the Igigi programmed thirteen faculties, or functions. The most important abilities were as follows:

6. move
7. sense danger
8. understand by association
9. memorize
10. see forms and shapes in four colors. These colors were bright yellow, representing gold; grey, representing minerals and rocks; blue, representing the atmosphere, air, and water; and a very strong red, representing heat and blood. Other colors such as green, purple, lilac, etc, were not visible or

known to the early and primitive form of quasi-humans."

"So they were not entirely primitive," I said.

"They were primitive enough… The first genetically created race could not speak, even the concept of Language was wholly unknown to them. Thousands of years later, the Anunnaki taught their own newly created race of humans to speak, read, and write. The Anunnaki's first genetically created human race was the seed of humanity as you know it; they began to populate the earth 25,000 years before the construction of the great pyramids. I am only citing the pyramids as a landmark in human history to give you a chronological perspective. Greater, taller and bigger monuments were erected centuries before the construction of the pyramids, and some ruins can still be found in Phoenicia (Modern Lebanon today) particularly in Baalbeck, and in Mesopotamia (Modern Iraq today). I have seen them all, at various stages of their development."

"How I would love to study like that. When I go back to earth, I will have to study the old fashioned way."

"It's a good start. Some day, when you come back to Nibiru, you will join the Academy and go on from there. Nothing is lost."

"Do you think I will ever learn to travel in time and see things in person?"

"Of course you will. We can easily teach you the skill, among others."

"How totally delightful that will be."

"You can visit endless points in time, learn the truth about so many things that are now obscure. And perhaps one day you will write a book about it, for your people, who knows?"

"I do so much hope so… I'd rather think about it than about my current mission."

"Do that, think happy thoughts. Your mission here is difficult, we all know that, but so important for the greater good. We honor you for accepting it."

I felt close to crying so I had to change the subject. "So tell me more about the real humans, please, Sinhar Inannaschamra," I said. "You know what we are taught. The scientists talk about evolution. The priests and rabbis talk about Adam and Eve. All of it so inaccurate."

"You are absolutely right," said Sinhar Inannaschamra. "As I mentioned before, they are not aware of so much of the truth of the matter. Contrary to all beliefs, including what Judaism, Christianity and Islam teach you, Eve was not created from Adam's rib. Men were created from an early female form that was fertilized by the leaders and the elite of the Anunnaki in a very special way that we will discuss later. These women lived in quarantined cities, and had both sons and daughters thus fathered by the Anunnaki.

Some of the most puzzling sites of these cities, due to their size and functionality, were in Ur, Amrit, Ougarit, Petra (Batra), Tyre and Sidon. Early humans called the quarantined cities of these women 'The Cities of Mirage', and 'The Cities of Beautiful Illusion,' and the quasi-humans who were made out of earth were *not* allowed to interact with these women.

Thousands of years later, the inhabitants of what is today the Arab Peninsula and the lands bordering Persia, the United Arab Emirates, and India, called these women 'The Women of Light', and those who were allowed to mix with them were called 'The Sons of Light.' From this early human race, all humans came to life. God had nothing to do with you. In other words, the God you know, revere, and fear today did not create you. Even the word or term 'God' did not exist in the early stages of the existence of the human race on earth. Instead 'Gods' or 'Heavenly Masters' were used. And thousands of years later, those terms were changed to 'Giants,' 'Elohim,' 'Nephilim,' 'Anakim,' 'Fallen Angels,' you name it... Incidentally, the Early Anunnaki who visited earth were extremely tall. Some reached the height of 9 feet, and lived as long as 400,000 years. These Anunnaki did not leave descendants on earth. Those who came to earth much later, before the regional deluge, and right after that huge Tsunami, left families behind them when they returned home. By home, I mean Nibiru, Zeta Reticuli and Ashartartun-ra. These families are the origin of the hybrids and/or extraterrestrial human beings living today among the people on earth. It is very important to learn and remember this.

Another important detail is the issue of population. For some reason, many believe that only grays or reptilians live on Zeta Reticuli, but this is not true at all. The Anunnaki had always occupied vast territories on Zeta Reticuli, and as you know they are not the grays or reptilians, as so wrongly described in Ufology literature."

"So many different races," I said.

"Indeed," said Sinhar Inannaschamra. "Some 300,000 years before the creation of the cities of 'The Women of Lights,' forty-six different races of humans and quasi-humans populated the earth. The greatest numbers were found in Africa, Madagascar, Indonesia, Brazil, and Australia. These races died out not because of famine, ecological catastrophes, or acts of war, but because of the disintegration of the very molecules and composition of their cells. The Anunnaki created the 'final form' of human beings, and all of you are their descendents."

"I am rather surprised that records do not exist."

"Actually, they do, but they are well hidden. There are those who know that the Sumerians, Ashurians,

Hyskos, and Phoenicians are the direct descendants of the Anunnaki, and that their descendants carry a rather clean genetic pool, like you, my dear; you are practically a full Anunnaki, genetically. But they don't want it known, now as well as in antiquity. For example, Eusebius, the Bishop of Cæsarea, Palestine, had genealogical records of the descendants of the Anunnaki who became Syriac. At the Council of Antioch in 363 CE, Bishop Eusebius intended to bring this subject in his *Theophania* to the attention of the members of the Council. But no additional information or manuscripts about what happened at the Council were provided. In the Syriac manuscripts of Zachariah of Mitylene, who frequently corresponded with Eupraxius, two references were made to the Anunnaki as the ancestors of the Ashurian-Syriac. Another bishop by the name of Proterius tried to destroy these letters. Fortunately, two hand-written copies were made, as the tradition of this era dictated, and were saved in the vault of a scribe. Those letters resurfaced in 1957 in a personal acquisition of Cardinal Maouchi, the Patriarch of the Maronite Church in Lebanon. After Maouchi's death, those files were kept in the secret vaults of Al-Kaslik Monastery in Lebanon. As for modern knowledge, the original language of the Anunnaki is still intact and is currently used by top American scientists and researchers who work in secret American-Alien military bases in the United States and Mexico. In 1947, the first attempt was made by American linguists, who previously worked at the OSS (Precursor to the CIA), to decipher it. They tried to compare it with the Sumerian, Hebrew, Armenian and Phoenician Alphabet, languages which are directly derived from the Anunnaki's written language. The problem they faced and could not resolve were the geometrical symbols included in the written Anunnaki's texts. But in 1956, they cracked the

93

code. Those mathematical figures hold great secrets regarding an alien advanced technology used for peaceful and constructive purposes. The American military intelligence and what's left from Dr. Fermi's group at Los Alamos wanted to use this alien technology for military purposes."

"The language is in use? Now?"

"Oh, yes. The American top military scientists who work in secret military bases and aliens' laboratories on earth have an extraterrestrial lexicon, and use it constantly. In that lexicon, or dictionary, you will find variations of Phoenician and Sumerian symbols. Some letters represent maritime and celestial symbols and measurements. The fact that the Americans are still using this extraterrestrial language should be enough to convince anyone that extraterrestrials, Anunnaki and Zeta Reticuli descendants, still live among you, otherwise why would anyone learn a language that cannot used to communicate with people who speak it and write it?"[1]

"Who else has a strong connection to the Anunnaki?" I asked.

"Besides the Sumerians, the Phoenicians, the Hyskos, and the Philistines, there are indeed others, such as the very early Etruscans, Druids, Minoans, and people of Mu. Later, the Ashurians resided among the last remnants of the Anunnaki who visited earth and lived there for 600 more years. After that, the Anunnaki left earth for good, to return only as visitors. One of the reasons for their

----

[1] On some of the manifestos of military parts used in anti-gravity secret laboratories underground in the United States, several letters were borrowed from the 'Enuma Elish' of Sumeria and regularly appeared on the top right corner of each document. In the eighties, those Sumerian numbers were replaced by an Americanized version.

departure was the discovery of the 'tree of life,' also known as 'The Tree of Knowledge' by humans – a metaphor for the acquisition of knowledge and understanding by the human race, on its own. The acquisition of this supreme knowledge caused the humans to rebel against the Anunnaki."

"What a mistake," I said. "Had we stayed loyal to the Anunnaki, we could have spared ourselves so much grief."

"Yes, but that is the way humans are, I am afraid... but as I said, we love you anyway."

"I understand that there is a close relationship between your language and your religion, is it not so?"

"Yes, it is. The Anunnaki have two kinds or styles of languages; one is spoken and the other one is written. The spoken language is the easiest one to learn, and it is used by the Anunnaki's population. The written one is used in books exclusively and consists of twenty-six letters. Seven of these letters represent the planets that surround our star. Many of the Anunnaki's letters cannot be pronounced by humans, because of certain limitations of your vocal chords. There are seven additional letters that are complete words, and these words represent the attributes of our 'Grand Leader.' Translated into terrestrial language, the Grand Leader is the creator of energy, in other words, 'God.' However, the Anunnaki do not believe in a God in the same sense you do, even though they were the ones who created and originated the early forms of religions on earth. However, those Anunnaki that have brought religion to earth were of a lower class. The god they brought was a vengeful and terrifying god, something that the Gnostics and early scholars of the Coptic Church in Egypt were fully aware of. The doctrines show their disdain for such a god, and consequently, they called him the

'Creator of Evil and Darkness.' Later on in history, the Gnostics began to spread the word that this earth was not created by the God of the Church, but rather by an evil demi-god. The early human beings who interacted with the Anunnaki shared similar beliefs."

"If humans learn about all this, the religious aspect would be most difficult to reconcile," I said.

"And yet, there is so much that is in common," said Sinhar Inannaschamra. "For example, your human ancestors borrowed many words from extraterrestrial languages, and learned the secret seven powerful names of God. Many of the Phoenician linguists and early creators of their Alphabet borrowed numerous words and expressions from the higher class of the Anunnaki. Ancient Phoenician texts and poems, recorded on tablets found in Tyre and Sidon, included reference to symbols and words taken from the written language of the upper class of the Anunnaki. Members of an early Anunnaki expedition to Phoenicia taught the Phoenicians how to develop their language, and revealed to them the secret powerful names and attributes of Baalshalimroot. They instructed them not to use these words for ill purposes. Particularly, the word 'Baalazamhour-Il' is never to be said, spelled, or written. Later on in history, the Hebrews religiously observed this instruction, and pronouncing the word of name of God became forbidden. However, the Anunnaki revealed to the Phoenicians and Sumerians seven positive and powerful names/attributes of the Grand Leader. If well used, these words can bring prosperity, good health, and salvation in moments of difficulty. The prophet Mohammad learned these seven words from an early Christian ascetic, a Sahara hermit called Raheb Bouhayra. Today, Muslims all over the world are aware of these seven words or names. They call them in written Arabic 'Asma' Al Lah Al Sabha' Al

Housna,' meaning the seven lovely names of God. Those names do not have numerical value or secret meanings as many scholars claim, simply because they were not originally written in a geometrical form. None of these words appeared in the so-called hieroglyphic measuring tape that the Americans found at the crash site in Roswell. The symbols and geometrical signs Americans found in Roswell were biochemical symbols.

Also, early names of the Hebrew God were of an extraterrestrial origin. It is true that the Sumerian ancient texts and records mentioned names of some of the Anunnaki leaders such as Utu, Ningishzida, Ninki, Marduk, Enki, Enlil, Inanna, but the greatest name of all remains Baalshalimroot, also referred to as 'Baalshalimroot-An'kgh.' Terah, the father of Abraham, mistakenly worshiped Baalshalimroot-An'kgh. Early Semites made the same mistake when they worshiped the leaders of the Anunnaki as gods who later became Bene Ha-Elohim, meaning the children of the gods. The Anunnaki never introduced themselves as gods. The words: El Elyon and Yahweh or Jehovah were taken directly from the Anunnaki's written language. The original word was "Yah'weh-El' Ankh" and El Elyon was "Il Ilayon-imroot."

"It's hard to understand the difference between lower class and upper class Anunnaki, not to mention the other races," I said. "It is, actually, quite bewildering."

"I know, it's rather difficult... some of your scholars equated the Anunnaki with the Nephilim. This is not totally correct. The lower class of the Anunnaki are the Nephilim, although many historians call them sometimes Anakim or Elohim. The higher class of the Anunnaki is ruled by Baalshalimroot, and his followers or subjects are called the 'Shtaroout-Hxall Ain,' meaning the inhabitants of the house of knowledge, or 'those who see clearly.' The word 'Ain' was later adopted by the early inhabitants of the Arab Peninsula. 'Ain' in Arabic means 'eye'. In the secret teachings of Sufism on earth, visions of Al Hallaj, and of the greatest poetess of Sufism, Rabiha' Al Adawi Yah, known as 'Ha Chi katou Al Houbb Al Ilahi' (The mistress of the divine love), and in the banned book *Shams Al Maa'Ref Al Kubrah* (Book of the Sun of the Great Knowledge), the word 'eye' meant the ultimate knowledge, or wisdom from above. 'Above' clearly indicates the heavens. Later on, it was used to symbolize the justice of God or 'God watching over us.' And much later in history, several societies and cultures adopted the 'eye' as an institutional symbol and caused it to appear on many temples' pillars, bank notes, money bills, and religious texts.

"I think even now these symbols are still around, Sinhar Inannaschamra," I said. "It is fascinating how such things stick around."

"Absolutely. Your Freemasons' and Illuminati's favorite symbol is the Anunnaki's eye. And as everything changes in time and takes on different forms and meanings, the 'eye' became a 'triangle,' a very secretive and powerful symbol. George Washington carried this triangle with him wherever he went, and wore it during official ceremonies. If you double and reverse the triangle, you get the Star of David. This very triangle is visible on many extraterrestrial spacecrafts, and on uniforms of military personnel in secret American military bases underground, working on alien technology and propulsion systems. And it will stay on, I am sure. [2] As an example, on February 17, 1953, an

---

[2] Sinharinannaschamra was right. The powerful Trilateral Commission was founded by David Rockefeller, the Chairman of the Chase Manhattan Bank of New York, in July 1973. It is recorded that In their first board meeting, Rockefeller proposed to adopt the

American millionaire by the name of Paul Warburg who was involved with the triangle issues shouted before the Senate of the United States of America: 'We shall have world government whether or not you like it, by conquest or consent.'"

"Sounds rather ominous," I said.

"Yes, the 'Triangle' can be a negative force," said Sinhar Inannaschamra. "When integrated without balance and cosmic harmony, in other words, spatial equilibrium, in architectural design and lining up territories, the triangle becomes a negative force on the map. If the three sides of the triangle are separated, such separation can cause serious health problems. The triangle becomes three lines of negative energy. This energy is not easily detected; nevertheless it runs strong and deep underground. People who live above these lines suffer enormously. In many instances, this negative power or current can negatively affect the present and future of many human beings. Similar to some Ufologists who can identify UFOs' hot

---

Anunnaki's triangle as the official symbol/logo of this world organization. According to an official statement issued by the Commission, the principal and official aim of the Trilateral Commission is 'to harmonize the political, economic, social, and cultural relations between the three major economic regions in the world.' The Commission divided the world into a triangle joining three regions consisting of the Far East, Europe, and North America, all within the perimeter of a triangle. Basically, the Trilateral Commission aims at controlling the world under the auspices of a centralized American power-group consisting of bankers, financiers, selected political leaders, top military echelon and members of the cabinet from each administration. Many members of the Trilateral Commission are descendants of a lower class of an extraterrestrial race. Some passed away, but many of them still live among us. It is impossible for ordinary people to recognize them. But the good and decent descendants of our extraterrestrial teachers can identify them very easily.

spots on earth, usually above ground, descendants of the extraterrestrials can identify and locate the negative currents underground. Each country has these negative currents or circuits underground. I do not wish to scare you, my dear, but I must inform you that some American states are located above these lines. For example, Mississippi, Alabama, the northern part of Washington, DC, and two areas in Brooklyn, New York share this misfortune."

"Scary," I said. "Poor people, suffering for no fault of their own."

"Many manage to overcome by sheer strength of character and goodness," said Sinhar Inannaschamra. "Life is full of challenges for everyone."

"Life here seems very pleasant," I said.

"Yes, in many ways it is," said Sinhar Inannaschamra. "And yet, we all have our burdens. But let's think of nicer things. How about a stroll in the garden? I would like to show you a nest of the most gorgeous new little birds; their parents trust me, I always feed them good things, so they will not object. We must take some of these almonds for them..." and so we went for a stroll in the magnificent garden, and the lesson was over for the day as soon as a tiny bird, all gold and red, flew clumsily out of the nest and perched on my finger. "She must be the first to take wings," said Sinhar Inannaschamra proudly, as the parent birds sat on her hands and delicately nibbled at the delicious almonds. The sky was turning purple as the three moons of Zeta Reticuli started to set, the soft light giving way to darkness, and the scent of the night blooming flowers began to permeate the air.

***   ***   ***

CHAPTER FOUR
An Irrevocable Decision

How I had to choose between giving up my child for the common good of humanity or be transported to another universe, away from everyone I loved.

And that, I thought, was that. The next day was my scheduled birth time. I was ready, and I was confident that I would not suffer under the gentle care of the Anunnaki physicians. I knew them all well now, they became my good friends, and whenever I needed to be examined, or have a little treatment, I was not even afraid and rather enjoyed visiting these ladies. I would feel nothing, that is, nothing physical. Emotionally, that was another question altogether.

The thought of giving up my baby was preying on me. Perhaps the psychological burden was even greater because I was an adopted baby myself, I really can't tell, but I was more and more uneasy about it. And yet, it was a point of honor to say nothing about my feelings. I did not want to distress either Miriam or Marduchk, who had invested so much time, effort, and work in the project. And so at dinner I made a special effort to be cheerful and pleasant, and I really thought I managed to cover my feeling and dupe Miriam and her daughters into thinking that all was well. Marduchk was not there; it somehow made me unhappy, I wanted to see him that evening before the great event, but according to Miriam he had to attend some function of great importance in the great library they called the Akashic Library, where all the knowledge of the universe was supposed to be accumulating for eons. I was promised that some day in the far future I could see it, and I was curious about it, but right now it was the furthest thing from my mind and I was sad not seeing Marduchk. I snuck out for a quiet walk in the garden while the Miriam and her daughters were admiring a new picture the girls created, telling them I wanted to do my meditation exercises.

I sat on one of the white marble benches, covered with gorgeous crimson and gold pillows, and really prepared to do my meditation exercises that the physicians taught me as a way to relax body and soul. I wish I could say I stuck with it, but instead, I started crying uncontrollably. After a short while, I felt a hand on my shoulder. Startled, I turned around and saw Marduchk.

"Marduchk! I am so glad to see you! I thought you will be busy all evening at the Akashic Library!" I sniffed and snuffled and tried to stop crying.

"I got away as early as I could. I wanted to see you before the big day tomorrow, and Sinhar Semiramicsh told me you were in the garden. But you are greatly distressed, Victoria. Let's talk about it, and see if I can help."

"I don't know, Marduchk," I said, wiping my eyes. "I don't even know how to explain… it's all so difficult…"

"Well, let's try to make it easier. There are always many options."

"Do you mean I can change my mind, even now?" I asked. "But the baby is due tomorrow!"

"Yes, you can change your mind," said Marduchk. "I will not lie to you and say that it will be easy, but it is doable."

"How?" I said.

"I can take you, still pregnant, to another dimension, another universe, and you will keep the baby."

"But what about my parents? They will not know what happened to me."

"They will have your former self. That one would have never met me, and life would go on as usual for the three of them." That was extremely confusing, but I thought I understood. Marduchk will travel back in time, and change the past. The girl that was I, the one that drove the car, would just go on driving, never meet Marduchk, while I, the offshoot, will be here, on Nibiru. Maybe. I could not concentrate on that, because the really important question was very different, and I needed to know that right away.

"Will I ever see you again, Marduchk?"

"No, you will not. That would be impossible, each of us will be living in different dimension." That thought really hurt, and his tone of voice and the look on his face told me it was irrevocable.

"So what would happen to me in the new universe?"

"I will find you a husband. You would believe that you married for love and that this man was the father of your baby, and you will live a normal human life there."

"And you will stay here."

"Yes, I will have to stay here, give you up, both from the point of view of the project, and worse, personally. That will be the price. That is why I said it would not be easy."

"You could not come with me to the new universe?"

"No. I cannot do so. I have only been here for thirty thousand years, Victoria, since my last branching. A blink of an eye in Anunnaki life. I have obligations, which cannot be left undone without enormous damage to many people, both Anunnaki and Human."

"Don't you care about losing me, Marduchk?"

For a long while he was silent, just sitting there, staring at ground. Then he said, "Yes, I would care very much. It will be more difficult for me than you can even begin to imagine. But an Anunnaki does not break his word, and does not walk out on his obligations."

"But humans do, right?"

"Sometimes," he said.

"And if I decide not to give up the baby, if I decide to move on to that new universe, I will be breaking my word to the Anunnaki."

"We will not hold it against you, Victoria. Never."

I took a deep breath and made my final decision. It was very hard, but it had to be done. I looked up at him and said, "I will not break my word either, Marduchk. The birth will go on as planned tomorrow, no matter how I feel. I have my obligations too."

The relief in Marduchk's black eyes was almost palpable. He could barely speak, it seemed. Finally he said simply, "Thank you, Victoria," and then put his head in his hands and was silent for a while. "I am very, very grateful," he added. "And since you made the decision yourself, after receiving honest information, I feel your free will was exercised without any coercion."

"I did exercise my free will, Marduchk." There was no coercion, but I have to admit, so many years later, that the thought of losing Marduchk was at least as strong in my decision as the idea of honoring my obligations. I am not as noble as Marduchk, probably never will be.

"I want to make your situation a bit easier for you, though. There is no need for you to suffer emotionally. Let me make you forget everything from this evening on. I will wipe your memory, take you to your room, and tomorrow everything will be done as planned. The next thing you will see will be the old Maine road as you drive home."

"So we will say goodbye tonight, Marduchk?"

"If you agree to this plan."

"I like the plan. It's quite merciful. But would you do me a favor, first?"

"Of course."

"Please try to explain to me, in the simplest fashion, this issue of branching and changing universes. Particularly, I want to understand the marriage you told me about."

"The marriage? Why?"

"Well, you see, in the future your personal life may be quite important to me, even the previous one. I will need to know such things, or they may burden my mind with questions and doubts. Now, I realize that if you explain everything now, I will promptly forget it, but as soon as my memory is returned, it will be there quite safely. And then we won't have to discuss the past, just move on into the future."

"That makes sense," said Marduchk. "As a matter of fact, this is a very mature and intelligent consideration. You are human, and the issue of trust is sensitive with humans, since their relationships are not as permanent as ours. Do you know, Victoria, we don't even have words for infidelity, or mistress, or extramarital affairs, or cheating? Once we make our choice, it is so permanent, it is as simple and as obvious as the air we breathe. But of course you need a different kind of reassurance. It's only natural, but it will all change. In a few hundred years, such thoughts will disappear from your mind altogether."

"So what happened to you?"

"Well, first you must understand the concept. The closest metaphor in human terms would be that sometimes,

105

you wish you could do something differently, change the past, change a life decision, right?"

"Yes, like, perhaps, going back in time to a point before you made a bad decision."

"Exactly. Or, if you think that you could do some good if you changed an entire event. Well, in our case, we do have the solutions for these dilemmas. We can split ourselves in two, or more if necessary, and move on to a universe that is very much like the one we are leaving."

"One universe which is like the one you are living in… does that mean there are so many universes, that some of them do not resemble this one?"

"Yes. There is an infinite number of universes. If you wish to branch and move, you have to study the matter very carefully and make the right selection."

"And the branching, or splitting, results in exact copies of the same person?"

"Yes, at the moment of separation. After that, each grows, spiritually, in a different direction, follows his or her own free will and decisions, and eventually the two are not exactly alike."

"So what do they do, first of all?"

"The old one stays where he is and follows his old patterns as he wishes. The new one might land one minute, or a month, or a year, before the decision he or she want to change or avoid."

"So let me see. Thirty thousand years ago, you decided that something was wrong in your life?"

"Not wrong, exactly. I was living a nice life with my wife and family. But I felt that I did not accomplish much, that I chose an easy life of playing with poetry and literature, and I suddenly wanted to be more active in the development of the universe."

"What do you think caused this change?"

"I witnessed a horrendous event, Victoria. A certain group of beings in our galaxy destroyed an entire civilization wantonly, killing millions of the inhabitants, in order to take over their planet for mining purposes. It happened while I was on a trip, and I actually saw the explosions while I was traveling. It was quite traumatic, and I thought, at that moment, that I must be active in preventing such events from occurring again, ever."

"So you told your wife, and what did she say?"

"My wife did not want to change our lifestyle, she was very happy just as she was, and if I changed my own life it would have caused her much pain. I would never want that to happen. But the restlessness was constant, and so my wife and I consulted, and together we decided that branching would be the perfect solution. I would go back in time to be in a spot before that fateful trip, branch out, and leave my former self, who was happy and content, to get on with his pleasant life. I, on the other hand, that is, the new person, would come to this universe, and start fresh, doing what I want to do."

"And you have accomplished what you wanted?"

"I have only just begun, but yes, I work hard."

"And for thirty thousand years, no one was right for you to marry, in this universe."

"Thirty thousand years are not a very long time to find the perfect life partner."

"Well, so now I understand," I said. "And do you hear from your wife and family?"

"At first, just to make sure all was well, I viewed them occasionally on one our viewing machines. Not any more, though. I don't want to spy on their privacy. They seemed as happy as ever, and that is all that matters."

"I think I do understand now, Marduchk," I said. "Not the technical parts, of course, that is beyond me. The idea of splitting a person, branching, is rather alien to me."

"I think you understand the principle, though," said Marduchk.

"You know, Marduchk, for someone who is 300,000 old, and so intellectually superior to me, it is amazing, and really pleasant, how much you treat me as an equal. At my age, you could have treated me as if I am a fly on the wall."

"But you are my chosen life partner, Victoria. Naturally I would treat you with all the respect you deserve. Besides, as you know, I have glimpsed into the future and I know the kind of woman you will be in a few hundred years, if you decide to come back to me."

"And yet, I am not allowed to accept or reject the marriage proposal."

"It won't be fair to you. You will not be exercising complete free will."

"Very well. But could you give me a small example of what it would be like to be married to you? I mean, show me what the merging of lights will be like? Now don't give me that alarmed look, as if I am breaking a horrible taboo. I don't mean the whole thing, of course, that is not allowed unless we are married, but just a little sample."

"But won't it influence your free will too?"

"I can't see why it should. It would not do more than a date, kissing me good night, could influence my choice of a husband years later."

"Even a small sample would be more than that," said Marduchk.

"Let's just take a chance for once," I said.

"It might influence your ability to choose and love a human man," said Marduchk.

"I certainly hope so," I said. "Do you realize what I will be missing if I meet and marry a human man?"

"But what about free will?"

"Free will may be overrated in this case, Marduchk. Besides, you will make me forget, deeply forget, one hundred percent forget. You know you can do it."

"I can't refuse it," said Marduchk. "I hope I am doing the right thing. But right or wrong, I simply can't refuse. So, just give me your hands, but sit as far away from me as you can. We don't want the light to catch on to the rest of our bodies, just the hands. And that, Victoria, must be our goodbye – for a while."

"You will make me forget after the lights merge?"

"Yes. Then, I will take you to your room, tell Miriam that you are not conscious to your surroundings, and tomorrow we will take care of business. I will be back for you, Victoria. Trust me on that."

I nodded and extended my hands, and he took them between his own. I felt a slight warmth, but for a while it seemed to be just the normal physical contact of hands. Then, I saw a glowing golden light rising from our joined hands. I am not sure if any words exist that could do justice to how this felt, try as I might. There was a sensation of magnificent physical well-being, mingled and combined with a sudden understanding that everything would be all right, that the universe is working as it should and that I could allow myself to be a part of it, totally and fearlessly. The pleasure that this combination of physical and spiritual joys produced was extremely intense, and I clearly remember thinking that if that was just a small sample of what marriage to an Anunnaki can be, well, the real thing was well worth waiting for... I felt as if my entire being was blazing, and then everything vanished, swept into a soft, velvety dark night that smoothly turned into an evening on a lonely stretch of road in Maine, and I was blissfully driving home from an afternoon study with my best friend.

But something remained. I am certain of it, and no matter how many times Marduchk later swore to me that my memory was completely stopped, still something remained, some remnant of this incredible feeling that would guide and keep me in the twelve years that were to follow until we met again. And if you ask me, that beats free will every time.

*** *** ***

CHAPTER FIVE
Marriage and Mingling of the Lights

> We complete the first three parts of the marriage ceremony,
> and I experience the incredible joy of the Union.

April 1977, Nibiru

It was a joyful day. My reunion with Miriam's daughters brought me much happiness, and this time, I met Miriam's husband, who was on a mission during my entire nine months of pregnancy. Sinhar Inlimekach was a very pleasant person, and he welcomed me heartily on my return to Nibiru. Of course, Sinhar Inannaschamra came to see me, and we were overjoyed to meet again. She promised that now I could see, study, and enjoy everything that was in her power to give at the Academy, and I was thrilled with the potential future studies. Yes, this was a very happy day. And yet, something very strange happened at the end of the day. After a festive dinner, which included many guests, Marduchk got up with the rest of the guests and left me at Miriam's place. I could not quite understand it, and to be honest, was extremely distressed about what seemed to me like abandonment. I simply had to understand this, so when the girls retired and Sinhar Inlimekach went to the library to prepare for something he needed the next day, I decided to consult Miriam.

"Miriam, what is going on? Has Marduchk changed his mind about marrying me?"

"Of course not, what would make you imagine such a horror? He has made his choice! It's final for him!"

111

"Well, he just got up, said good night, and left me in your house. Not that I object to being with you, you know how much I love all of you, but I imagined I would be living in his house, since we are getting married!"

"No, of course you can't live in his house! You are not married yet!"

"I see... so why doesn't he mention it? Shouldn't we make some arrangements, do something?"

Miriam laughed. "You know, my dear, my brother is a loveable creature, but sometimes he forgets that humans don't know everything we do and have no clue to our traditions. Why he assumes you understand it all is beyond me, but that is Sinhar Marduchk all over. He has made all the arrangements, Victoria. He had plenty to do even to persuade the Council, show them you were of age even though you are only thirty..."

"Only thirty? Women marry at a much earlier age on earth."

"But the council is rather rigid, and they have their code. You must remember that you are a child, on Nibiru, until you are seventy-one years old."

"*WHAT*? He won't marry me for forty-one years? Are you all mad?"

"No, no, you are to be married right away, with your permission, and he talked the council into everything he wanted. Sinhar Marduchk can be quite persuasive, and all is arranged. Why does he assume that you know everything, I could not say. As for me, I said nothing because I thought he explained."

"So, what are we waiting for?"

"We are waiting for tomorrow, when he is going to present you with a formal proposal."

"Heavens, how rigid your traditions, rules and regulations are... I suppose it is because you are such an ancient race. But also, he seemed apprehensive, if an Anunnaki can be said be nervous. What is it?"

"He did not exactly explain to me, but I suspect he is indeed apprehensive. He is probably not sure if you know how we are constructed, physically, and what our marriages are really like. I mean, of course you know about the Union, the mingling of lights, but are you aware that Anunnaki do not have sex organs like humans?"

"Of course I am aware of it. I saw a whole lot of little children swimming in the ponds, quite naked, when you took me to our swimming trips. I know exactly how you are constructed physically."

"Well, does it bother you?"

"Why should it? Miriam, the night before I left, your brother gave me a tiny sample of the mingling of lights. Nothing much, we just held hands and kept apart when he activated our lights, so it involved only the hands. That was all he thought would be appropriate and fair to my free will. So I respected that, but let me tell you, this slight touch was better, a million light years better, than any sexual activity we have on earth."

"So it would not hurt you in any way that as the centuries go by, and you become more and more an Anunnaki, you will lose the sex organs?"

"I would not bat an eyelash."

"You know, Victoria, I believe that your Anunnaki genes influence you considerably already."

"Quite possibly. Also, you must understand that single women in my world usually experiment with sex from their late teens and on. I had a couple of experiences in my twenties."

"Well, I must say I am glad Sinhar Marduchk is too ethical to have spied on you. He would not have enjoyed these experiments, I suspect."

"He might have been made rather happy about them, Miriam. They were nothing to me. Something inside me retained the memory of the mingling of lights with Marduchk, because I really did not like any of these men or what they tried to give me. Sex, as I told an old earth friend just before you brought me here again, is highly overrated... After experiencing the mingling of the lights, it is a minor thing indeed, a mere physical sensation at best. I don't have to tell you that the mingling of lights involves mind, body, and soul. Just don't tell that to Marduchk... he might feel I needed thirty more years to make sure my free will is intact, and I am *NOT* waiting to be sixty before I marry."

"Since I have never experienced sex in the earth way, or ever had sex organs, of course I can't tell the difference. The mingling of lights, to me, is highly spiritual. But do you know, Victoria, that your species is the only humanoid one in the known universes that has sex organs, which were given to you to match the animals and the plants on your planet? I personally think it was a mistake, it deprived you of true unity with your mates and created much frustration. No other species share this aberration. Anyway, I am so glad you feel this way, Victoria. I have looked upon you as my sister from the moment you came here the first time, and I would not want to lose you to the earthlings."

"You never will. I will grow and become more Anunnaki every day, and I, too, see you as my sister."

"I am so very happy about it. All of us love you, Victoria."

"I will always stay with you. And now that you explained Marduchk's bizarre behavior, I will not fret, and I will be as formal as any Anunnaki when he comes to take me to the library. But Miriam, there is something else on my mind."

"What is it?"

"Did you know Marduchk's previous wife?"

"No, of course not, she is in another universe which he has left. I see the problem, but Victoria, don't let such human concerns distress you. She is not his previous wife, she is married to another version, not to the Sinhar Marduchk you know."

"This business of multiple universes and duplicate versions is quite confusing."

"I know. We spend years in school, trying to internalize the concept."

"I wish I understood it better. There must be some master version, the one from which all the other versions are copied, right?"

"Exactly. You understand it better than you think. But we never meet the master version, only the copies."

"And Marduchk can remember his other versions, but he is separate from them."

"Right again. And they become remote after a while, each pursuing his or her own destiny and mission. Everyone has a mission, or a life work."

"Will I be given one, too?"

"All in good time. First, the marriage, then, a fabulous wedding trip, then, plenty of time to settle down with your husband, your new home, your extended family. When you are ready, you will know, and then you shall meet with the Council representatives and choose your mission."

"Choose? So it is not simply assigned?"

"Assigned? Of course not! Your are only asked to do what is a deep wish in your heart already. They will just help it develop and blossom. With us, Victoria, free will is everything. There is no exception to this rule, ever."

"Indeed, I can accept that. Marduchk is simply obsessed with it. I still can't get over the fact that he was willing to risk losing me because of it. That is almost frightening."

Miriam laughed. "Well, don't worry about it. True, tradition and free will are extremely important to him, but I am sure he will relax as soon as you are married and resume his loveable, if sometimes annoying, self."

In the morning, Marduchk came early. I was in the garden, waiting for him, while everyone else was still in their rooms. The morning was beautiful, butterflies fluttered in the dense flower beds and every tree was full of singing birds. The roses were blooming so intensely that their scent was incredibly strong. I felt that the occasion meant a lot to both of us, even if I had no idea what was to take place, so I dressed in a semi-formal fashion, and wore a long cream-colored dress with a beautiful red belt. Marduchk seemed to have had the same thought, since he, too, wore something that seemed more afternoon than morning to me. He was glad to see me up already and asked me to come to the library.

Inside, he approached a shelf, but instead of taking one of the usual conical books, he removed an ancient wooden box and brought it to one of the tables. Inside was a scroll that seemed ancient, probably hundreds, if not thousands of years old. "Is this Egyptian papyrus?" I asked.

"Yes, it is. A few thousand years ago, we had to copy the original manuscript. It lasted for eons, but finally it was beginning to crumble. We decided we wanted to make an exact replica, since it was so beautiful, rather than reproduce it on a cone, as many families do."

It was truly beautiful, written in a language I could not understand and illuminated with small, magical pictures, many of them seemingly some kind of symbols. I longed to touch it and see what the texture was, but I did not dare to do so.

"This is our marriage record book where all our marriages are kept. Now is the time to make your final decision, Victoria, if you can. Will you marry me?"

"Of course I will," I said, surprised. "Did you have any doubts about it?"

"I have to ask you formally, no matter what I think. It is part of the ceremony."

"Marduchk, I know nothing about it. Would you please explain to me what the ceremony is all about?"

"It has four parts. The first is a verbal consent and a statement of free will. The second is signing the marriage record. The third is the mingling of the lights. The fourth is a conclusive ceremony officiated by three representatives of the Council."

"And a party? With beautiful dresses, and music, and food?"

Marduchk laughed. "Of course," he said. "Right after the ceremony."

"Then let's get on with it, Marduchk! It's not all solemnity, you know, we should have some fun!" Marduchk smiled. "Indeed," he said. "We shall now continue, then. Let's start again. Will you marry me?"

"Yes, I will marry you, Marduchk."

"Are you certain, and ready to sign this book?"

"I am certain."

"Can you see, imagine, visualize, or even fantasize any other option than our marriage?"

"No, I cannot."

"And do you realize, that once you sign this book our union is irrevocable?"

"I realize that."

"Is anything other than complete free will is at all employed in your consent? Was any form of persuasion, coercion, promises, or any other such behavior employed on my part?"

"There is only free will."

Marduchk unrolled the scroll and picked up a writing implement from the table. It was shaped like a pen, but from previous experience, I knew it worked with energy, not ink. Nothing could erase it, ever. Under a text paragraph, he signed his name in the Anunnaki language. He then handed me the pen, and I signed my name, in plain English. To my surprise, each of our signatures, though done by the same pen, had a different color. And what's more, under my English signature appeared what seemed to be a translation into Anunnaki, but it kept my signature's color.

"Are we married now?" I asked.

"Yes, we are. For eternity." He seemed suddenly relaxed.

"And then, can I move to your house? Or do I stay at Miriam's house like a nice little virgin until the Council blesses me?"

"No, you move to my house. It is now your house, we are married."

"It's about time," I said, and we both laughed.

Everyone congratulated us when we came back to Miriam's living room. They were all there, waiting for us.

"And now we must take your things to your home," said Miriam, after a good breakfast, where everyone was relaxed, happy, and full of plans. "Would you believe your husband would not allow me to take your dresses, all the accessories my daughters designed, shoes, and all the jewelry, until after the marriage was accomplished? I knew you will stay, but he just won't allow it, tiresomely refereeing again to free will… but we will try to forget his annoying ways. We will take everything now, or teleport it, rather, into your closets. Come see all the stuff."

"He does stick to tradition," I said, following her out of the room.

"Ah, well," said Miriam with resignation. "We must accept the fact that all over the known universes, the female of the species is more realistic."

Marduchk heard us, and laughed. "Very true," he said. "Wait one second, Victoria. Once the ceremony and celebrations are all over, where would you like to go for our wedding trip?"

"Why, Paris, of course," I said. "Where else would one go for a honeymoon?"

"What a charming idea," said Miriam. "I was thinking about a planet on the Alpha Centauri system where so many people go for their wedding trips, but Paris will be very nice."

The wardrobe they prepared for me was so incredible, I had to gasp. Closet after closet, full with the most beautiful gowns for all occasions, from casual to formal. Entire shelves full of shoes in all colors, accessories that were everything from hair decorations to belts and scarves, and jewelry that can only be described as breath taking. "Later, we must decide on the wedding dress," said Miriam. "I have about six or seven for you to choose from."

After I could finally manage to tear myself away from the enchanting wardrobe, everything was quickly teleported without the slightest physical effort, and finally

Miriam and Marduchk took me to my new home to get settled. Marduchk's home, which, as I have explained before, was attached with a corridor to his sister's home, was just as beautiful and comfortable as Miriam's. I remembered it from my last visit, since of course I have seen it many times, but it turned out that the brother and sister decided to change everything and make it perfect for a new bride, more elegant, less masculine. The theme they decided upon was an indoor garden. The living room retained the structure of smooth levels and high ceiling, of course, but it was now filled to the brim with indoor roses, both bushes and trailing, and parts of the floor grew the softest, greenest grass where previously they were covered with carpets. Other trailing and hanging flowering plants undulated with the soft breeze that came from the opened windows, making the room look like a miniature magical forest. Tiny ponds, surrounded with ferns and supporting water lilies were on every level, and miniature waterfalls twinkled delicately as they softly fell into the ponds. Tall willow-like trees and bamboo grew behind the furniture. The couches were all covered with green and gold silk, and the red hibiscus flowers here and there completed the enchanting color scheme. This was the most beautiful room I have ever seen.

The dining room, the guest rooms, the bedrooms all followed the garden idea. Each guest room was decorated with a different flower theme, one of them all lilies of the valley like flowers, another one like an orchard of flowering plums and almonds. The bathrooms were small rainforests. Our bedroom was Zen like, with the bed in the middle and a few trees behind it and before it. A couple of small tables had each a vase with one white lily, and all the storage for clothes and beddings was hidden behind wooden screens. One large pond with papyrus growing right in it was placed in a corner, and was surrounded with gray, moss-covered rocks. It was a place of serenity and peace.

As Miriam and Marduchk were conducting the tour of the house, I simply could not stop admiring and exclaiming over everything. It felt to me like something of a childhood's dream or fairy tale. "I am so happy you like it," said Miriam. "After you live in it for awhile, you may want some changes, some things to make it more comfortable or more suitable for your personal taste. Nothing will be easier. You will tell me, and I'll teach you how to manipulate objects with your mind."

"For the moment, I don't want to even think of changes," I said enthusiastically. "What a place..."

"And now I must go and let you settle. Come for lunch tomorrow, and we'll choose the dress." She left and Marduchk and I were left in our home, finally married and alone in this green paradise. We were now free to bring about our Union and mingle our lights.

Marduchk stood up and said most formally, "Victoria, would you do me the honor of accomplishing our Union? This will be the third part of our marriage."

Tears came into my eyes. "Do you the honor, Marduchk? No, you are doing me the honor. You, and your family who accepted me as one of them, and the Council who is willing to bless our marriage despite the fact that I am, truly, a member of an inferior species. I am honored."

"You are not an inferior, Victoria. You are one of us in every way. You have been brought up on earth, and that changed a few things, but nothing fundamental. Your genetic makeup is ours, and most important, your spirit and your soul is ours. And the Council will prove it to you by honoring you, during the wedding ceremony, by giving you your very own Anunnaki name."

"The greatest honor is your wanting to marry me, Marduchk, waiting for me, and allowing me the centuries of learning and growing to be like you. And to answer your question, in the formal style that is needed, yes, I will now happily come with you and accomplish our Union."

There are certain things that cannot be described, things that human language has no words for, and I am afraid that the mingling of the lights is one of them. I can describe the physical procedure – and unlike human sexual behavior, there is nothing in the Union that is embarrassing or disturbing to even the most traditional and old-fashioned people, but the experience itself is impossible to relate.

We went into our bedroom, which traditionally had no windows. That is because it is not seemly to have the lights, which can be intense, be seen by people who may be walking in the gardens. We sat on the bed, and I said to Marduchk, "I have no idea how the lights are to be activated."

"You don't have to do anything, since the lights are not activated. They emanate from our beings, and just sitting here together will do it. Do you remember how the light grew around our hands, just before you left?"

"Of course I do," I said. I did not want to add that the experience lived in my mind, if unconsciously so, enough to make me come back to him. So I kept it to myself and smiled inwardly with complete happiness.

"Just sit near me, Victoria, close your eyes, and imagine the same light emanating from your entire body." I did as he said, and imagined golden light surrounding me like a soft, flowing veil. For a few minutes nothing happened, and then I felt a change and opened my eyes to see each of us surrounded by a bubble of the most brilliant light. The bubbles came together, touched each other exactly like floating soap bubbles do, and merged together into one glowing orb. The light grew stronger and stronger until the whole room was illuminated by undulating, flowing strands of light, a little like the strands that can be seen in the sky during the aurora borealis. And the sensations I felt were the incarnation of beauty, at once mental, physical, and spiritual, since it cannot be anything but a combination of the three, and it mounted and increased until the light exploded into a shower of stars and the Union was achieved.

And that is all I can really say, because as I said, human language is too limited. In Anunnaki, there are many words to describe the Union in all its aspects. I do want you to understand, though, I am doing my best. So if you can recall the most wonderful sexual experience you ever had, with someone for whom you had pure love and respect, perhaps you may have an inkling, but only that. I suspect that until humans evolve mentally, spiritually, and physically, until such time as they can shed all the negative traits of infidelity, jealousy, and fickleness, all they can have is a pale imitation of the Union. I hope that some day it will happen, because the Union, unlike human sexual relations, can only ennoble and enrich you, can never be negative, can never cause pain or embarrassment. It is the essence of purity and happiness.

After all was over, and we were resting on our bed, I told Marduchk that I remember smelling the scent of a certain flower I knew from my childhood, which grew only in the hothouses. Marduchk was sure it was part of the experience, and tried to understand which flower it was, but I forgot the name, and could not describe it to him adequately. So Marduchk smiled and said, "Well, make a shower of these flowers fall on us."

"Make a shower of flowers? Me? How do I do that? Don't you forget I am a mere human?"

"Having gone through the Union already started you on developing special powers. Just close your eyes, and imagine the flowers, as you remember them, falling on us like a steady rain from the ceiling. Make heaps and heaps of them."

I laughed at the idea, but to indulge him, I closed my eyes and imagined the flowers doing that. Suddenly I felt something landing on me softly, like a snowflake. I opened my eyes, and to my total amazement I saw a few flowers falling from the ceiling. White and yellow and smelling like an earthly paradise, the rain of flowers got thicker and thicker and they covered us with their scented petals. I was speechless with amazement at my new gifts and the impossibility of what I was creating, but Marduchk just picked up one flower and said in a total matter-of-fact way, as if no miracle had been taking place, "Oh, I see, Plumeria. Of course. I should have recognized them from your description; they grow here all over the place." I laughed. "What next?" I said. "Will I fly to one of the moons on my own silver wings?" Marduchk looked at me seriously and said, "Sure, if you like. There are no limits, really... wings are easy enough to make, any color you want." What a place, I thought, what a life... and I sank into a blissful sleep under the soft and warm blanket of the delicate while and yellow flowers.

*** *** ***

CHAPTER SIX
The Unthinkable Horrors

How I was taught the truth about alien abductions, saw a monstrous experiment, viewed a non-physical demonic dimension, and visited the horrific laboratory of the Grays.

We were going to our wedding trip in Paris in a few days. Marduchk had some business with the Council, regarding a new assignment which he planned to work on after our return, so I had a few days to settle down and prepare for the trip. But there was nothing to prepare, really, since everything was ready, packed, and arranged in the spaceship in a few minutes. Therefore, I decided to take Sinhar Inannaschamra at her word and make a little visit to the Academy. I asked her if it were convenient, while she was having dinner with us one evening, and she was delighted to oblige.

The next morning I went to the Academy. It was a huge, sprawling complex of buildings, all of them connected in the traditional Anunnaki architecture, and when I first saw it, during my previous visit, I remember thinking how amusing it was that even on another planet, places of higher education had the same look as our own universities. The gray stones, the ivy-like climbers, the winding walks among ancient trees. You simply could not mistake it for anything else but a place of learning. Sinhar Inannaschamra took me to her own office, which was a very pleasant library with thousands of conical books and desks cluttered with more cones and ancient manuscripts. The light that filtered through the climbers by the windows tinted the air with green, and soft armchairs made you wish you could settle for a good reading session that would last for hours.

Sinhar Inannaschamra was pleased with my admiration of her place. "Yes, I love working here," she said. "I cannot imagine myself working anywhere else. I have been here for ages, ever since I have decided on my mission, which in my case was teaching future generations about the history of the Anunnaki and its relationship to the universe. And the more I teach, the more I learn, and the more I realize how infinite is the field... which brings me to a question I really wanted to ask you but did not think, yesterday, that it was a topic for a dinner conversation. Did you devote some thoughts to your own future mission?"

"Not really," I said, a little embarrassed. "Miriam said I should not rush into it. She suggested I concentrate on the four parts of the ceremony, then the trip, then settle down for awhile, and only then start thinking about it."

"Oh, of course, there is no rush whatsoever," said Sinhar Inannaschamra. "I was thinking about it merely because if you have something in mind, I would start your studies by introducing you to it, rather than go randomly at various subjects."

"Well," I said, considering. "I know one thing. I am a beginner, a stranger, and rather young. I don't think I would do very well with species I am not familiar with, and I don't think I can feel comfortable, at this stage, with shape-changing. In addition, I have a very strong interest in the fate of the hybrid children on earth, considering that this was what I was asked to do when I had just started my relationship with the Anunnaki."

"Do you think, then, that you may be willing to work with the hybrid issue? Some of it is very nice, like your situation, because the Anunnaki treat the people they contact with utmost respect. But other species are not exactly like that. Some of it is even gruesome."

"I think I can only make such a decision if I am to know what really happens with the hybrids," I said. "Even if it is gruesome, I am aware that not everything I will encounter in my life here is wine and roses, even though it sometimes does seem like a paradise."

"You display an excellent attitude," said Sinhar Inannaschamra. "I am sure that if I show and tell you a few things, you will have a better base on which to form an idea and eventually to make a decision. The first thing we must talk about is the situation with the Grays."

"The small extraterrestrials with the bug eyes, right?" I said.

"Yes. They do not contact people like we do, on your planet. They abduct them. You are probably familiar with many stories that come from the people that they have abducted, but much of what these people say is inaccurate, and based upon mind control that the Grays exercise on them. I am going to tell you a bit, and then, if you feel up to it, we will take a short trip on my spaceship and visit one of their labs."

"Would they let you in? Aren't they dangerous?"

"Dangerous? Very. But not to an Anunnaki. We are much stronger and they are afraid of us. If I come to their place and demand to see a lab, I will see a lab. In addition, I want to show you a few things on a monitor. Some will be extremely unpleasant, but it cannot be avoided if you want to learn something."

"What do they want of us on earth?"

"There are a few things that they want. First, they want eggs from human women and use them to create hybrids. Let's take a look at this monitor, and I'll show you how they do that. But Victoria, steel yourself. This is pretty horrible, even though I have seen even worse. You will also be able to hear, it is like a television."

The monitor blinked and buzzed, and a small white dot appeared on the screen. It enlarged itself, moved back and forth, and settled into a window-like view of a huge room, but the view was still rather fuzzy. I heard horrendous screams and froze in my seat; these were sounds I have never heard before.

After a few minutes the view cleared and I saw what seemed to be a hospital room, but it was elliptical, not square. Only part of it was revealed, as it was elongated and the far edge was not visible. The walls on the side were moving back and forth, like some kind of a balloon that was being inflated and deflated periodically, with a motion that made me dizzy; they seemed sticky, even gooey. The room was full of operation tables, of which I could see perhaps forty or fifty, on which were stretched human beings, each attached to the table and unable to move, but obviously not sedated, since they were screaming or moaning. Everyone was attached to tubes, into which blood was pouring in huge quantities. I noticed that some of the blood was turning into a filthy green color, like rotting vegetation. At the time I could not understand what that was, but later that day I found out. This blood was converted to a suitable type for some of the aliens that paid the Grays to collect it, and it was not useful in its raw condition.

The creatures who operated these experiments were small and gray, and they had big bug eyes and pointy faces without any expression. I thought they looked more like insects than like a humanoid species. They wore no clothes, and their skin was shiny and moist, like that of an amphibian on earth. It visibly exuded beads of moisture which they did not bother to wipe away.

Each operating table had complicated machinery that was poised right on top of the person who was strapped to it. On some of the tables, the machinery was lowered so that needles could be extracted from them automatically, and the needles reached every part of the human bodies, faces, eyes, ears, genitals, stomach. The people screamed as they saw the needles approaching them, some of them fainted. Many of the people were already dead, I could swear to that. Others were still alive but barely so, and some had arms and legs amputated from their bodies. It was clear that once the experiment was over, every single person there would die.

I don't know how I could continue to look, but somehow I managed. I looked at the ceiling of this slaughter house and saw meat hooks, on which arms and legs and even heads were hanging, like a butcher's warehouse. On the side of the tables were large glass tanks where some organs were placed, possibly hearts, livers, or lungs, all preserved in liquids.

The workers seemed to be doing their job dispassionately and without any feelings, moving around like ants and making buzzing sounds at each other as they conversed. They were entirely business-like and devoid of emotion. At least, their huge bug eyes did not convey any emotion to me, neither did their expressionless faces.

I watched until I could no longer tolerate it, and finally covered my eyes and cried out, "Why don't you stop it? Why don't you interfere?"

Sinhar Inannaschamra turned the monitor off. "This event is a record from decades ago, Victoria. It is not happening now as we look. And even though often we do interfere, we cannot police the entire universe or even the entire earth. They know how to hide from us. And you must understand, that often the victims cooperate with their abductors."

"Why would they?"

"Basically, through mind control. The Grays have many ways to convince the victims. The Grays can enter the human mind quite easily, and they find what the abductees are feeling and thinking about various subjects. Then, they can either threaten them by various means, or persuade them by a promise of reward."

"Reward? What can they possibly offer?"

"Well, you see, they show the victims images through a monitor, just like this one. They tell them that they can send them through a gate, which is controlled by the monitor, to any number of universes, both physical and non-physical. That is where the rewards come in. For example, if the abductees had originally reacted well to images of Mary or Jesus, the Grays can promise them the joy of the non-physical dimensions. They show them images of a place where Mary and Jesus reside, where all the saints or favorite prophets live, and even the abode of God. They promise the abductees that if they cooperate, they could live in this non-physical universe in perpetual happiness with their deities. Many fall for that."

"And if they resist?"

"Then they show them the non-physical alternative, which is Hell. Would you like to see some of it?"

"You can show me Hell?" I asked, amazed.

"No, there is no such thing as Hell… it's a myth that religions often exploited. But I can show you what the Grays show the abductees, pretending it is Hell; they are quite devious, you know. You see, some creatures live in different dimensions, where our laws do not apply. Sometimes, they escape to other dimensions. These beings have no substance in their new dimensions, and they need

130

some kind of bodies to function. At the same time, the Grays can tap into numerous universes, because they can control their own molecules to make them move and navigate through any dimension. Well, a cosmic trade had been developed. The Grays supply the substance taken from human abductees, and from the blood of cattle. You must have heard of cattle mutilation, where carcasses of cows are found in the fields, entirely drained of blood? The Grays do it for their customers."

"How do these creatures pay the Grays?"

"By various services. Once they get their substance, they are incredibly powerful in a physical sense. The old tales of genies who can lift buildings and fly with them through the air were based on these demons; the Grays often have a use for such services. But let me show you a few of these creatures. Of course, you can only see them when they have already acquired some substance from the Grays."

The monitor hummed again as Sinhar Inannaschamra turned it on. The white dot expanded into its window, which now, for some reason, was larger and took over the entire screen. All I could see was white fog with swirls floating through it. Sometimes the fog changed from white to gray, then to white again. I started hearing moans. Not screams, nothing that suggested the kind of physical pain I saw before, but perhaps just as horrible, since they voices where those of hopelessness, despair, and emotional anguish. Every so often I heard a sound that suggested a banshee's wail, or keen, as described in Irish folklore.

"It will take a while for someone to show up," said Sinhar Inannaschamra. "Most of them have no substance, and therefore they are invisible. Others have a shadowy substance. Then, there are the others… but you will see in a

131

minute. Once they notice they are being watched, they will flock to the area, since they are desperate to get out. Incidentally, it was never made quite clear to me how they produce sounds without bodies, we are still trying to find out what the mechanics are, but it's not easy, because we would rather not go there in person."

"They sound horribly sad," I said.

"This is what makes it so Hell-like. In many cultures, Hell never had any fire and brimstone and tormenting devils, but rather, it was a place of acute loneliness, lack of substance, and alienation from anything that could sustain the individual from a spiritual point of view. Think of the Greek Hades, or the ancient Hebrew Sheol, before the Jews made their Hell more like the Christian one. Look, here comes the first creature. Poor thing, he is a shadow."

I saw a vaguely humanoid shape in deep gray. It seemed to have arms, which it waved in our direction. It was fully aware of the monitor. Then another shadow, then another, all shoving each other and waving desperately at the monitor. Then something more substantial came into view, and I jumped back as if it could reach me. It seemed to be a severed arm. Cautiously, I came back, and then saw that the arm was attached to a shadow body. I looked at Sinhar Inannaschamra, speechless, and she said, "Yes, here you see one that managed to receive an arm. It wants to complete its body, of course, so that it can get out of this dimension and serve the Grays, but the Grays keep them waiting until they want them."

More and more came, clamoring for attention. "Do they think we are Grays?" I asked.

"Yes, they do. They can't tell the difference, all they know is that they are watched, and they try to get the attention of the watchers. It's incredibly cruel, but if you feel for them, which I still do, remember that at the same time they become murderous, cruel creatures themselves as soon as they escape their dimension and join the Grays."

Another half thing came into view. It had eyes stuck in the middle of a half-formed face, each eye different. The face seemed mutilated, somehow, until I realized it had no nose and no chin. Floating heads, arms, legs, torsos – they all jostled in front of the monitor, each more horrible than the other. And then I saw the worst thing imaginable.

"Sinhar Inannaschamra!" I screamed. "This is a baby's head! A floating baby's head! What in the world it is attached to?"

"Another shadow," said Sinhar Inannaschamra. "They don't care what age the substance comes from. Sometime the babies' heads or limbs get attached to big adult bodies."

"They use babies," I said, sobbing. "Babies…"

"Yes, this is the kind of creatures we have to tolerate," said Sinhar Inannaschamra sadly. She looked at me and realized I could not take any more of this Hell, and so turned off the monitor.

"This was something," I said, shivering and trying to recover.

"Indeed," said Sinhar Inannaschamra. "So you see, they can easily show them horrific pictures of Hell, enough to frighten them to such an extent, that they are sure to obey. Interestingly, the abductees, under such threats, often develop physical, psychosomatic effect in the form of scratches, burns, or even stigmata, on parts of their bodies. Of course, sometimes the Grays burn them with laser beams as a form of punishment or of persuasion, and sometimes the wounds are produced simply by the radioactive rays emanating from the spaceship, like what sometimes happens in nuclear plants on earth, or during

133

nuclear explosions. But most often it is the mind reacting to the image."

"How horrible…" I said weakly.

"It gets worse," said Sinhar Inannaschamra. "They can show them the physical universe as well. They would project, on screen, well-known events that occurred during times in which humanity was utterly cruel, or when war, famines, and plagues ravished the earth. They might show them the Crusades, or Attila the Hun, or the Nazi concentration camps, or the famine in Ireland, or the black plague in Europe, and threaten them that they can open a gate through the monitor, and abandon them there for the rest of their lives."

"The poor things. No wonder they obey," I said.

"Yes, you see, the Anunnaki tell you the truth when they contact you. They let you know that they cannot change the past, nor can they interfere with the future. But the Grays lie. They tell the abductees that they can change events in the past, from day one, and that they could project and change life at two, five, or ten thousand years in the future of humanity."

"I wish you would just wipe them of the face of the universe," I said.

"We don't do such things. Some of us recommend it, but we just don't. Anyway, they have other systems of persuasion. Some women have a very strong reaction to the images of children. The Grays catch it, of course, and then they tell the women that they have been abducted before, years ago, and were impregnated by the Grays. Then they show them a hybrid child and tell them that this is their own child. Many of the abductees who are thus psychologically influenced fall into a pathological attachment to the hybrid child. Then the Grays tell them that if they don't fully cooperate, they will take the child away. The woman cooperates, the experiment takes place, and then the Grays make them forget the child and place them back in their beds at home. Usually, some vague memory remains, since the Grays don't care about the well being of their victims and don't bother to check if the memory is completely cleaned out."

"But it is not really their child?"

"Sometimes it is, sometimes it isn't. You must realize that normal impregnation and the nine months of carrying the baby does not occur. The Grays take the eggs out of the woman, the way you just saw it on the monitor, put them in a tube, fertilize it by an electric or sometimes atomic way, and the hybrid grows in the tube until it is of term. No woman has ever given birth to a hybrid."

"This is beyond words," I said. "And I thought most of the extraterrestrials would be like you."

"There are many species," said Sinhar Inannaschamra. There are those humans call 'The Nordic,' they look and behave much like humans, they are rather kindly, and other kinds are reasonable as well. But there are a lot of horrible species. The closer any species get to the demonic dimension, and particularly if they trade with them, the worse they become. Some look reptilian, some insect-like. Some eat human beings and other sentient species, in what we see as almost cannibalistic behavior. Some make sacrifices of sentient beings to their deities. The reptilians have a specialized digestive system. They don't eat solid food, but only suck blood through pores in their fingers. That is why some researchers on earth connect the extraterrestrials with vampirism. The Grays sell them cattle blood, since the reptilians don't particularly care where the blood comes from. But anyway, are you ready for your field trip? Let's go and visit a Grays' lab."

I thought I was ready. I thought I was tough. But what I saw on this field trip would remain with me for eons.

Sinhar Inannaschamra took me to her spaceship, and informed me that the trip would be very short. She had been to this lab before, and knew the conditions very well. Just before we landed, she pulled out a suit that was needed to protect me from any radiation. Apparently, for this trip, she needed no protection herself, but she could not tell as yet if I could tolerate such conditions or not, due to my human existence for the last thirty years. The suit was made of lightweight, soft metallic material that was actually rather comfortable and moved easily with me. Then, I put on a helmet, which was entirely transparent and allowed me perfect vision.

We landed on a bleak field covered with some material that looked much like cement, gray and unpleasant, but with a smoother finish. Right before us was a huge building which looked like an ugly airport hangar, completely utilitarian without any ornamentation. The entire area around it was an empty prairie-like field with stunted, grayish vegetation, stretching into the horizon without any feature like a mountain or a city. The sky was gray but without clouds. We walked to a large door, tightly closed and made of metal.

Sinhar Inannaschamra put her hand on it, and it slid immediately to the side and allowed us to come in. "They know my hand print," she said to me. We entered a small hall, empty of any furniture, and from there, a door opened into a long corridor, brightly lit and painted white. On each side there were doors, also painted white, all closed, and it was entirely empty of any occupants. Sinhar Inannaschamra lead the way to one of the doors, and again placed her hand on it. The door slid open silently, and we entered an enormous room. It was so huge that I could not see the end of it, and had gray walls and a white ceiling. Round, bright lights of large circumference were placed in the ceiling, emanating a very strong illumination. The impression the room gave was that of a hospital ward, or a surgical hall, but there were no beds or operation tables, only large tanks containing some objects I could not as yet see. And while the place was scrupulously clean, the smell was nightmarish. I recognized the stench of formaldehyde, mingled with some other malodorous liquids. I was surprised I could smell anything through the helmet, but Sinhar Inannaschamra explained that they deliberately made the suits and the helmets allow as much interaction with the environment as possible.

"It smells like that because this is the warehouse, where they keep all the spare parts," said Sinhar Inannaschamra. "Come, look at this tank."

We approached an enormous tank, transparent in the front parts and increasingly opaque as it extended further into the room. Inside floated a large number of severed arms and legs, all human. I recoiled in horror, but quickly recovered. We went to the next tank. It was arranged in the same manner, but inside floated severed heads and torsos. And so it went on, each tank filled with body parts, some even with full bodies. Smaller containers had interior organs, such as livers, hearts, and some others I was not sure of. In addition, there were containers of blood, some red, some green. I already knew that the green blood became like that after preparation for sale to species that needed the adjustments.

Suddenly I heard sounds of conversation, as if a group of people were approaching us from somewhere. The sounds were in a language I could not understand, and uttered in a metallic, screeching way that was almost mechanical. To me, it sounded demonic and inhuman. A group of five Grays approached us. After what I have seen on the monitor, I was about to escape in terror, but the group bowed to Sinhar Inannaschamra, and went on about their business. One of them approached a tank. He looked at what seemed to be a chart, like a hospital chart but in a language I could not understand, that was positioned above the tank, and just stared at it for a short while. A line on the chart lit up, and some equipment that was build above the tank came down, entered the tank, and using a robotic hand pulled out a specimen and placed it in a tube, along with some of the liquid. Then the robotic hand came up, moved forward, and handed the tube to the Gray. The Gray took the tube, looked at the chart, and the robotic hand withdrew.

The Gray took the tube to a wall and placed the tube against it. To my amazement, the wall sort of swallowed the tube and it disappeared. I looked at Sinhar Inannaschamra for explanation, and she said, "The walls are not solid. They look solid, of course, but really they are constructed of energy. The Grays can move things back and forth, and even pass through it themselves. Some of the walls contain drawers, where they place equipment."

The other Grays were all communicating among themselves in their demonic language, mostly ignoring us. "Let's go to the next room, where I can show you what they do with their specimens," said Sinhar Inannaschamra. We went to the wall and she put her hand on it while holding me with her other hand, and I found myself passing through the wall as if it was made of thick molasses.

The room we entered was designed just like the others, architecturally, but had work tables instead of tanks and containers. Hundreds of Grays stood there, each at his table, doing things to the limbs, torsos, and blood. The smell of formaldehyde was so intense that I almost fainted. "Here," said Sinhar Inannaschamra. "Let me adjust the helmet so you don't have to smell the liquid." She did something at the back of the helmet, and I felt better.

"And now, let's go to the area where they fit the spare parts on the creatures I have shown you, the ones that want to buy substance," said Sinhar Inannaschamra.

We stepped into a third room, again through the wall, and this was a much smaller room. On the walls, there were a number of monitors, just like the ones in Sinhar Inannaschamra's office, but much larger. Before each monitor stood a Gray. We walked to one of them, and the Gray bowed to Sinhar Inannaschamra, and returned to his work. The Gray adjusted something, and a swirling shadow attached to one leg appeared on the screen. Behind him were numerous other shadows, but the Gray managed to separate the first creature from the others with some walls of energy that looked like white fog. The creature waved desperately at the Gray, who had before him a torso in liquid. A large robotic hand came from above the monitor, picked up the torso, and allowed the liquid to drain into its container. Then, he passed the torso through the screen, which now I realized was made of energy, like the wall, and placed it on the shadow. The shadow shivered, as if in pain, and I heard a deep moan or sigh, as the torso attached itself to the swirling gray form. I had a glimpse of a shadowy face, contorted in agony, but whether it was physical or mental pain I did not know. The shadow seemed utterly exhausted by the bizarre procedure, and floated away.

"What will happen to it now?" I asked.

"It will be back again and again, and when the Gray decide, they will give it more parts, allowing it to adjust and become more substantial."

139

"Are there any of them ready to leave and serve the Grays?"

"Yes, but I think this would be too dangerous to visit in person. The demonic creatures don't have the restraints the Grays have, regarding the Anunnaki, and often they are too stupid and just lash out as soon as they are brought into our dimension. Their transport, therefore, is done in a different part of the lab, under tremendous precautions. Besides, we don't want to stay much longer, since I think you had seen enough for one day…" I could not agree with her more, and we retraced our steps back to the spaceship.

"Some time I will show you how the creatures are taken out and put to service," said Sinhar Inannaschamra. "Only not in person." This sounded good to me. I was already so shaken from my day's adventures, I did not think I could take much more instruction, nor did I have a wish to meet such creatures in person. But, of course, I knew that one day I would have to do exactly that.

*** *** ***

CHAPTER SEVEN
The Wedding Ceremony

How I encountered and learned about shape-shifting, and
all about the fourth part of my wedding ceremony.

In the middle of the night I suddenly woke up. Even
thought the room had no windows, it was not totally dark,
since the nights on Nibiru always maintain a soft dusk-like
illumination, and the large door between our bedroom and
the room next to it was wide open. During our Union, the
door was closed for the sake of discretion, so I figured
Marduchk must have opened it; the Anunnaki are very fond
of fresh air. I moved around, preparing to go back to sleep,
when something caught my attention.

A huge mirror that decorated one of the walls
reflected something red. I looked at it and froze in terror.
Two orbs of bright red light were reflected in the mirror;
they seemed to glare at me. I could swear these were eyes.
What sort of horror entered our room? What kind of
monster lived on Nibiru that no one has ever mentioned to
me?

Trembling with fear, I extended my hand over to
awaken Marduchk. He was not there. Here I was, totally
alone on another planet, with some creature with red eyes
in my bedroom. And where was Marduchk? Naturally I
imagined the worst, and decided that the creature ate
Marduchk. But then I thought that an Anunnaki would not
allow himself to be eaten so easily. Probably he went to the
garden before the creature gained access. All the Anunnaki
are light sleepers, and they often love to walk in the

moonlight. Marduchk was probably quite safe, but I was about to die.

As I began to get adjusted to the dusk, and I saw a shape that made me even more afraid, if that was possible. What became visible was huge form, hunched and heavy-shouldered like an oversized gorilla. He was at least seven feet tall. The creature was looking at itself in the mirror and doing some strange movements that convinced me it was a sort of ape. It bent over and touched its knees, which were bent, then straightened up and shook its head from side to side, as if admiring himself. Then, he tapped his chest like a gorilla from an old Tarzan movie, and danced about. I heard it cough, then growl softly.

I simply could not move and had no idea what to do. Obviously, I could not get out of bed and run to the garden, since the creature was between me and the door. Staying in bed seemed the only option, perhaps pretending to sleep, so the creature would not be disturbed. But then, my plans came to nothing because the creature turned away from the mirror and started ambling toward the bed, still growling softly to itself. As it moved toward me my control broke down and I screamed, shutting my eyes as tight as I could so as not to see the face of this thing.

"Victoria, it's me, it's all right!" I heard Marduchk's voice. Where did he come from? I thought, forcing myself to open my eyes, shivering with terror. "Victoria, it's me, I am just practicing for my new assignment!" All the lights were turned suddenly on, and I saw the revolting creature, all covered with dirty brown hair and with the face of an ape, as I suspected, and talking to me with Marduchk's voice! I could not talk, and watched with horror as the creature started to change his shape, his eyes turning from red to black, his fur disappearing, and slowly turn into the form of my husband.

"I am so sorry," he said, looking distraught. "I thought you were asleep, and I was wide awake, so I figured I'd try to shape-shift into the form of the people on my new mission."

I found my voice. "In the bedroom? In the dark? You turn into a monster? If I told your sister you did that, what would she say?"

"She would be furious... I know... I seem to make it into a habit, frightening you with my shape-shifting, like what I did when we met. I may be a member of an intelligent race, but sometimes I act like an Igigi... I truly apologize."

"Ah, well," I said resignedly. "I might as well get used to monsters in my bedroom. What are those things, anyway?"

"Believe it or not, they are the nicest people. These ape-like creatures are kind, enlightened, compassionate, and highly intelligent in a non-technological kind of way. Highly intellectual but without physics or chemistry, and very little mathematics. They read long epics to pass the time, and sing songs without a tune. We love them, and now they are threatened by a very technological species from a different planet, who apparently have discovered some metals that they could use on the apes' planet. The usual story. I will have to go there and tweak their history a bit in preparation for a better technological approach that would allow them to defend themselves against those would-be invaders."

"Will you encounter any danger?"

"None whatsoever."

"I am glad you can help them, then. Well, what now? It's the middle of the night and both of us are wide awake."

"Let's go for a walk in the garden. The moons are glorious at this time of night."

"Great idea," I said. "Would you kindly manifest some cappuccino?"

"Consider it done."

We took our cups and walked out. The garden was enchanting indeed, all the white flowers were opened and the white moths fluttered from flower to flower.

"Tomorrow I am to choose the wedding dress," I said to Marduchk. "Miriam said she had six or seven to choose from."

"Yes," said Marduchk. "The girls were creating and manifesting any number of things. They were so excited about the wedding. It should be a very nice ceremony, you will love it, and a huge number of people will attend it, not to mention the reception afterwards."

"I can't wait."

Choosing the wedding dress was not an easy task. All seven dresses were so gorgeous I simply did not know what to do. Finally, with the help of Miriam and her daughters, and emotionally strengthened by the promise that I could keep all the dresses and wear them for important occasions, the wedding dress was chosen. The Anunnaki brides don't wear white to weddings, incidentally, but rather ornate and rich colors. The dress was made of heavy silk that started out being deep cherry red, but would change colors according to the person who was near it, and I thought it would make quite a sensation as I walked down the isle, and the dress would take on the hues that matched the people sitting next to it. It was designed like a Renaissance dress, with long, flowing sleeves and tight around the waist, a style that was the latest fashion on Nibiru. The trimming was gold, and I was to wear heavy gold jewelry around my neck and in my ears, and gold satin shoes. Marduchk was to wear a suit consisting of pants and tunic of the same color, deep saffron-gold. This type of suit was the formal male wear on Nibiru, but again in different colors.

I was told that all was ready, the Council representatives chose the date, and in a couple of days I found myself dressed and ready. To get to the Assembly Hall, which was at some distance, no one teleported but chose the ancient way of traveling by the beautiful canals, using highly decorated gondola-style boats, each accommodating six to eight people. There was no need to row, of course, the Anunnaki moved the boats with their minds, but it looked traditional and rather enchanting. The boats came from all sides, and when our boat reached the Assembly Hall a large crowd was already sitting inside the enormous room. We waited a few minutes under a canopy of flowering wisteria, and everyone settled in their seats.

I have mentioned before that cats were highly regarded on Nibiru, and could converse with their people. I did not know until that day that they would accompany us to the wedding, but when I found out, I was very happy about it. Many other people brought their cats, too, and they were sitting sedately next to their people, watching everything with their huge, intelligent eyes. As we walked into the Assembly Hall, the three family cats walked first, and then came Miriam's daughters, carrying flowers. Then came Miriam and Sinhar Inlimekach. After them came Sinhar Inannaschamra with her husband, Sinhar BaalNippur. All of them stood near the front of the Assembly Hall, near a large podium that was as yet empty. Marduchk and I followed, and indeed I was pleased to see that my robe changed colors from one row of guests to another. It moved subtly from red to blue, gold, green,

145

looking more wonderful all the time. As we were walking, roses were raining on the audience and accumulating on the floor, just like the Plumeria rain I produced after our Union.

As soon as we approached the podium, three individuals suddenly materialized on it. I was so startled I wanted to scream, but I controlled myself and wondered why Miriam did not mention it. Then I remembered, that of course she would assume that Marduchk would tell me, and of course he would forget that I did not know... as usual. Ah well, I thought, and forgave him because he looked so devastatingly handsome in his saffron-gold suit. The three individuals were dressed in long white robes, beautifully decorated in silver, and as their faces were covered with translucent white veils, I was not sure who was male and who was female. They greeted us by bowing their heads toward us, and the ceremony began.

The ceremony was conducted in the Anunnaki language, which I did not understand yet, but a few words in Aramaic here and there, or what seemed close to Aramaic, made it more pleasant and familiar. Each of the three individuals said his or her piece in a sing-song voice. In a way, the whole thing was not too different from the churches I have been familiar with all my life. It made me think how closely humans resemble the Anunnaki, after all. The ceremony continued by Marduchk putting a ring on my finger, a heavy gold ring set with a magnificent ruby, very different from the wedding bands we use on earth. I have been wearing it ever since. Then, the three individuals chanted in unison: Sinhar Ambar-Anati! Sinhar Ambar-Anati! Sinhar Ambar-Anati! The whole room clapped their hands joyfully, and I realized that this was the final acceptance, that they have bestowed upon me my Anunnaki name. I was now one of them, for ever, and the fourth part of the marriage had been accomplished.

146

The three individuals dematerialized, and I have no idea if they returned to their own abode or decided to remove the white robes and veils and mingle with the guests. I rather suspect that they mingled, since the party was spectacular. We all boarded our boats again, and traveled, under the willows that so gracefully grew near the canals, to our home, where Miriam had prepared a feast the likes of which I have never seen before. It took no effort, she told me, since all was done in the mind, but it certainly took a sense of beauty and sumptuous hospitality. The party lasted the whole afternoon and very late into the night, and included dancing to the stately Anunnaki music, which really fitted the Renaissance fashions very well. The tall, handsome, and elegant Anunnaki, all young, all graceful, presented a scene which cannot be done justice to in describing it. The cats, who came with their humans, were invited to partake of their own special foods which were arranged on low tables for their convenience. Many of them came to congratulate me, and after saying what they had to say in their interesting language, also emphasized their approval by rubbing against my legs in the eternal cat fashion, making it clear that a little ear scratching would be well-received under the happy circumstances. The little children formed circles with their own special type of dancing, and looked like fairies from the old folktales I used to love. It was the most beautiful gathering I have ever witnessed and I enjoyed it tremendously. And all the while the inner joy of knowing that I was married to Marduchk for ever never quite left my thoughts. I had the first sense of what eternity was all about.

*** *** ***

CHAPTER EIGHT
Honeymoon at the Domain of the Dead

> About how a charming wedding trip to Paris can end up in one of the most frightening underground places on earth, about experiencing alien spirit possession, and learning something new and unexpected about my husband.

May 1977, Paris

Having lost my sense of time on Nibiru, I didn't know if Marduchk made a deliberate landing in spring, tweaking time for the purpose, nor did I care. All I knew was that we landed in a city full of blooming chestnut trees, and every store window was decorated with lilies of the valley and violets. The whole place was permeated by their scent, which to me will always embody spring. But in truth there was no need to tweak anything – nothing is as perfect as Paris in May.

One morning we were sitting in a little café, ready to order breakfast and plan the activities for the day. We have already done many wonderful things, such as going on top of the Eiffel Tower (by teleportation, of course, since Marduchk did not believe in standing in line), strolled over the Champs-Élysées, and spent an entire day of splendor in the Louvre.

"How about Malmaison?" I asked. "I always wanted to see Joséphine's roses; I heard many of the existing plants are still related to her own flowers."

"Not really," said Marduchk. "It would be better if I took you to Malmaison during Joséphine's real time, don't you think? You can see the real thing. It was quite a garden in her time, and she could show you yourself."

"Sure, I would like that."

"But I have another, rather interesting idea for today, let's see what you think," said Marduchk. "When you get into your studies at the Academy, you will have to pass three tests as time goes by. One of these tests takes place right here in Paris, and I have a feeling you can pass it with ease. Why not give you a head start and see how you do? It's a fascinating place anyway."

"But what if I don't pass the test? After all, I did not do any real studies yet."

"Oh, it would not matter one bit," said Marduchk. "If you don't pass this time, you can always have another chance later."

"Then sure, I would love to try!" I said, getting into the spirit of the thing. "What is it?"

"It's the Paris Catacombs. Have you heard of them? Miles of catacombs under the city, and a big part of them is lined with bones and skulls."

"Sounds creepy," I said.

"Yes, it is, but it does have a certain grim beauty. They are extremely old, even older than many people suspect."

"How were they created?"

"When the Romans were here, they quarried for limestone under the city, and left a huge system of underground passages. Many bodies were tossed there for burial for centuries, including some by the Knights Templar, but the real thing started in the late eighteenth century. The city was overcrowded and filthy, the high level of disease brought on early death for many of the inhabitants, and in short, the cemeteries became so crowded it was impossible to give anyone a proper burial. The area around the cemeteries actually smelled, the air was poisonous."

"How revolting," I said.

"Yes, people could not keep milk and wine from spoiling, can you believe it? And then disaster struck, and the cemetery of Les Innocents collapsed under its dead in 1780. Homes were destroyed, people were killed, and finally the authorities decided to evacuate the cemetery and dispose of the dead elsewhere."

"So they brought them into the catacombs. Good idea, I would say."

"Right. Starting in 1786, the disinterment and removal took over fifteen months, the area, of course, being first consecrated by the Church. Other cemeteries followed, and over the next decades millions of bodies, or rather the bones, were transferred. Many people who were executed during the French revolution found their way there, by the way. And we also know that Lavoisier, Montesquieu, and Madame de Pompadour were taken there."

"And you can visit?"

"Over the years, sometimes it was permitted, sometimes it was forbidden, and sometimes only parts were allowed to be explored, since people did get lost and died there, and sometimes parts of it collapsed. We can go in these days, in a limited fashion, but of course I can go anywhere we want. We should be perfectly safe if we touch nothing."

"And what is the test?"

"You will have to look at these thousands of skulls, and identify, by visual contact only, at least two ancient Anunnaki skulls," said Marduchk, looking over his shoulder for the waiter. We had tried to get the waiter's attention without success for quite a long time.

"But Anunnakis' bone structure is not that much different from humans' bone structure," I said. "How am I supposed to recognize them? Are there some clues?"

"Yes, you will get some subtle signs, but they must be strictly visual. You are not to touch any of the skulls."

"You bet I won't touch them, Marduchk. They may have the world's worst germs on them after all those years in the damp catacombs."

"Germs, yes, and worse things as well," said Marduchk casually. "You know, Victoria, I am tired of waiting for this waiter. What will you have?"

"I would like some café-au-lait and a croissant," I said, assuming that Marduchk intended to go to the counter and order. I should have known better. Marduchk simply materialized two steaming cups of café-au-lait and a basket of croissants. I laughed and started eating. Half way through our breakfast, the waiter came to our table, and looked, confused, at the food. The cups and the basket were identical to those on the other tables, but he knew perfectly well that he did not bring them. I waited patiently for development, and sipped my coffee. Of course, I took a quick cone-book lesson in French before we came, so I was just as fluent in French as Marduchk, and I was ready to enjoy the scene.

"We are not quite ready to pay," said Marduchk innocently. "May we have two more cups?"

"But monsieur, where did these cups come from? I am the only waiter here this morning, unfortunately, and I did not speak to you, or to madame…" He seemed bewildered.

"Well," said Marduchk, considering, "they did not come out of thin air, did they? You must have brought them. And we waited a long time for them, too…"

"But…"

"So, if no one brought them, then we don't have to pay for them or leave tip, do we?"

On hearing the word "tip" the waiter gave up. "I am desolated you had to wait, Monsieur. I'll bring more coffee right away…" he scurried off.

"Poor boy," said Marduchk, laughing. "I must leave him a very generous tip to compensate for this harassment."

We went out and quietly teleported to the entrance of the catacombs. One of the entrances has a charming sign saying, "Stop! This is the Empire of Death!"

We went down a long spiral staircase, deep into the earth. The corridor leading down felt like a mine, and smelled dank and musty. The walls dripped occasionally, and the water disappeared into invisible holes. The place was so silent that the only thing you could hear were these rivulets of water. No one else was in sight, and the lights were dim. And then the walls of bones came into view, miles and miles of very orderly bones stacked very high on top of each other. There were femurs, neatly arranged, and some other bones which I could not recognize, and the skulls were artistically arranged between all that, sometimes with a weird pattern, like a heart or a cross or an arch. I could see miles of bones, stacked very high.

Side corridors were barred by chains. It would not have occurred to me to cross such a barrier, but Marduchk simply removed one chain, stepped into the dark and forbidding corridor, and said, "Yes, this is the one. I can sense the test at the very far corner. Let's go in there."

I don't know why I was not terrified, perhaps because it was so interesting, or perhaps something deeper than that spoke to a similar thing in my soul. I found the place grimly fascinating. And what I really wanted was to see if I could pass the test, whatever it was.

"Okay, enough fun and games," I said. "Let's get serious and start with the test." I stood for a moment, considering what was expected of me, and suddenly I knew exactly what I needed to do. I started looking at the skulls in a slightly different way, not staring at them directly, but rather looking at them in an oblique angle. I had no idea why I was doing it that way, but I suppose I had this knowledge instinctively through the Anunnaki part of my DNA. For a while, however, I saw nothing unusual.

"Who are these Anunnaki I am looking for?" I asked, hoping for a clue.

"They are a very low rank of Anunnaki, vicious creatures," said Marduchk, "and very, very ancient. Even when they have departed from these bones, there is still a residue, a connection between their souls and the skulls, which is why you should not touch them, but at the same time this connection would give you the clue you need."

I went on looking, moving slowly from one set of bones to another. After a long walk which began to tire me out, I suddenly saw a faint red light coming from a short distance away. I walked toward it, trying to control my excitement. Marduchk was following right behind me, but I did not want to say anything, wishing to be certain of my findings first. I approached the red light and again, looked at it obliquely, avoiding a direct stare. The light became stronger. It came from a square where about five or six skulls were jammed together. I turned my head away, to clear my vision, then glanced sideways, to see that the light became very strong, emanating from the empty eye sockets of one of the skulls.

I was so excited I forgot everything, and shouting "I got it!" grabbed the skull with my hand.

"Victoria, don't!" Marduchk cried, "don't touch!" but it was too late. My hand was resting squarely on the skull, the light shining between my spread out fingers. I hastily drew my hand away, and the light died. I looked at

Marduchk with apprehension, and to my horror, his face showed fear, even despair.

"Let's go back to the hotel," he said, and grabbing my elbow, teleported us right into our room. We stood in the middle of the room, looking at each other without word.

"I am going to talk to the hotel manager, Victoria, and settle the bill. We must return to Nibiru immediately." I shook my head silently. "Don't do a thing until I come back. This is an extremely dangerous situation."

I sat on the bed, too weak to pack by hand, and not as yet able to do the neat teleporting-style packing that the Anunnaki could achieve so easily. My head was splitting with pain and fear. I knew Marduchk was in a desperate hurry, but I wished he would have explained to me what I had to expect. He said not to do a thing. Well, I won't do anything, but if I could just take a shower and relax under the warm water, I would certainly feel better. I got up and went into the bathroom, and started up the shower so it would heat up properly when I got in. Like most European showers, the water took a few minutes to heat. As I tried to withdraw my hand from the faucet, it got wet, and suddenly I could not move it and the water continued to pound it, wetting my hand and my arm and my sleeve. I could not move. The water became bright orange-red and shone as if electricity was going through it. I tried to scream but could not open my mouth. The bath was filling as the water came too fast for it to drain properly, and suddenly a huge figure materialized in an instant before my eyes. I have never seen such an evil face. Even the horrendous Grays at their lab did not reach such heights of viciousness in their looks. He was well over eight feet tall, powerfully built, and wore a long robe that was tied around his waist, of the same red-orange color. The monster laughed at me, and his teeth were as red as his eyes in his enormous face.

155

At this minute Marduchk came into the room to witness the scene. In an instant, he jumped next to us and pulled a small object from his pocket, directing it toward the monster. But the creature was holding me tightly, and whatever Marduchk would do, he knew he would hit me as well. I could see the helplessness on Marduchk's face; the ancient Anunnaki was stronger than him and more cunning, and I was his hostage. With another triumphant laugh, he grabbed me by the neck with his other hand, causing me great pain, and somehow the pain broke the paralysis and I screamed loudly. The monster dragged me into the shower and violently threw me on the bottom, and as I touched the water I fainted.

I don't know how long I was unconscious, I never really found out, but I suspect time did not really play a part here. I woke up to find myself in a small tight room, all alone; it was bare and dark, and neither the monster nor Marduchk were to be seen. I started running from one wall to another, trying to find a door, a window, an opening of any sort. There were none. To say that I panicked is an understatement. I screamed until I was hoarse and then sat on the floor and started shaking, attempting to accept death as inevitable. I was not even sure how long the oxygen would last in this box. And at that moment Marduchk passed through the wall and stood next to me. He was covered with blood.

"Let's go," he said. "I killed three of his versions. I must find his Master Being, or he will come back to haunt us for the rest of our days."

Killed three versions? What was he talking about? I was not sure I understood, but I said nothing. At this moment, I would have done anything to get out of this box-like room. Marduchk held me and we passed through the wall. I cannot explain where we went, exactly. I think we

156

passed through alien dimensions that I hope I will never see again. Howling things, bits of people, faces that are better not described, all were there, floating in the thick air. It was much like the Hell-like dimension Sinhar Inannaschamra showed me; perhaps it was the same. And then we came into a hole in this atmosphere, a sort of a rounded sphere, and something that looked like the monster stood there, similar but not quite the same. He did not seem to notice us at all, and Marduchk pushed me behind him, pointed the small object I saw before, and a huge flame-like light, blue and gold, came out of it and engulfed the monster. The monster lunged at Marduchk, and tried to grab him, but Marduchk sent a second light, and a third, and a fourth, and the monster burned to a crisp. I stood there looking at the charred, oily substance that was all that remained of the thing. Marduchk put the object in his pocket and turned to me, smiling through the blood and soot that covered his face.

"He is dead, Victoria. All of him is dead now. If any versions still existed before I killed the Master Being, they are dead now; we are safe."

I said nothing. I was too shocked to think. Various creatures came out, whimpering softly, and took the oily, charred remains away, I don't know where. Marduchk did something and we were back in the hotel in Paris, washed up, teleported ourselves and our stuff to the well-hidden spaceship, and flew back to Nibiru. I still could not talk. Marduchk tried to speak to me, but all I could do was shiver and when I tried to answer, I choked and coughed. So he sat me on a comfortable chair and covered me with a blanket, telling me to try and rest. I closed my eyes and saw nothing but the burning image of the monster.

When we got to Nibiru Miriam came over right away, and put me to bed. She knew everything, Marduchk must have spoken to her telepathically when we were still on the spaceship. She sat next to me and held my hand and told me to sleep. But I could not. At least, I was finally able to find my voice and spoke.

"Miriam, this was horrible."

"Of course it was, love. These ancient low level Anunnakis were demonic. You are lucky to be alive, both of you."

"That is not what I mean, Miriam. I know Marduchk saved our lives, but something about it frightens me very much. I never imagined Marduchk could kill, and with such ease... he did not bat an eyelash, Miriam. He actually smiled... And he is usually so gentle and kind..."

"I am not sure I understand, Victoria. Would you prefer it if he let you die?"

"No, of course not. Of course he had to kill the monster. But Miriam, he did it comfortably. It did not seem to bother him at all. I would have probably tried to kill it, too, but I would be shocked even if I succeeded. For Marduchk, it was all in a day's work, or so it seemed."

"I see," said Miriam, and smiled at me. "But killing is sometimes quite necessary. I have killed myself, many times, when I felt it was needed. It was a simple choice to make."

I sat up in bed, staring at her wildly. "You killed? How many?"

"I am not sure, really. Quite a few, during many missions. My dear Victoria, you must adjust to the Anunnakis' ways. Some things in the multi universes are pure evil, and they must be disposed of. As humans, you often kill the innocent. You even kill and torture animals, children and the elderly. You declare war on people who have done nothing wrong to you just so that you can get their wealth. Why be hypocritical? We never kill the

158

innocent; we never kill for greed. We only kill when needed, we kill that which is evil. We don't wait, we don't have a so-called justice system like humans do, a flawed system that so often hurts the innocent in the name of legal games. When something is evil, it is killed. And so it is, and so it shall be."

I lied back in my bed and looked at my beautiful sister-in-law and dear friend. I was horrified, but she was right and I had to admit it. I think this is when my true education really began.

*** *** ***

CHAPTER NINE
At the Anunnaki Academy

> I am given an orientation at the Academy in preparation for discussing my mission, and I undergo the purification and the creation of the all-important mental Conduit.

It took some time, and many discussions with Marduchk, but I finally managed to put the trauma of the fight with the ancient Anunnaki behind me. It is never easy to adjust to a new culture. It is even more difficult to do so when your own spouse is part of this new and incredibly different culture. Think what it is like if you are adjusting not only to that, but to life on another planet. I have to admit that I succumbed to a form of depression. It was not the danger that so much affected me, but I was wondering if I really understood Marduchk. My commitment to him never wavered – I am too much of an Anunnaki to have doubts about my husband once I have made my choice – but I felt helpless and alone and terribly inadequate. However, I received much help from Marduchk, who understood my feelings completely and was willing to support me through this hard time, and also from Miriam and Sinhar Inannaschamra, who advised me of how to manage my feelings from the female point of view. In addition, the spiritual value of the Mingling of the Lights makes a person more and more attuned to the feelings and thoughts of his or her spouse. I grew to understand Marduchk's motives and behavior better every day. And one morning I woke up to feel that life seemed good again, and I was ready for whatever was in line for me next.

"Time to go to work," I said to Marduchk over breakfast. "I think it will be good to start thinking about my mission."

"In this case, then, I think you might want to start your orientation at the Academy. You can't do a thing without it," said Marduchk.

"Just what I would love to do," I said enthusiastically. "Shall I go to Sinhar Inannaschamra and see about the test for admission into the orientation?"

"You have already passed the test," said Marduchk.

"But I only identified one ancient Anunnaki skull," I said, surprised. "You said I had to identify two."

"You had to go through an extended fight with a threatening, evil life form, traveled to other dimensions, rejected the attempts of a monster at possession, and survived his locking you at this deathtrap of the box-like room, not to mention seeing your husband destroy a Master Being and all his versions for the first time," said Marduchk in his matter of fact way. "It counts as identifying a second skull, I should think... anyway, Sinhar Inannaschamra thinks you passed, and that is all that matters. She said to me that as soon as you are ready to start, you will be most welcome to the orientation."

"How thrilling! When shall I go?"

"Tomorrow will be fine, since there are never any official dates for that, as they have on earth. I'll just tell Sinhar Inannaschamra."

"Fantastic. Do I need to bring anything with me? Supplies, copybooks, etc.? Or do I get the supplies there, on the spot?"

Marduchk laughed. "No, there is no need for supplies. The students do not have to write or copy anything. No pens or pencils required, no copybooks. We don't even have desks in the classrooms, come to think of it. You see, the lessons are entered directly into the cells of the students, and become a permanent part of their learning acquisitions."

"How in the world would they do that?"

"It's hard to explain. It will be a lot easier for you to follow it step by step and get the background information as you go along. I could tell you that the acquisitions, or depot of knowledge, will become an integral part of the intellectual, mental-scientific program of the students, but it may not mean much to you until you experience it, I suspect."

"Indeed it means nothing at all... I'll just take everything as it comes, and most likely enjoy it enormously. So, in the meantime, would you kindly manifest another cup of coffee for me before you go off to the Akashic Library? After I drink it, I must go and consult Miriam. She can help me decide what to wear for my day in school. I can't an imagine Anunnaki having to wear a school uniform."

"A uniform? An Anunnaki wearing a uniform? How funny!" said Marduchk, amused and mildly shocked by the idea.

"It might interfere with free will, won't it?" I asked, a little maliciously.

Marduchk laughed. He had begun to notice his own extreme attachment to the notion of free will, not as yet entirely shared by his wife.

The next morning I went to the Academy. I have always loved this magnificent edifice, with its sprawling complex of buildings, all connected to each other in the traditional Anunnaki's architecture. I never failed to be amused by the similarity of all places of higher education, even on another planet. You could have taken this complex, with its lovely old stones and ivy-like climbers, just as it was, and place it next to Harvard, Oxford, or La Sorbonne, and it would fit right in.

A few other students were approaching the particular building where Sinhar Inannaschamra held her classes, and we were all welcomed very cordially by one of her apprentices and sent to our various classrooms.

I entered a large, beautiful room. Later I found out it was 220 meters long by 70 meters wide,[3] dimensions that represent very elegant proportions like all Anunnaki architecture. Huge windows allowed in delicate green light, filtered through the climbers. All the wall space between the windows was covered with shelving, on which many conical books were arranged. The classroom was divided into three sections. The apprentice that was my host explained the section system to me. It was rather complicated, since the sections were not only constructed for the convenience of teaching, but had deep symbolic meaning. He started by asking me a question that at the time I found very strange. "Are you, by any chance, a Freemason?" he said.

"No, why?" I asked, intrigued.

"Well, you see, if you were a member of the Freemasons, much of what I have to tell you about the symbolism would have already been known to you."

"Really? How come?"

"The Freemasons, with their extremely ancient Phoenician heritage, have acquired much information from the Anunnaki, and it is still in use by them. But no matter, in no time at all you will know more than any of them. I will fully explain the matter to you, and I might as well tell you about the Freemason and Phoenician connections,"

---

[3] Approximately 772 X 230 feet.

said my guide pleasantly. "After all, you are from earth, and I understand you are extremely interested in history and archaeology." He appeared to be highly knowledgeable and extremely happy to share information, traits that seem to serve the Anunnaki well.

"Indeed I am," I said. "Thank you so much for your instructions."

"My pleasure," said the apprentice, and launched into the most informative discourse.

"Section one is named Markabhah-Ra, and its code is '3'. There are three rows, each seating one beginner, since this section is reserved for new students or recruits. In freemasonry, the code of the new recruits is also '3'. Markabhah-Ra in Anakh[4] means 'traveler.' It is exactly the same name given to a new recruit or member in a Freemason lodge. In the ancient Hiram[5] Brotherhood Society, number '3' was originally number '1.' Later on it was changed to '3' because number '1' was considered the first attribute of Baal,[6] henceforth no human was worthy of receiving this sacred number.

Section two is named Kah-Doshar-Ra, and its code is '18.' There are eighteen rows, each seating one apprentice. It is reserved for the mid-level Anunnaki's students. Kah-Doshar-Ra in Anakh means Holy, or more exactly, 'Students of the holy energy or source of life.' In Freemasonry, it is exactly the same thing. Mid-level Freemasons receive the degree '18.' With them, Kah-Doshar-Ra became Kadosh. Many Semitic and ancient Near East/Middle East languages have a word much like it, including the Hebrew and Aramaic Kadosh, the Coptic

---

[4] The name of the Anunnaki language
[5] A Phoenician king, mentioned in the Bible
[6] A Phoenician god, also worshipped by other people of the region

165

Kakous or Kouddoup, the Syriac Kouddous and the Arabic Kouddoup or Moukadass.

Section three is named Wardah-Doh-Ra, and its code is '33.' There are thirty-three rows, reserved for the Masters, each seating one Master. Wardah-Doh-Ra means the Flower of Knowledge. Same terminology applies to several Middle East languages, Western languages, and most particularly to Latin and French. And all have the same meaning. Wardah means Rose in Arabic. In Hebrew, it is Vered, and a female name was constructed from it, Varda. In Europe, the organization of the Rosicrucians took its name from the Rose. Annunaki's masters are given the degree '33' just as they do in Freemasonry where the highest level in 33. Incidentally, the number three is important to all these people. For example, in the ancient calendar of the Anunnaki-Phoenicians, the month was divided into three weeks. Each week was composed of eleven days. The month consisted of three weeks, totaling thirty-three days."

"How fascinating," I said. "A few minutes into the Academy and I have already learned more about the truth than in months at the University on earth."

"It's not the professors' fault," said the apprentice. "Their knowledge is limited because so much has been done to obscure the truth, by so many different authorities. Sometimes I marvel how much the earth scholars did manage to learn, despite all the obstacles. But we must come in now, you have your purification ritual to do."

"Purification ritual? Why?" I asked.

"All Anunnaki students are required to purify their bodies before their orientation or their regular course of studies. Lots of people do. You might remember that the Jewish scribes, since earliest times, had to purify their body before adding the name of God into the Torah? It is the same principle. The only difference is that our purification does more than purify the body. The substance we use purifies the mind and spirit as well. It's all very pleasant."

"Is it like the Jewish Mikvah? They have these communal baths that women visit, much like a swimming pool, where they purify themselves each month."

"No, ours is private, each student must purify his or her own being alone, since if we did it together, the mixing of the impurities might produce a barrier to the proper purification. Incidentally, remember the Essenes, these Judaic sect members of the Second Temple era? At first, they used our style of purification, but as time went by, and their numbers grew, they changed into a Mikvah-like, communal purification."

"What about the Christian baptism?"

"Of course, it is all the same idea of purity and cleanliness. And the Christians believe that the mind and spirit are indeed cleansed by the baptism."

He lead me to a door at the end of the room and opened it. Inside was a small room, entirely made of shimmering white marble. In the middle of the room was a basin, made of the same material, and filled with something I could not define.

"It does not look like water," I said, eyeing the glowing substance with suspicion.

"No, it is something else. This is Nou-Rah Shams, an electro-plasma substance that appears like 'liquid-light.' It actually means, in Anakh, The Liquid of Light. Nou, or Nour, or sometimes Menour, or Menou-Ra, means light. Shams means sun. Nour in Arabic means light. The Ulema in Egypt, Syria, Iraq and Lebanon use the same word in their opening ceremony. Sometimes, the word Nour becomes Nar, which means fire. This is intentional, because the Ulemas, like the Phoenicians, believed in fire as a symbolic procedure for the purification of thoughts. This created the word Min-Nawar, meaning the enlightened or surrounded with light. In Anakh it is: Menour-Rah. Which, if you know any Hebrew, you might remember that Menorah means a lamp. It's all connected. Later, the Illuminati used it as well. Anyway, to complete the first phase, all you have to do is spend a little time in the basin and enjoy the purification. I will knock on the door shortly."

He closed the door gently behind him, and I removed my clothes and entered the basin. This bath was the most pleasant cleaning experience I have ever encountered. Every minute made me feel lighter, happier, more complete within myself and sparkling clean. I was sorry when the apprentice knocked on the door and asked me to get dressed and join him.

"Now," said the apprentice, "You are ready for the second phase of the purification. It is called the Nif-Malka-Roo'h-Dosh" Ritual"

"Heavens, what a name," I said. "What does it mean?"

"Nif means mind. Centuries later, it was used by terrestrials as Nifs or Roo'h, meaning Soul or Spirit. Since the Anunnaki did not believe in a 'separate soul,' the mind was the only source of creation and mental development, while humans continued to interpret it as 'Soul.' It means the same thing in Akkadian, Hittite, Aramaic, Hebrew and Arabic.

Malka means kingdom or a higher level of knowledge and mental development. Humans changed Malka to Malakoot or Malkout; and the same, or very similar word, was again used in Aramaic, Hebrew, Syriac, Coptic, Arabic, Phoenician and so many other languages.

Roo'h is the highest level of mental achievement. The Arabs use the same word, while the Hebrew word is Ru'ach. However, the meaning changed in both languages, to represent soul, not mind. And Dosh means revered. Now, let's go into the room where we can proceed." He opened another door, and we entered a moderately sized room off the classroom. In the room was a cell, shaped as a cone and transparent. The cell floated in the air, approximately twelve centimeters above the ground.[7] The top of the cell seemed to be connected to a beam originating from a grid attached to the ceiling, but the interesting thing was that the ceiling, too, floated in the air. It was totally suspended on its own.

"Please step into the cone," said the apprentice. A door opened and I entered the contraption, much intrigued. I stood and waited, and suddenly, a clear fog formed in the center. After a short while, the fog's color changed from white to silver-blue in form of waves. I felt nothing at all, but to my amazement, I saw something registering on an information board that was posted on the right side of the cell. I looked at it, bewildered, and suddenly I knew, with absolute certainty, that these were my thoughts that were registering on the machine. These thoughts began to take physical shape, which was instantly copied to a screen. The screen transformed the thoughts-form into a code, which I could not decipher, but very quickly the code was transformed into a sequence of numerical values. I was not sure what this mysterious sequence meant, but later I found out that the sequence then is prescribed as a Genetic formula. This genetic formula is the "Identity Registration" of the Anunnaki student. In terrestrial terms, you can call it

---

[7] Approximately 4.7 inches

DNA. But it is more than that. It is the level of mental readiness for the next stage.

At this point, I heard a direction in my head, as clear as if someone was talking to me directly. Obviously, I was approached on a telepathic level, something I was not as yet too accustomed to.

I was told to free my mind from all thoughts. It is something like what the Japanese call "Koan," or "Kara," a state of "mind nothingness." Surprisingly, I managed to do so with great ease. I imagined this had something to do with the purification rituals, because in the past, when I tried to do the same in order to meditate, I failed miserably. Then, something began to happen. Rays of various densities and colors surrounded me in a cloud. It is tempting to compare it to the aura in terrestrial terms, but this is not the case. It is not an aura, because it is not bio-organic. It is entirely mental. What happened next took only one minute, and at the time I could not understand what was really happening, but later it was made extremely clear. This was the most important procedure done for each Anunnaki student on the first day of his or her studies – the creation of the mental Conduit. A new identity is created for each Anunnaki student by the development of a new pathway in his or her mind, connecting the student to the rest of the Anunnaki's psyche. Simultaneously, the cells check with the "other copy" of the mind and body of the Anunnaki student, to make sure that the "Double" and "Other Copy" of the Mind and body of the student are totally clean. During this phase, the Anunnaki student temporarily loses his or her memory, for a very short time.

This is how the telepathic faculty is developed, or enhanced in everyone. It is necessary, since to serve the total community of the Anunnaki, the individual program inside each Anunnaki student is immediately shared with everybody. Incidentally, this is why there is such a big difference between extra-terrestrial and human telepathy. On earth, no one ever succeeds in emptying the whole metal content from human cells like the Anunnaki are so adept in doing, and the Conduit cannot be formed. Lacking the Conduit that is built for each Anunnaki, the human mind is not capable of communication with the extra-terrestrials.

However, don't think for a moment that there is any kind of invasion of privacy. The simplistic idea of any of your friends tapping into your private thoughts does not exist for the Anunnaki. Their telepathy is rather complicated.

The Anunnaki have collective intelligence and individual intelligence. And this is directly connected to two things: the first is the access to the "Community Depot of Knowledge" that any Anunnaki can tap in and update or acquire additional knowledge. The second is an "individual Prevention Shield," also referred to as "Personal Privacy." This means that an Anunnaki can switch on and off their direct link, or perhaps better defined as a channel, to other Anunnaki. By establishing the "Screen" or "Filter" an Anunnaki can block others from either communication with him or her, or simply prevent others from reading any personal thought. "Filter" "Screen" and "Shield" are interchangeably used to describe the privacy protection.

In addition, an Anunnaki can program telepathy and set it up on chosen channels, exactly as we turn on our radio set and select the station we wish to listen to. Telepathy has several frequency, channels and stations.

When the establishment of the Conduit is complete, the student leaves the conic cell and heads toward the section assigned to him or her at the classroom. In my case, I was just about to finish my orientation with the all

171

important conversation with Sinhar Inannaschamra, discuss my mission with her before it was to be communicated to the Council, and make a few important decisions for the future, both personal and professional.

*** *** ***

CHAPTER TEN
Surprises and Decisions

A Startling revelation about the Grays, my future mission is considered, and a personal decision of great moment is made.

Sinhar Inannaschamra took me to her office and we settled in two of her comfortable armchairs. "How did this session affect you?" she asked. "Are you tired? Would you prefer to postpone our discussion for another day?"

"I am not at all tired," I said. "On the contrary, these procedures made me feel energized. My head feels so clean."

"Excellent," said Sinhar Inannaschamra. "So just tell me your thoughts and views about a possible mission, and remember, there will be no rush in taking it up. Rather, we would like you to prepare for it for a while, get your bearings."

"I do have a notion of what I want to do, but perhaps I lack the necessary knowledge."

"I don't think so," she said. "You see, Victoria, your situation is unique, regarding studying, and it has certain advantages. At your age, people born on Nibiru would not be considered adult; our children are considered mature at age seventy-one, and until that time they go regularly to the Academy, studying things like ecology, history, etc. for many years. Their Conduit until that age is partial. Then, at the age of seventy-one, they graduate, and receive the complete Conduit. You, on the other hand, are ready to be considered a graduate right away."

"So am I not missing something precious because of my being an adult at age thirty?" I asked, a little apprehensive.

"Not at all, on the contrary. Everyone here knows that graduating from the Academy is just the beginning of a life-long course of studies. I am four hundred thousand years old, and I have been learning and refining my studies every day of my life. You are now prepared for independent studies – your Conduit, and your capacity to absorb knowledge from the cones, are complete – so there is no limit to what you can do. And of course, if something interests you at the Academy, all you have to do is show up. All adults do that."

"How I love your ways," I said. "How wonderful to acknowledge the need to learn throughout life. Yes, I would love to start preparing for my mission, if you and the Council will approve, and if I have the support of Marduchk."

"Our approval, and your husband's support, are so certain that there is nothing to worry about. Just tell me, then, what is this potential mission that has occurred to you? You realize, there is no commitment, this is just the preliminary, very preliminary, discussion," said Sinhar Inannaschamra.

"I want to help the Hybrids," I said. "I know by now that there are many Hybrids on earth, the result of the Grays' experiments. And I would also like to help those people who are half human and half Anunnaki, like my son; I am sure he is not the only one that has been adopted by earth families."

"This is an excellent choice for your first mission," said Sinhar Inannaschamra. "I completely understand your motives and your choice, both professionally and personally."

"I think I am tuned to the Anunnaki connection to humans," I said. "After all, I am part of one of the situations. But I know very little about the Grays."

"Yes," said Sinhar Inannaschamra meditatively. "Very few people, on any planet, really understand the Grays. I have made it my business to learn all I could about them, and I will be able to help you."

"In my trip to their lab, I felt nothing could be worse than these beings," I said. "They seem to me to be a constant menace to everyone."

"They are cruel," said Sinhar Inannaschamra. "But I am thinking about something else. Unless you know their problem, all you see is this technological, highly qualified race without heart or feelings, vicious, violent, and engaged in senseless, merciless experiments. But there is more to it than that. They are a dying civilization, desperately trying to save themselves."

"Dying civilization? How come?" I asked, surprised. With all their activity they seemed very much alive to me, and extremely dangerous.

"Have you ever heard of Progeria? On earth they also call it Hutchinson-Gilford Syndrome, after the two scientists who discovered it in 1886."

"Yes, I have heard a little of it. Progeria victims are children who age, really become old people, before they even reach puberty. A parent's nightmare, but very rare, I should say."

"On earth it is indeed very rare. Only one Progeria-stricken child is born out of four to eight million births. It is a rare, very frightening genetic disease, resulting from spontaneous mutation in the sperm or egg of the parents."

"Yes, this is what I have always heard," I said.

"The horror of this disease is that it has no cure. The child is born, starts showing early symptoms, and begins to age right away. The children remain tiny, rarely over four feet, both boys and girls become bald, and all develop a large cranium, a pointy nose and a receding chin, resulting in an amazing resemblance to each other, almost as if they were clones... And then they die of old age, mostly in their teens but often before, and there is nothing anyone can do for them. They develop old age diseases – such as hardening of the arteries – and often die of strokes or coronary disease, while their poor parents have to watch helplessly. The name Progeria is very appropriate. It means 'before old age,' and expresses it very well."

"But what is the connection of the Progeria children to the Grays?" I asked, a frightening suspicion beginning to form in my mind.

"The civilization of the Grays is millions of years old, and for eons, they have been degenerating. A huge percentage of their population has Progeria, in varying degrees, and because of that, they are threatened with extinction. No one knows how many Grays are affected, and how many are Progeria-free. We only meet those who are, at least for the present, able to carry on their duties, with the help of their advanced medical technology. For all we know, there are millions of sick individuals hidden from view on their home planet."

"This is incredible," I said, shuddering.

"You must also remember that the Grays do not reproduce sexually. They used to, but not anymore. Also, they don't reproduce like the Anunnaki, either. For thousands of years, they have been relying on cloning. And that has damaged their DNA even further, creating more and more cases of Progeria. They are dying out."

"An entire civilization destroyed by Progeria... it is almost impossible to believe," I said.

"If you study the two groups, you will see strong similarities between the Grays and the Progeria children. I won't go into all of them, the list can take days, but let's consider the most prominent ones. For one thing, Progeria does not produce any form of dementia. Both groups maintain their excellent mental faculties, usually with high IQ, until they die. That is a very important clue, but here are the others for your consideration:

- Neither group ever grows much beyond four feet.
- Both have fragile, weak bodies, with thin arms and legs; all their bones are thin, as a general rule.
- Both groups are bald.
- Grays have no sexual reproduction, most have no genitalia at all. Progeria children never reach puberty.
- Both have large heads by comparison to their bodies.
- Both have receding chins and pointy noses. Within their groups, they closely resemble each other. The Grays are cloned; the Progeria children look as if they could have been cloned.

"So will the experiments they do help them survive?"

"That is what they hope for. They take the eggs and the sperm from humans and combine them with Grays' DNA. Thus, they create the Hybrid children."

"Those poor children. I pity them so."

"They are not exactly what you think, Victoria. I pity them too, but you must realize that they are closer to the Grays in their character and behavior than they are to humans."

"What are they like?"

"The first generation Hybrids are smaller than human children. They tend to follow the growth pattern of the Gray parent – and by now you know this is a very fragile one. They are even smaller than Progeria babies. The retardation of growth begins before birth."

"When you say 'first generation' does it mean that they go on mixing the genetic material?"

"Yes, that is exactly what they do. The Hybrids may or may not have Progeria, but naturally, the more human DNA is mixed into the species, the more chances of eliminating the bad genes exist. So they breed the Hybrids with more human DNA, always hoping to eradicate the disease, never quite succeeding. That is why they have to get fresh human specimens all the time."

"Do you think they have a chance of survival?"

"No, personally I don't think they have a chance. I think they are doomed. But many Anunnaki disagree with me. At any rate, there is nothing we can do either way."

"Do you think the authorities on earth know about all that? Like various governments? Why isn't something done about it?"

Sinhar Inannaschamra looked at me silently. Her big black Anunnaki eyes were suddenly full of such sorrow, such deep sadness, that I did not know how to react. Finally she said, "Yes, they do know. I have to tell you the truth, Victoria, even though it breaks my heart to do so. Almost all earth governments have made a deal with the Grays. They supply them with humans."

I jumped on my feet, completely horrified. "They do that? They sell humans to the Grays for torture and killing? What do they gain?"

"Can't you guess?" said Sinhar Inannaschamra quietly. "The Grays give them the technology they crave. They have learned so much from the Grays, and they mostly use it for military purposes. Humans are not kind to each other. Look at wars, torture, genocide, holocausts… all part of human history, and still taking place."

"Unfortunately, this is true," I said.

"Anyway, there are various places on earth where such activities can be studied, various military bases, underground mostly, in many countries. One day you will spend some time there, I am sure."

"Well," I said, trying to recover from the shock. "I can't answer for the earth's governments, but I can try to help."

"Indeed you can. We are trying, in many ways, to alleviate the situation, even though, as I once explained, we cannot police the whole universe, or even the entire earth."

"Do you think I should go and look at the Hybrids, as part of my education?"

"Yes, I think the best thing to do will be to take you on a field trip. You must meet these Hybrids face to face before you make your decision about the mission. But there is something else I wanted to talk to you about. Such missions will have to be on earth, you know. There are no Hybrid bases anywhere else, certainly not on Nibiru. You will be alone for long periods. We don't go back and forth to earth very often, which means that you may have to spend years on earth, except from short vacations."

"Marduchk told me he had committed himself to work with those apelike things he shape-shifted into and scared me so much after our wedding. That means, I am sure, that he will be away for extended periods of time as well, doesn't it?"

"Yes, that is how we all live. My husband is on missions all the time. Most of us are. I used to go to distant places, also, even though currently my mission is fulltime teaching at the Academy."

179

"But are Marduchk and I going to be completely isolated from each other for all these years?"

"No, of course not. Now that you have your Conduit, you can talk to each other every single day of the time you spend apart, and every few years, you can meet for vacation."

"That does not sound too bad," I said. "I will miss Marduchk and all of you very much, but what are a few years? You have given me the hope of living a very long and useful life, and Marduchk has begun to teach me about the next phase of eternity, which is not yet entirely clear to me but very comforting, nonetheless. I am trying very hard to absorb it. In that light, I would be willing to make the effort without any regrets. There is only one thing… I am not sure if you will think it is a good idea…"

"I can sense what it is, Victoria. You want a child."

"Was I that transparent?"

"It was to be expected. Anyone who has had to give a baby for adoption, the way you so heroically did, would want another baby. That is natural. But why should you not? Why do you think it is an idea that will not appeal to me?"

"Because I will have to leave the child on Nibiru when I finally go on missions. Another abandonment."

"First of all, you did not abandon your son. You insisted on knowing all the conditions, you were assured of the loving family and wonderful future he was going to get. And as for the next child, surely you see that our system here is extremely family oriented. When you go on your mission, let's say when the child is somewhere between five and ten, you will have an entire family ready to take over. Think about it – the baby's father, aunt, uncle, nieces, not to mention her loving great-great-great-grandmother ten times removed, namely me – will all be there, taking care of this child. And you can talk to the child every single day through the Conduit, see each other during vacations, and come back long before the child graduated from the Academy. I don't think any of your missions will take seventy-one years, and frankly, I see no abandonment here at all."

"What will Marduchk think?"

"Probably love the idea. He likes children. Not all Anunnaki choose to have children, you know. Some never do, some only have one or two and then spend thousands of years without further reproduction. It's entirely a matter of free will. Those who want children are of course encouraged to have them whenever they please, since they make excellent parents. Those who do not wish to raise children are never pressured into the task. And remember, Victoria, you can have more children after you come back from your mission, if you choose to do so. It is always your choice, and time does not play any part in it."

I was quiet for a few minutes. Being raised on earth eroded so much of the self-confidence and poise all Anunnaki possess. Well, I will have to work on becoming more like them, that is all.

"This time I will have the baby Anunnaki style," I said, feeling better every minute, "in the tube. So I can freely study and travel during the time before it is ready for its birth."

"Incidentally, you can decide in advance if you want a boy or a girl," said Sinhar Inannaschamra in the most matter of fact way.

"I'll consult Marduchk about that," I said. "He may have a preference. I don't care if it is a boy or a girl. I just want a healthy baby."

"Well, that is a given. You will have a perfect baby, every time. And tomorrow, come back and I'll take you on the field trip. I think meeting the Hybrids will be a very interesting experience."

I went home, and as I was waiting for Marduchk to come back from the Akashic Library, I strolled a little in the garden, breathing in the evening air and the scent of the opening night blooming flowers. I saw Marduchk approaching and waved at him.

"You got the Conduit!" he said right away. "I can sense it."

"Indeed," I said. "Shall we try to communicate telepathically? Let's see if I am good at it."

"Do you know how to start it?" asked Marduchk.

"I do." I did something in my mind, which regrettably I cannot explain to anyone who had not received the Conduit, and the Conduit opened, first a little hesitantly, then fully. It was a surprisingly easy and extremely pleasant, effortless way to conduct a conversation. I related to Marduchk everything that happened, in detail, and a conversation that would have taken about an hour was accomplished in a few minutes. As for the great decision (namely the child, not the mission…) Marduchk was charmed by the idea. "A daughter," he communicated, meditatively, "if you don't mind. I had two sons, but I have never had a daughter… it would be a nice experience."

"Fine with me," I communicated back. "And when I come back, we might consider having more. I love children."

"Certainly, if you wish," Marduchk communicated. "I find raising children extremely nice." And so the decision was made, and I felt very, very happy.

This is a good time to explain something regarding Anunnaki fatherhood. Earth readers might wonder about how the Anunnaki male feels about the children, since he does not contribute sperm, and the fertilization of the eggs, as I have explained in a previous chapter, occurs by the activation of the specialized light. Does the Anunnaki male see himself as a father of his wife's natural children? The answer is a resounding "yes." The Anunnaki does not put much weight on trifling physical matters, such as the use of sperm. The Anunnaki couple is an inseparable unit, and whichever way a child comes into their lives, the child is secure of a loving father. I wish the same could be said for all human fathers – whether they do or do not contribute sperm.

*** *** ***

CHAPTER ELEVEN
Visiting the Hybrids

My first encounter with the hybrid children, and my first glimmer of understanding of what eternity is like.

"The base we are visiting today is under water," said Sinhar Inannaschamra. "We are about to descend way down into the Pacific."

"What about air?" I asked, a bit apprehensive about the idea. Surely Sinhar Inannaschamra won't forget I could not breathe under water, but still…

"We pass through a lock that is safe for both water and air," said Sinhar Inannaschamra, "and inside, it's geared for the hybrids, which, just like humans, need air." In a few minutes, we stopped and I assumed, correctly, that we were already inside the base.

"They are expecting us," said Sinhar Inannaschamra. "Don't worry about them. They know I can blow the whole place up if they dare to give me any trouble."

The spaceship's door opened and I saw that we were inside a huge, hangar-like room. If I had expected a beautiful, aquarium-like window, showing the denizens of the deep playing in their blue environment, I would have been disappointed. But knowing the Grays, I expected nothing of the sort, and so the beige and gray room, all metal and lacking any windows, did not exactly surprise me.

"This base is enormous, you know" said Sinhar Inannaschamra. "It is used for many operations, but we will just concentrate on the hybrids today."

I was pleased to hear that, since I was secretly apprehensive about the possibility of stumbling on one of the Grays' hellish laboratories. I will never forget, or forgive, what I saw in their lab. But I said nothing and waited to see what was going to happen next. Sinhar Inannaschamra walked me to a solid wall, put her hand on it, and the wall shimmered a little and then moved, allowing a door to form and open for us. We entered a long corridor, illuminated by stark, white light, with many regular doors on each side. Sinhar Inannaschamra opened one of the doors and we entered a large room, obviously a refectory since it contained extremely long tables, all made of metal. The room was painted entirely in beige – tables, chairs, walls, and ceiling, and had no windows. It was scrupulously clean.

Suddenly, the tables opened up, each table revealing a deep groove on each of its long sides. Plates of what seemed to be normal human food were released from the grooves, and placed each before a chair. At this moment, a few doors opened at various parts of the room, and from each door an orderly file of children came in and settled at the table. They were completely silent, not a word was heard, as they picked up their forks and began to eat. None of them paid any attention to us, even though we stood in plain view.

The children seemed to range from six to twelve, but it was difficult to be sure of that. On one hand, they were small and fragile, so I might have mistaken their ages. On the other hand, their eyes gave the impression of almost old age. They seemed wise beyond their tender years. Their hair was thin, their skin was pale to gray, and they all wore white clothes of extreme cleanliness.

Despite these similarities, which made them look as if they were all related to each other, I could tell some

186

differences between them that seemed rather fundamental. It was almost as if they fitted within three distinct groups. I mentioned it, in a whisper, to Sinhar Inannaschamra, and she nodded.

"Yes, you got it," she said. "They consist of early-stage hybrids, middle-stage hybrids, and late-stage hybrids. The first group is born from the first combination of abductees' and Grays' DNA. They closely resemble the Grays. Look at their skin – the grayish color is very close to that of the Grays, and so is the facial structure. The second group, the middle-stage hybrids, are the result of mating between these early-stage ones, once they are old enough for reproduction, and human abductees. The resulting DNA is closer to humans, and so they look much more like humans, and many of them lose the Progeria gene. The third group, the late-stage hybrid, is the most important. Middle-stage hybrids are mated with humans to create them – and they can hardly be distinguished from humans."

"Yes, I can tell who the late-stagers are quite easily," I said. "But there are not too many of them here, right?"

"This is true, not too many are here. A large number of these hybrids, who represent the most successful results of the experiments, are placed for adoption with human families."

"Are the human families aware of the origin of their children?"

"Yes, in most cases they are. Generally, they are adopted by a high-ranking United States military person, who had worked, or still works, with extraterrestrials, in secret military bases. This happens much more often than most people suspect... the spouse of the military person may or may not know, depending on circumstances and character traits. These lucky hybrids lead a much better life than whose who are raised in places like this one, communally."

"Are they badly treated here? Are they abused by the Grays?"

"No, the Grays don't want to lose them, they are too valuable. But they receive no love, no individual attention, there is no real parenting, and the environment is barren and depressing. They live like that until they are old enough to be of use in the experiments. Not a very nice life for any child."

"And what about Progeria? I mean, for the adopted ones."

"Only the hybrids who are entirely free of Progeria are adopted by human families. We even suspect, though we are not sure, that many of the Progeria stricken late-stagers are killed, since their Progeria gene is too strong. The Grays believe that after these three attempts, it cannot be eradicated by further breeding."

"And so they kill the poor things... what is the motive for all these atrocities?"

"All for the same reason I have mentioned. They think they somehow will save their civilization. But they are doomed."

"But in the meantime, they harm, torture, and kill so many people. I don't understand why it is tolerated." Sinhar Inannaschamra did not answer.

The children finished eating, still in complete silence. Each child, as he or she finished his meal, leaned back into the chair, and as soon as all of them were leaning back, the groove from which the plates came opened up, and re-absorbed all the plates. "They now go to an automatic dishwashing machine," explained Sinhar Inannaschamra.

The children got up, and left the dismal room in the same file arrangement they came in. As soon as the room was empty, large vacuum cleaners emerged from the wall and sucked up every crumb, every piece of debris. Then they sprayed the tables and floor with a liquid that smelled like a disinfectant. The room was spotlessly clean again, ready for the next sad, depressing meal.

"Shall we go to the dormitories now?" asked Sinhar Inannaschamra. I nodded. We followed the children through one of the doors, and entered a place that was a combination of an old-fashioned orphanage and military barracks. It was a very large room, but the ceiling was not high, only about twelve feet. Again, everything was beige and gray, and there were no windows to relieve the monotony. The room was full of beds, arranged above each other in groups of three, like in a submarine. Dozens and dozens of such rows seemed to stretch to a very long distance. The beds were made of some metal, very smooth, and of silver-gray color. They seemed to be assembled like prefab furniture.

"Sinhar Inannaschamra," I said, "there are no ladders. How do the children reach the upper levels?"

"They can levitate," said Sinhar Inannaschamra. "Look at this. Part of each bed is magnetic, so each child can have his or her toys attach to it. As for the lower beds, the toys are stored next to them."

"So they have toys," I said. "That's a mercy."

"Yes, the Grays discovered that mental stimulation is highly important to the hybrids' development. There are plenty of other activities, mostly with abductees, that relieve their lives of the tedium, at least to a certain extent."

"But they have no privacy at all."

"None whatsoever, they only get their own room when they are more mature, but they have one thing that

189

pleases them. If the children want to, they can put their things in their bed, close the bed with a panel, and hide it inside a wall. They like that."

"I wonder, too, if it is not a comfort for them to be together, after all."

"Their feelings and emotional climate are not exactly human… it's hard to explain. I think it's time for you to see them interact."

"Where are all the children now?"

"They are attending various activities," said Sinhar Inannaschamra. "Come, I'll show you."

We entered a room that opened directly from the dormitory. To my surprise, it was really a glass bubble. You could see the outside, which was an unpleasant desert surrounding. I found it nasty, but I figured that to the children it might have represented a pleasant change. About ten children, seemingly between the ages of six and eight, sat on the ground, which was simply the desert sand. They were playing with normal human toys – trucks, cars, and trains. They filled the things with sand, using plastic trowels that one usually sees on the beach. They were also building tunnels from the sand, wetting it with water from large containers that stood here and there. They seemed to be enjoying their games, certainly concentrating on them, but their demeanor remained quiet and subdued, and they did not engage in the laughter, screaming, yelling, or fighting that children of this age usually produce.

"They also have rooms with climbing equipment, and places to play ball," said Sinhar Inannaschamra. "It is needed to strengthen their bones and muscles."

I approached the children, a little apprehensively, worrying that I might frighten the poor things. They looked up at me, seemingly waiting for me to do something, but I was pleased to realize that they were not afraid. I sat on the

190

sand, took some stones that were scattered around, and arranged them so that they created a little road. The children stared at me for a minute with their strange, wise eyes, as if trying to read my thoughts, and almost instantly grasped the idea and continued to built the road together. None of them smiled, but they seemed very much engaged in the new activity. Once all the stones were used, they looked at me again, as if trying to absorb information, and sure enough, after a minute they took the trucks and make them travel on the little road. I got up and let them play.

"So they can read minds," I said to Sinhar Inannaschamra.

"To an extent," she said. "At this age, they basically just absorb images you project. You probably thought about the trucks going on this road, and they saw it."

"And everything was done together, as if they were mentally connected," I said. "Do they do everything together?"

"Yes, everything is communal, even the bathrooms where they clean themselves. But don't be too upset about it. If they are separated from each other before their adolescence, they are extremely upset. It is almost as if the onset of puberty makes them an individual, and before that they have a group mentality."

"Horrible," I said.

"They are not unhappy," said Sinhar Inannaschamra. "Only as adolescents, when they break off the communal mind, they understand how unhappy they are. But we will visit the adolescents on another occasion."

"Very well," I said.

"Would you like to see the room where they keep the fetuses?" asked Sinhar Inannaschamra.

I followed Sinhar Inannaschamra to the corridor, and we walked quite a distance before opening another door. We entered another one of the hangar-sized rooms, full of tanks.

"Each tank contains liquid nutrients," said Sinhar Inannaschamra. "This is where they put the fetuses, as soon as they are removed from the abductees. The tanks are arranged in order, from the youngest fetuses to those that are almost ready to be removed."

"Do they separate them into their stages?" I asked.

"Yes, this room is for early stagers only. In other rooms, they have the middle stagers. But the late stagers remain in the mother's womb until birth, to make them as close to humans as possible."

"And what are the babies like?"

"Quiet, not as responsive as human babies. Many of them die as soon as they are removed from the tank. Those that survive are generally mentally well developed, physically weak, and emotionally subdued."

"And who takes care of them?"

"Both Grays and abductees. The Grays perform most of the physical requirements, but the abductees supply the human touch. We can't go there yet."

"How come?"

"We need to prepare you to interact with abductees. They are very complicated. We shall have a few sessions about interacting with them at the same time we teach you how to work with the adolescents. Also, you wanted some instructions of how to contact and help those people that are children of humans and Anunnakis, like your son. This should take some teaching, too."

We went back to our spaceship, not saying much. I remember thinking that if I were a member of the Anunnaki Council, I would vote to kill every Gray in the known universe. Of course I did not say it to Sinhar Inannaschamra, but I am sure she knew how I felt. Back home, I went to my beloved garden and sat under a tree that constantly showered tiny blossoms on me, like little snowflakes. I did not even know I was crying.

"What is the matter?" said Marduchk, who suddenly appeared next to me. I told him about the visit with the hybrids.

"The hybrids are not abused," said Marduchk. "Something else is bothering you."

I thought for a moment, and then decided I might as well be honest with him. "Yes," I said. "I cannot understand the Anunnaki's casual attitude about the fact that thousands of human beings are tortured and killed all the time. Neither you nor Sinhar Inannaschamra seem to be as shocked as I am about the fact that the Grays engage in such atrocities."

Marduchk was quiet for a minute, thinking. At this conversation, we did not use the Conduit, because at my agitated state I found it difficult. I was not entirely used to it as yet. So I waited for him to say what he thought.

"I see your point," he said. "You think we are callous about it."

"Yes, I do, to tell you the truth. Why don't you destroy the Grays? Why do you allow so much death, so much pain? Are you, after all, cruel beings? Have you become callous because you have lived so many years, and became thick-skinned about suffering?"

"No, we are not cruel. It's just that we view life and death differently than you do. We cannot destroy all the Grays, even if we wanted to. We don't commit genocide, even if they try to do it. But we don't want to kill them. We know that they will die on their own."

"And in the meantime, suffering means nothing to you?"

193

"It means a lot, but destroying the Grays would not eliminate suffering in all the universes we go to. There are other species that are even worse, you just don't know them because the objects of their behavior are not humans."

"It seems to me, that even though you are so much more sophisticated than the humans, the fact that you deny the existence of God may have deprived you of your ethics, after all."

"Deny God? What makes you think we deny God?" asked Marduchk. He seemed genuinely surprised.

"Marduchk, you have told me, more than once, that the Anunnaki created the human race, not God. So where is God if He is not the Creator? Your statements are contradictory."

"Not at all," said Marduchk. "The Anunnaki view of God is similar to human religions in many ways, but contains much more information. The term we use to describe God is 'All That Is.' To the Anunnaki, God is made of inexhaustible mental energy, and contains all creation within Itself, therefore representing a gestalt of everything that has existed, exists now, or will exist in the future, and that includes all beings, all known universes, and all events and phenomena. God's dearest wish is to share in the lives of all Its creations, learn and experience with them, but while they are imperfect, God Itself is perfect, which is why It can only be seen as a gestalt."

"Why are you calling God *It?*" I asked.

"Because we do not attribute gender to God."

"I see," I said. "So in essence, the Anunnaki God is not all that different from ours. What else should I know?"

"It is possible that other primary energy gestalts existed before God came into being, and actually created It. If so, then the possibility exists that there are many Gods, all engaged in magnificent creativity within their own domains. We are not certain if that is so, but we do not dismiss this beautiful possibility."

"That is vastly different from human thought," I said, meditating. "But how does it tie up with the life and death issues, and with the fact that you have created us?"

"The individuals that exist within God, though part of God, have free will and self-determination. In life and in death, each is a part of God and also a complete and separate individual that will never lose its identity. The Anunnaki are indeed the creators of human beings, but since each Anunnaki is a part of God, there is no conflict in the idea of their creation of humanity. Creation is endless and on-going, and human beings, in their turn, create as well – for example, great art, literature, and service to other people, animals, and the planet Earth – though they do not exactly create life as yet. We are all part of the grand gestalt, and that makes All That Is such an apt name for God."

"So how does that make the situation with the Grays' atrocities any better?"

"It is better because the lives that they take are not disappearing into a void. Each individual is eternal, and even if killed as a child, will go on into other domains. I am not saying that this justifies the Grays' atrocities. I am merely pointing out that even though these atrocities do exist, the individuals affected will have another chance."

"Yes, this does make a difference, and I can see how it would affect your thinking. But for me, after seeing what the Grays do to humans in their labs, it is still very disturbing."

"I can understand that, Victoria. It is not something you are accustomed to. Tell me, do you still want to do this mission?" he asked his question in a very neutral way, obviously not wanting to influence my free will.

"Yes, more than ever," I said. "Maybe I can do some good for these sad children."

"I have a suggestion, then," said Marduchk. "I don't see it as a long-term mission, since you cannot change the ways of the Grays from within. I think you will find it a springboard to other missions, as it is obvious to me that you have some thoughts about making the Anunnaki do something about the Grays and force them to stop the experiments. Doing this mission will be extremely good as a learning experience, right from inside the Grays' base. As for contacting the people who are the children of humans and Anunnakis, that will not take much of your time. There are very few of these around, these days."

"How long do you think this mission will take me?"

"Exactly nine months," said Marduchk. I stared for a minute and then laughed.

"I see what you mean, Marduchk. You think I should start our daughter, allow her to grow in the tube in the Anunnaki fashion, and while she is in the tube, concentrate on my mission. Then, I should come back and spend some time with you and the baby, before embarking on other missions."

"Doesn't it sound like a good plan? While the baby is in the tube, there is nothing you can do for her other than look at her as she grows. And you can easily do that with a monitor from earth, right from the Grays' base. And we will talk every day, so if you have any concerns about her, I can take care of it."

"This is a wonderful idea," I said. "I will have the orientation regarding the abductees and the adolescent hybrids, and of course the human-Anunnaki people, and when I am ready to go on my mission, I will first stop at the hospital and start the baby!" This plan made me feel a little better, but I knew I must give the issue some more thought, and perhaps further discussion. So when I went to see Sinhar Inannaschamra the next day, to arrange for orientation, I brought the subject up with her, and told her honestly how I felt.

"Yes, I do understand how you feel, Victoria," she said. "Before we do any more work with the hybrid mission preparations, I would like to give you a little background about our relationship to life and death."

"I would very much welcome it," I said.

"So let's start with the concept of An-Hayya'h," said Sinhar Inannaschamra.

"I have never heard the word mentioned," I said.

"This word, which is also used as A-haya and Aelef-hayat, could be the most important word in Anakh, our language, as well as in the written history of humanity, because it deals with several extremely important issues. These are:

- The origin of humans on earth.
- How humans are connected to the Anunnaki.
- Importance of water to humans and Anunnaki.
- The life of humans.
- Proof that it was the original woman who created man, Adam and the human race, via her Anunnaki identity.
- The return of the Anunnaki to earth.
- Humanity salvation, hopes, and a better future for all of us, our gifts to you, as your ancestors and creators."

"Complicated concepts," I said.

"I will try to explain the whole concept as clearly as possible, because it is extremely difficult to find the proper and accurate word or words in terrestrial languages and vocabularies. Let's start with the word itself. The word An-Hayya'h is composed of two parts.

197

The first part is 'An' or 'A' (Pronounced Aa), or 'Aelef' (pronounced a'leff). It is the same letter in Anakh, Akkadian, Canaanite, Babylonian, Assyrian, Ugaritic, Phoenician, Moabite, Siloam, Samaritan, Lachish, Hebrew, Aramaic, Nabataean Aramaic, Syriac, and Arabic. All these languages are derived from the Anakh. Incidentally, the early Greeks adopted the Phoenician Alphabet, and the Latin and Cyrillic came from the Greek. The Hebrew, Aramaic and Greek scripts all came from the Phoenician. Arabic and most of the Indian scriptures came from the Aramaic. The entire Western World received its language from the Phoenicians, the descendants of the Anunnaki. Anyway, the 'An in Anakh means one of the following:

- Beginning
- The very first
- The ultimate
- The origin
- Water

On earth, this word became Alef in Phoenician, Aramaic, Hebrew, Syriac and Arabic. Alef is the beginning of the alphabet in these languages. In Latin, it's 'A' and in Greek it is Alpha. In Hebrew, the Aleph consists of two yuds (pronounced Yood); one yud is situated to the upper right and the other yud to the lower left. Both yuds are joined by a diagonal vav. They represent the higher water and the lower water, and between them the heaven. This mystic-kabalistic interpretation was explained before by Rabbi Isaac Luria. Water is extremely important in all the sacred scriptures, as well as in the vast literature and scripts of extraterrestrials and Anunnaki. Water links humans to the Anunnaki. In the Babylonian account of the Creation, Tablet 1 illustrates Apsu (male), representing the primeval fresh water, and Tiamat (female), the primeval salt water.

These two were the parents of the gods. Apsu and Tiamat begat Lahmu (Lakhmu) and Lahamu (Lakhamu) deities.

In the Torah, the word 'water' was mentioned in the first day of the creation of the world: 'And the spirit of God hovered over the surface of the water.' In the Chassidut, the higher water is 'wet' and 'warm,' and represents the closeness to Yahweh (God), and it brings happiness to man. The lower water is 'cold,' and brings unhappiness because it separates us from Yahweh, and man feels lonely and abandoned. The Ten Commandments commence with the letter Alef: 'Anochi (I) am God your God who has taken you out of the land of Egypt, out of the house of bondage.' The letter 'Alef' holds the secret of man, its creation, and the whole universe, as is explained in the Midrash. In Hebrew, the numeric value of Aleph is 1. And the meaning is:

- First
- Adonai
- Leader
- Strength
- Ox
- Bull
- Thousand
- Teach.

According to Jewish teaching, each Hebrew letter is a spiritual force and power by itself, and comes directly from Yahweh. This force contains the raw material for the creation of the world and man. The Word of God ranges from the Aleph to the Tav, which is the last letter in Hebrew. In Revelation 1:8, Jesus said: 'I am Alpha and Omega, the beginning and the ending.' In John 1:1-3, as the Word becomes Jesus, the Lord Jesus is also the Aleph and the Tav, as well as the Alpha and the Omega. In Him exists all the forces and spiritual powers of the creation. Jesus is

199

also connected to water, an essential substance for the purification of the body and the soul, which is why Christians developed baptism in water. In Islam, water is primordial and considered as the major force of the creation of the universe. The Prophet Mohammad said, as can be read in Quran: 'Wa Khalaknah Lakoum min al Ma'i, koula chay en hay,' meaning: 'And We (Allah) have created for you from water everything alive.' The Islamic numeric value of Aleph and God is 1. To the Anunnaki and many extraterrestrial civilizations, the An or Alef represents number 1, also Nibiru, the constellation Orion, the star Aldebaran, and above all the female aspect of the creation symbolized in an Anunnaki woman 'Gb'r, whom you know as the Angel Gabriel on earth."

"The Angel Gabriel was a woman?" I asked, amazed.

"Unquestionably so," said Sinhar Inannaschamra, smiling. "She certainly still is."

"How interesting," I said. "But do go on. What about the second part of the word An-Hayya'h?"

"The second part, namely the Hayya'h part, means:
- Life
- Creation
- Humans
- Earth, where the first human, which was a female, was created.

In Arabic, Hebrew, Aramaic, Turkish, Syriac, and so many Eastern languages, the Anunnaki words Hayya'h and Hayat mean the same thing: Life. But the most striking part of our story is that the original name of Eve, the first woman, is not Eve, but Hawwa, derived directly from Hayya. You see, Eve's name in the Bible is Hawwa, or Chavvah. In the Quran it is also Hawwa, and in every single Semitic and Akkadian script, Eve is called Hawwa or Hayat, meaning the giver of life, the source of the creation.

Now, if we combine An with Hayya'h or Hayat, we get these results: Beginning; The very first; The ultimate; The origin; Water + Life; Creation; Humans; Earth, where the first was created; Woman. And the whole meaning becomes: The origin of the creation, and first thing or person who created the life of humans was a woman, or water. Amazingly enough, in Anakh, woman and water mean the same thing. Woman represents water according to the Babylonian, Sumerians and Anunnaki tablets, as clearly written in the Babylonian-Sumerian account of the Creation, Tablet 1."

"Well, no wonder then that God has no gender in the Anunnaki concept," I said. "I found it very interesting, when Marduchk told me about All That Is as the name of God."

"Yes, it all ties together rather nicely, even if it is a little complicated," said Sinhar Inannaschamra.

"A little?" I said, laughing. "I will have to think about this for a long time before I am comfortable with the concepts. But it is fascinating. I would like, moreover, to understand a little better how the Anunnaki created the human race."

"Well, it happened around 65,000 B.C.E," said Sinhar Inannaschamra. The Anunnaki, at that time, lived in the areas you now call Iraq, which was Sumer, Mesopotamia, and Babylon, and Lebanon, which was Loubnan, Phoenicia, or Phinikia. We taught your ancestors how to write, speak, play music, build temples, and navigate, as well as geometry, algebra, metallurgy, irrigation, and astronomy, among other arts. We had high hopes for this race, which we have created in our image. But the human race disappointed us almost from the beginning, for human beings were, and still are, cruel, violent, greedy and ungrateful. So, we gave up on you and left earth. The few remaining Anunnaki living in Iraq and Lebanon were killed by savage military legions from Greece, Turkey and other nations of the region. The Anunnaki left earth for good, or at least that was the plan at the time. Other extraterrestrial races came to earth, but these celestial visitors were not friendly and considerate like the Anunnaki. The new extraterrestrials had a different plan for humanity, and their agenda included abduction of women and children, animal mutilation, genetic experiments on human beings, creating a new hybrid race, and so on."

"But you are still there, Sinhar Inannaschamra. And you are still trying to help. Obviously, you would not have projects such as you had with me if you had forgotten us…"

"No, we did not totally forget you. We could not... After all, many of your women were married to Anunnaki, and some of our women were married to humans. Ancient history, the Bible, Sumerian Texts, Babylonian scriptures, Phoenician tablets, and historical accounts from around the globe recorded these events. You can find them, almost intact, in archeological sites in Iraq and Lebanon, as well as in museums, particularly the British Museum, the Iraqi Museum and the Lebanese Museum."

"So how did you keep in touch with human civilization?"

"Before leaving you, we activated in your cells the infinitesimally invisible multi-multi-microscopic gene of An-Hayya'h. Yes, this is how it is all connected… It was implanted in your organisms and it became a vital component of your DNA. Humans are not yet aware of this, as they were not aware of the existence of their DNA for thousands of years. As your medicine, science and technology advance, you will be able, some day, to discover that miniscule, invisible, undetectable An-

202

Hayya'h molecule, exactly as you have discovered your DNA. An-Hayya'h cannot be detected yet in your laboratories. It is way beyond your reach and your comprehension, but it is extremely powerful, because it is the very source of your existence. Through An-Hayya'h, we remained in touch with you, even though you are not aware of it. It is linked directly to a 'Conduit' and to a 'Miraya' (monitor, or mirror) on Nibiru. Every single human being on the face of the earth is linked to the outer-world of the Anunnaki through An-Hayya'h. And it is faster than the speed of light. It reaches the Anunnaki through 'Ba'abs' (star gates). It travels the universe and reaches the 'Miraya' of the Anunnaki through the Conduit, which was integrated in your genes and your cerebral cells by the Anunnaki some 65,000 years ago."

"The same Conduit I have now?"

"Yes, that same Conduit. Of course, humans cannot use it, since it was not activated like yours. But hopefully some day they will be able to."

"And how do the Anunnaki receive the content of a 'Conduit' to allow them to watch over the humans?" I asked.

"Through the 'Miraya' which we created to function with the Conduit and the An-Hayya'h, even though we felt that you do not deserve it. The Anunnaki have been watching you, monitoring your activities, listening to your voices, witnessing your wars, brutality, greed and indifference toward each others for centuries. We did not interfere, at least not very much."

"But from my experience, you are returning?"

"Yes. We will, because we fear two things that could destroy earth and annihilate the human race. The domination of earth and the human race by the Grays, and the destruction of human life and planet Earth by the hands of humans. The whole earth could blow up. Should this happen, the entire solar system could be destroyed. For we know, should anything happen to the Moon, the earth will cease to exist."

"Is there hope that we will change?"

"There is always hope. We are trying to change you. The most delightful and comforting aspect of it, is the hope for peace, a brighter future, and a better life you can accomplish and reach when you discover how to use it without abusing it. Every one of you can do that."

"I wonder how many humans I know will see such change in their lifetime," I said wistfully.

"Even when people die, their An-Hayya'h will always be there for them to use before they depart earth. It will never go away, because it is part of you. Without it you couldn't exist. Just before you die, your brain activates it for you. Seconds before you die, your mind will project the reenactment of all the events and acts, good and bad, in your entire life, past, and 'zoom' you right toward your next nonphysical destination, where and when you judge yourself, your deeds, and your existence, and where you decide whether you wish to elevate yourself to a higher dimension, or stay in the state of nothingness and loneliness, and for how long. Everything is up to the individual."

"So there is no death. Our minds live forever."

"Indeed, there is no death. Your minds live on, and make all the individual decisions about their future."

"What about reincarnation? Do we return to earth, ever?"

"No, you will not return to earth, nor will your 'soul' migrate to another soul or another body. From evidence, we know, not just believe, that there is no such thing. And why would you wish to return to earth, anyway? Earth is the lowest sphere of existence for humans; everything else is an improvement!"

"It's good to know that you have not deserted us, Sinhar Inannaschamra. It makes me feel safer, for myself and for humanity."

"My dear Victoria, you are now a full Anunnaki, you will never, ever, be alone. But I understand your attachment to your previous fellow humans. There is no reason to worry about them. The humans are always connected to the Anunnaki in this life and the next, and in the future, we plan a much closer communication. So please, go on to your mission with a lighter heart. There is plenty of bright hope for everyone, even the hybrids, I dare say." I went home, feeling much better about life, the universe, and my mission. As a matter of fact, I began to look forward to it as a new adventure. And soon I will have a baby girl, too!

*** *** ***

CHAPTER TWELVE
Reporting to the Council

My return to Nibiru at the end of my mission, the Akashic Library, and my report to the Council. I am now waiting for my daughter's arrival, and planning an astounding time-travel trip to meet one of the most important persons in human history.

"Marduchk," I said into the monitor, during our daily conversation, "I am finished here. I have done all I could, and I would like to return to Nibiru and make my report to the Council."

"Will you be ready later this evening?" asked Marduchk. I was now used to Nibiru-like speed, so I got my stuff ready in advance. "I am ready now," I said.

"Very well, I'll be there shortly, so you can say your goodbyes to anyone you want." The monitor flickered off and I sat waiting for Marduchk, looking at the notes I prepared for my report to the Council. There was, quite literally, no one to say goodbye to – a sad statement after spending eight months on the Grays' base. But precisely this situation was, anyway, an important part of my report. I was more than ready to return to Nibiru.

I cannot tell you how happy I was to be home again. In a couple of days I was supposed to meet the Council at the Akashic Library, and I spent these days in complete idleness, except for my happy reunion with everyone in my family, and my daily visits to the incubator, where my darling baby was almost ready to emerge, with only four weeks to go. Her big black eyes were wide open, staring at the big world outside with interest and curiosity, and she had soft black fuzz on her precious little head. I was wondering if she knew who I was. And of course, seeing Marduchk again was a joy. Naturally, I missed him very much, and living alone with the Grays and hybrids was not what could be considered a comfort.

I was a little apprehensive about meeting the Council, since I felt that my mission was not a glowing success, but I knew I could not ask Marduchk to come with me when I went to give the report. Anunnaki women do not ask their husbands to protect them – they are completely equal to any man in their ability to take care of themselves, physically as well as emotionally. I was not going to lower my credibility before the Council by acting like a human woman, who, we must admit, sometimes shows such occasional weakness. But Marduchk, always sensitive to my moods, must have noticed something or read a passing thought, because when we were having dinner on the evening before my dreaded meeting with the Council, he said, "Did Sinhar Inannaschamra tell you that she decided to come to your meeting?"

"No, I had no idea," I said, relief practically flooding my entire being. "How come? Of course I know she is a member of the Council, but this is not the area she works with, these days."

"She is interested, I suppose," said Marduchk in a very neutral way. "Any member of the Council can choose to come." I would have bet my right arm that Marduchk asked her to be there for me, but since he would not admit it, or even mention it, preferring to let me believe that he thought of me as a full Anunnaki, I decided not to inquire any further. We took our coffee and went to sit peacefully in the garden, and soon Miriam came to wish me luck with my presentation, and somehow the whole thing did not seem so menacing after all.

Until this time I did not have the opportunity to tell you much about the Akashic Library, which is really a very important part of the Anunnaki culture. Marduchk spent a large amount of his time there, doing research for his various missions, and I suspect, simply enjoying himself as well by immersion in all sorts of information. And since I am about to tell you about the meeting, this is a good opportunity to describe the Library.

The reason it is called the Akashic Library is that it has equipment that allows the researcher to connect to the Akashic Record – the vast compendium of knowledge encoded in a non-physical plane of existence, in a substance that is called Akasha. The Akashic Record has been described as a library, a universal computer, the mind of God, the universal mind, the collective unconscious, and a dozen other metaphors, but in the end it is a collection of records of everything that has ever been thought of or experienced, every word, every action. The individual records in it are constantly updated.

On Nibiru, each Anunnaki has access to the Akashic Record through the Akashic Libraries, which are located in every community. The libraries everywhere have the same appearance, and they are built very differently from the normally classical architecture of the Anunnaki. Usually, the houses are built of various types of stone, marble, or bricks, but the libraries are constructed from materials such as glass, fibreglass, or other plastic-like materials; they give the impression of a modern, industrialized edifice.

One enters through a huge door, that is never closed, day and night. It opens into a huge hall, seven hundred to one thousand meters in length, by five hundred meters in width. The hall is empty of any furniture, and is lit by windows that are placed very high, near the ceiling.

The windows were designed in such a way that the shafts of light that enter through them are very sharply delineated and look like solid beams of light. At night, the same effect is achieved by enormous spot lights placed near the windows. The result is incredibly impressive.

Extremely large billboards hand on each wall, and on the floor, in front of each billboard, there are hundreds of pads. When visitors enter the library, they approach the billboard, stand each on a pad, and think about their destination within the building. The pad has the capacity to read minds, and as soon as it does so, it begins to move, and slides right through the billboard, which is not really solid but is made of a form of energy, carrying the visitor with it. Behind the billboard is the main hall of the Akashic Library.

But the Anunnaki Akashic Library is not a library in the traditional sense, because it contains no physical books on shelves, and not even cones, that are the normal format for an Anunnaki book. Instead, the visitors find themselves in the presence of an immense screen, made of materials that are not found on Earth. The screen is hard to describe; it can be compared to a grid, with a multitude of matrixes and vortices of data. The screen is contacted through the Conduit – it can read minds – and it knows right away what information the visitors seek. All the visitors have to do is stand still in front of the screen, and the data will be displayed.

Of course, the data is not represented by lines, sentences, or paragraphs, but rather by codes. Each code contains particular information related to an aspect of the subject. For example, if you would like to visit Iraq, 2000 B.C.E., 300 C.E. and 2008 C.E., all you have to do is to focus on the these requirements, and three codes will

210

appear on the screen, waiting for your command to open them up.

From this moment on, the Conduit and the Screen are communicating in the most direct fashion. The three files will open up. The nearest description of these files would be digital, for the lack of the proper word; each one will contain everything that had happened pertaining to that particular date in Iraq. The Conduit will sort out, classify, and index the particular data for the part of the information the visitor is most interested in. Then, the information will be stored automatically in the cells of the visitor's brain, increasing the size of the depot of knowledge in the brain. And because Anunnaki are connected to each other and to their community via the Conduit, the data recently absorbed is sent to other Anunnaki to share it, which is extremely beneficial, because if the data received from the screen is difficult to understand, the Anunnaki community, or an individual Anunnaki, will send, also automatically, the explanation needed. This is quite similar to an online technical support on earth, but it is much more efficient since it functions brain-to-brain.

As mentioned before, each Anunnaki community has the same kind of center for these mirrors of knowledge which are the Akashic files. The complexity of the centers, though, is not the same. Some of the Akashic Libraries include more perplexing and complicated instruments and tools, which are not readily available to other communities. These tools include the Monitor, which is also called Mirror, or Miraya in Anahk. Each Miraya is under the direct control of a Sinhar, who serves as custodian and guardian. It is very important to protect the privacy of every member of the community, because individual Anunnaki could attempt to tap into the data of the Miraya and have access to the codes of the telepathic communication of other Anunnaki, thus enabling them to read the mind of all the community members, something that is considered highly unethical and absolutely must be avoided.

The screens, by the way, can expand according to the number of codes that the Anunnaki researcher is using. Seven to ten codes are normal. If a larger number of codes are opened, the screen is fragmented into seven different screens, which are only visible to an Anunnaki mind. An amazing phenomenon occurs at this moment – time and space mingle together and become unified into one great continuum. This enables the researcher to grasp all the information in a fraction of a second.

An added convenient aspect of the Akashic files is the ability of the researchers to access them in the complete privacy of the researchers' homes or offices, since part the files can be teleported there. But since the private screen is not as complicated as the central one in the Library, no multiple screen will open up, only the original one.

It is important to understand that the data received is not merely visual. There is much more to it than that. By the right side of the screen, there are metallic compartments, as thin as parchment paper, which serve as a cosmic audio antennae. These compartments search for, and bring back, any sound that had occurred in history, in any era, in any country, and of any magnitude of importance. This includes voices of people, preachers, prophets, etc., and this is just the tiny part of it which is human, because it also brings sounds made by many other civilizations. According to the Anunnaki, every single sound or voice is never lost in the universe. Of course, it may not traverse certain boundaries. For humans, if the sound was produced on earth, such a boundary is the solar system. Each of these antennae-compartments will probe different galaxies and star systems, listening, recording, retrieving, and playing back sounds, voices, and noises.

A combined asset of the visual and audio systems is the ability to learn languages that is afforded by the Akashic Library. This applies to any language – past, present or future, and from any part of the universe. The researcher can call up a shining globe of light that will swirl on the screen with enormous speed. As it rotates, the effect blends with an audio transmission that comes from the metallic compartments. In an instant, any language will sink into the brain cells.

On the left side of the screen, there are conic compartments, that bring still images of certain important past events. This display informs the researcher that these particular events cannot be altered. In other words, the Anunnaki cannot go back into the past and change it. The Anunnaki are forbidden to change or alter the events, or even just parts or segments of the events represented on the conic compartment, because these images represent events created by the Anunnaki themselves. This restriction works as an essential security device. For example, a young Anunnaki cannot visit earth sixty five thousand years ago, enter the genetic lab of the Anunnaki in Sumer or Phoenicia, and change the DNA and the genetic formula originally used by Sinhar Enki, or Sinhar Anu, to create the human race, or the seven prototypes of the human race created by Sinhar Inanna. Sinhar Inanna herself can go back and change it, but not for use on earth as we know it. She has to transpose it and transport it to another dimension, parallel to the original dimension where the event occurred.

This safeguard means that Sinhar Inanna cannot recreate a new race on our earth by the device of sending the current living humans back in time, remolding us, and then bringing us back to the twenty first century as a new species. This would be unethical. All she can do is recreate her own experiment in another dimension.

More options are available for research, and one them is a sort of browsing. Inside the screen, there is a slit where the mind of the Anunnaki can enter as a beam. This will open the Ba'abs, or Stargates, to other worlds that the researcher is not even aware of; they appear randomly as part of the discovery or exploration. In each slit there is an Akashic file that belongs to another civilization, sometimes more advanced than the Anunnaki themselves, where the researcher can retrieve important information. It is like going back into the future, because everything present, or occurring in the future, has already occurred in a distant past and needed time to surface and appear before the current living Anunnaki.

And there is also the option of simply having fun, some of which is not so ethical. Sometimes an Anunnaki will go back in time, let's say 400 C.E., choose a famous historical figure, and at the same time bring over another important person, one thousand years older, simply to see how they would interact. They can easily deceive these personages, since every Anunnaki is an adept at shape shifting. Or they can transpose people, move them in time, and see how they will react to the new environment. These games are strictly forbidden, but some low class Anunnaki occasionally try it as a game. Sometimes they interfere with our daily affairs, and temporary loss of memory may be a result of that. Anunnaki children, though usually extremely well-behaved, may also play silly games, such as deliberately misplacing objects and then returning them, to the amazement of the human. These games, while they can be quite annoying, never harm any one seriously. One unpleasant result may surface in therapy, though. A psychiatrist might tell a person complaining of such an event that his or her mind is playing tricks. Well, it is indeed a trick, but not created by the mind. It is performed by the Anunnaki people. Ah, well. Nobody is perfect, not even the Anunnaki.

Early in the morning, as directed, I entered the Akashic Library. I was informed ahead of time precisely to which room I had to go for my meeting, and what was the etiquette, so I was ready. I wore a formal white long gown, following Miriam's instructions of what was the right outfit for the occasion. The door was always open at the Akashic Library, so I just walked in, stood on a pad before one of the great billboards, sent a message saying "Council" and went through the billboard to the other side. The pad glided to a side door, which opened into a large room. The pad would stay there until my business was finished, and then retrace its steps back into the front room, unless given different instructions.

The room was entirely empty, with no windows, but had a glass ceiling, creating the atmosphere of an atrium. The walls were off white, made of the same material as the outside, smooth and clean. It was a little intimidating, but as soon as I stepped in, a comfortable armchair came out of the floor, and turned itself toward me, as if asking me to sit. Right away, a few other armchairs sprouted from the floor, and in an instant five members of the Council, including Sinhar Inannaschamra, materialized in them. I stood up and bowed to them, following the etiquette, and the whole group got up and bowed back to me. That apparently concluded the formal part, and they all smiled at me in a most encouraging manner, and very kindly asked me if I was ready to tell them about my mission with the Grays. Of course, our entire conversation was conducted telepathically, but I will report it as if we were talking

215

verbally. Come to think of it, there is very little difference, except that the telepathic conversations take very little time by comparison to verbal conversations. My fear disappeared completely, I pulled out my papers, and told them the whole truth about my mission, which I have found rather distressing.

There was little I could do for the hybrids, no matter how hard I tried. Emotionally, the children were severely damaged goods. None of them could be referred to as a normal child; in my opinion, they were all showing symptoms of serious personality syndromes, autism, and various mental illnesses. Those children who had the advantage of meeting the abductees on a regular basis, that is, those abductees who came specifically to play with them, were somewhat better, but not much. Their mentality, as I have suspected from the start, was entirely communal, much like ants, or bees, and they tended to do just about everything together. If separated from their group, they showed signs of severe distress.

However, something happened at the onset of adolescence. Up to that point, all the activities were geared toward socializing the children and getting them acquainted with earth, and with humans' day-to-day activities, mainly through games, but at adolescence they were given new tasks, geared toward reproduction. Unlike the Grays, the adolescent hybrids were interested in sexual activity, and as soon as they showed signs of their interest, they were encouraged to mate. The hybrids can imitate human emotions, since they have a limited amount of telepathic ability that allows them to acquire quite a bit of information from the abductees. The results can be devastating, since a male hybrid could actually persuade a female abductee that he is in love with her, mimicking human emotions and style of communication. As a result, she may form very strong

216

feelings for the hybrid, but in reality he does not feel love at all, being incapable of true feelings toward humans. The same can happen with a female hybrid and a male abductee. The only strong feeling an adolescent hybrid has is a sense of loss, sadness, and depression about his or her own life, and nothing can alleviate this type of suffering. All this can lead to many cases of abuse, both physical and emotional, mostly because the hybrids do not know how to deal with their feelings, and often lash out against their partners. One bad case of physical abuse caused me to tell the abductee that she could come with me out of the base – that I could take her to freedom and make sure the Grays never bother her again – but by that time, her mind was so warped that she refused to leave, telling me how much she loved the hybrid who mistreated her, and how she hoped that he will be changed, some day, by her love.

Another aspect of my mission was truly devastating. I knew that the abductions took place for thousand of years, there is even Biblical evidence to such doings. But during my stay I have learned that the rate of abductions was greatly accelerated at certain times, including the present. Having investigated these periods, I saw the correlation between a larger number of hybrids introduced into human society, while propagating their genes of cruelty, indifference, and lack of ethics or morality, which are much worse than those of normal human beings, and human events. Each time the abductions accelerated, they created the worst times humanity ever experienced. The accelerated abductions corresponded to the Inquisition, for example, to the Holocaust in Nazi Germany, and even were related to specific people, such as Vlad Dracula, Stalin, Genghis Khan, and many, many others. Torquemada, Hitler, and the others mentioned above were loaded with the Grays' DNA. We are now experiencing an accelerated period. It has started in the 1920s. We can see the results already, but the next few decades will be even worse.

I also told the Council that I had very little success with the human/Anunnaki offspring. There were only seven of them on earth, and none needed my help at all. Most of them were extremely successful in their chosen fields. Ironically, one of them was a famous writer of science fiction, who thought that his ideas came to him out of his own imagination, while in truth he retained an enormous amount of Anunnaki knowledge, which worked very nicely as fiction... So this part of my mission was not a success either. One thing I did do – I naturally watched over my son and his family, via the Monitor, and I had the supreme luck of saving them from a car accident. They were driving on a narrow road, a car came toward them very fast, and in an instant, I lifted the car off the ground, made it hover in the air until the other car passed, and then let them gently down again. Of course I made them forget the whole incident, something that by now I knew how to do. But that was a personal triumph, and the mission was a failure.

"Not at all, my dear Sinhar Ambar-Anati," said one of the Council. "We consider your mission a huge success."

"Why?" I said, perplexed.

"First of all, you may have saved the life of your son. We have tremendous hopes for his future, we think he will be instrumental to our plan for humanity. Had he been killed by a car accident, all our plans for him would have failed to materialize."

"But what about the hybrids?"

"That, too, is a great success. You must realize that the Anunnaki have serious distaste to being with the Grays. You are the first, the absolute first, to live with them, learn their way with the hybrids, and basically, see how they function. We will read your notes very carefully, Sinhar

218

Ambar-Anati, and we will meet again and again to learn more from you. Your analysis of the periods of acceleration is a particularly important find, something we did not know but we must study very carefully. It is extremely significant."

"I am very happy if this is so, Your Honor," I said.

"It is so. And what is more, it opens many roads for you for the future. We understand how you feel about the Grays' activities, and even though in the past we did little about it, your view brings fresh insights. We may change our entire treatment of the Grays, and of humanity, because of your findings. And we think that as we develop a new policy, you will very likely be asked if you would consent to act as an envoy to some of the human governments which are collaborating with the Grays, and make a stop to the atrocities."

I was so stunned by this statement, that I stared at them, speechless. Sinhar Inannaschamra laughed. "My great great granddaughter is overwhelmed, my friends. We will allow her some time to absorb all that, and I hope all of us meet regularly over the next few years, to develop a solid plan for her new mission."

"We are grateful to you, Sinhar Ambar-Anati," said another member of the Council. "I know you are about to have a daughter. I suggest you rest for a while, enjoy your family, but still spend some time with us. We will introduce you to various subjects through the Akashic Library, where you will have the opportunity to study at your leisure, and prepare for your new mission as an envoy to earth. Would that please you?"

I found my voice. "That would make me exceedingly happy, your Honor," I said. It was all I could do not to cry with the happiness for these results. If indeed the Anunnaki would rise to end the atrocities and save the lives of humans, not to mention prevent more of the Grays' DNA from contaminating the earth, it will be worth every effort, every sacrifice.

All the Council members smiled at me, bowed again, and vanished, except Sinhar Inannaschamra. She stayed with me, signalled a pad to come and carry her, and we glided back to the large hall and then strolled home together.

"My goodness, Sinhar Inannaschamra," I said. "Here I thought my mission was a failure, and yet they were so pleased! I will never understand."

"Well," said Sinhar Inannaschamra, "you might as well enjoy the glory and start visiting the Akashic Library."

"Did they really mean it? Me, an envoy?"

"Why not? You are the perfect advocate for humanity, with your dual nature and affiliations. You got them thinking in a new way, quite an achievement."

"I must start my studies right away," I said.

"Yes, you should get acquainted with the Library, learn how to navigate it, and how to utilize the tools. Is there something you would like to learn? Something that interests you? I think anything would do, it's just for practice, and I will help you."

"Yes," I said, musing. "There is one thing I would like to do, and it involves a bit of time travel. There is a person I always wanted to meet, a person from the deep past... I wonder if it can be arranged?"

"Who is the person?" asked Sinhar Inannaschamra

"Mary Magdalene," I said.

"Really?" said Sinhar Inannaschamra. "Jesus' wife? Yes, she was an interesting woman. Yes, of course you can meet her. We will need to do a little shape shifting, and go and visit her; I imagine you would want to see both of them in France, right? Perhaps meet their children?"

"I have heard the theory of her being Jesus' wife, but I don't know much about it, and there is so much conflicting evidence. But France? Didn't she live out her life in Judea? And I always assumed Jesus died in Judea, too, on the Cross. Was I wrong on that?"

"They'll have plenty to tell you, I can see that," said Sinhar Inannaschamra, laughing.

*** *** ***

CHAPTER THIRTEEN
Jesus and Mary Magdalene

My first shape shifting and time travel; how I met Jesus and Mary Magdalene – who turned out very differently than expected.

It is impossible to describe my feelings regarding my expected visit with Mary Magdalene. I always had a deep interest in her and thought she must have been a most complicated personality, and her place in history, next to Jesus himself, was enough to make me revere her. The thought of seeing her, and soon, was an emotional whirlwind, particularly since Sinhar Inannaschamra was quite sure that I will be able to meet Jesus as well. Having been brought up a Christian, it was difficult for me to accept the possibility that Jesus not only did not die on the Cross, but lived happily in Massilia (modern Marseille) with his wife and family. But the Anunnaki had never been wrong in anything they had ever told me, so I decided to put my disbelief and shock on hold, keep an open mind, and learn as much as I could.

I assumed I would have to use a cone to learn the language spoken in ancient Gallia Narbonensis, the part of France where Massilia existed, prepare my clothing, and practice shape shifting, but it turned out I was wrong. All I had to do, said Sinhar Inannaschamra, was to wear my Monitor around my neck, exactly the way I wore it when I went to my mission at the Grays' base, and use the same code, so she could keep an eye on me. She was going to check on me periodically, and if anything went wrong, come and get me. But she expected everything to go smoothly, and as always, I trusted her. She gave me exact

223

directions as to what to do and how to behave, and indeed, it seemed so simple I could hardly believe it.

"How do I get back?" I asked.

"Very easy," said Sinhar Inannaschamra. "Just speak the code to the Monitor and think of Nibiru. It will do the rest, you will hardly feel it. This trip should be very comfortable, it's just training, you know."

Next morning I went to the Akashic Library, wearing normal clothes and carrying nothing other than the Monitor around my neck. I repeated the steps I took when I met with the Council, only this time requested the Departures Room. The pad took me to an octagon-shaped glass pavilion that stood out of the main building, surrounded by ancient conifers. The glass was transparent, so I could see that the room was entirely empty, other than one stool in the middle of it. The room was not very big, and it had a glass door, also transparent. I entered, and to my amazement, I could not see anything outside, because the glass became opaque. I had no idea at the time what caused it, since Sinhar Inannaschamra forgot to tell me about it. Later I found out that the air in the room has a special quality that made the glass opaque. As instructed, I sat on the stool, and that started the action. One of the panels opened up, and millions of charts with codes started to flicker on a screen. At the same time, all the other panels turned black. The whole room darkened, and only the front panel, which showed the charts, had any light on it.

At this moment, the screen seemed to release a plasma-like substance, and it came toward me and circled my body. I began to spin around myself, feeling very dizzy and strangely heavy. I am not sure how long it lasted, but it seemed that in an instant I found myself in an ancient town by the sea. To me it seemed not much larger than a fishing village, but this was only because I was not used to first century towns and had the prejudices of a modern person as to what a town should look like. This was Massilia, the Roman name for present day Marseille, a thriving, growing Roman trading port, and I knew it did well because it was the first town of Gallia Narbonensis to have a public sewer system. Actually, it was already an old town, since originally it was built by the Greeks and had archaeological remnants of the Greek settlement. But the Romans had added quite a lot of buildings, streets, and roads since Julius Caesar conquered it.

I knew what to expect, but the experience was nevertheless incredibly bizarre. Most people seem to think that time travel is simply going to the time and place you wish to visit, and entering it as if it were a normal place. This is not so. When time traveling, it is almost as if one travels in virtual reality, and the experience has to build upon itself, to materialize. Therefore, the place was entirely empty, with only a few fishermen standing at a distance on the shore. But they were not moving, they were like statues. The rest of the town was completely empty of people. I felt the town was alive, as if expecting something to happen, but no one was in sight. All of a sudden, people started to appear in the street, but they came from nowhere, from the empty space in the air. Materializing one by one, they filled the town; it felt as if I was meeting apparitions. Then, in a few minutes, I adapted, and started experiencing real life in a real town. Everything became normal.

I decided to take a short walk to just study the town a little. Massilia was a bustling town. The houses were made of stone fixed with mud, low and sturdy, but a few houses were truly elegant. Walking toward the opposite direction from the sea, I entered the open market, full of little stores and workshops. Each workshop was a small, rather dark room, that opened into the street with a large, open doorway. You could see the craftsman working on the goods he hoped to sell, or the merchant surrounded by his goods. Most of the stores were devoted to foodstuffs, such as stores of neatly packaged spices, or one devoted to cheeses and pickles. But there were also some shops that sold fabrics and various notions needed for weaving, sewing, and embroidery. The market, with its noisy cries of the merchants, the interesting smells, and colorful sights, was extremely appealing. After enjoying strolling in the market, I turned back and walked to the shore. The whole place smelled like fresh fish, but it was not terribly unpleasant despite my growing dislike for animal food. Those fishermen who were not at sea were mending nets, cleaning their catch, and doing other chores. Some little fishing boats were turned upside down, being mended. The sun was shining, the light Mediterranean breeze was blowing, and beautiful, big white shells were strewn everywhere. I picked a little warm sand in my hand. Having been brought up in Maine, I was very fond of the sea. The place felt like home and I felt a twinge of homesickness, remembering how my mother used to bring me to the shore and help me collect shells and smooth sea glass and pebbles.

I decided the time came to drag myself away from nostalgia and go visit Mary Magdalene, fully aware that I was postponing this very thing I wished to do because I was quite nervous about it. Resolutely, I turned away and went into the town proper. Many women were carrying baskets on their way to the market, and to my relief, as I looked at myself, I was assured that I was wearing the same clothes as any of the better dressed women who walked the streets. I had on a long woollen outfit, white with multicolor stripes on the sleeves and on the hem, soft leather sandals, and a thin silk scarf loosely covering my head. Obviously, I matched the upper class ladies, just as Sinhar Inannaschamra told me I would. I took my Monitor, which was still hanging around my neck, and looked at my face in the mirror that was part of the Monitor. I looked different than the usual, in a subtle way. The spinning that turns into shape shifting, really affects all the molecules in one's body, even helps one fit into the climate and environment one travels to. Sometimes one does look different for the duration of the trip. I looked a little older, I thought. That was good, I would inspire confidence in Mary Magdalene as an older woman. I must say I liked the ornate silver earrings I was wearing, just showing under the white silk scarf. Very nice, I should get something like that when I was back on Nibiru, I thought. The only thing left was to rehearse the language. At the moment of arrival, I did not know the language, but all it took was hearing one or two words spoken on the street. This is because the spinning opens up the Conduit, and triggers the part of the knowledge depot which is the seat of all languages. As soon as I heard those words, I knew the language as if I had spoken it all my life. I rehearsed a few words, just in case, and felt comfortable. But I was determined to speak to Mary Magdalene in Aramaic, her own language.

I looked at the Monitor, got directions to Mary Magdalene's house, and strolled there, still enjoying the sights and sounds of the busy town. I did not have far to go to the small, neat house, well maintained, and standing in a little garden planted with herbs and flowers. Like all the other houses, it was made of stone and mud, and two stories high.

I stood on the other side of the street, wondering how to approach Mary Magdalene. I was so excited about the meeting, that I did not think about what lines to use to persuade her to talk to me. But everything worked out very well. As luck would have it, I saw a woman approaching the house, carrying a basket. One look and I knew it was Mary Magdalene, because Sinhar Inannaschamra showed her to me on the monitor. She was not beautiful, exactly, but nevertheless was extremely attractive. She must have been in her late thirties, small and slight but with an elegant figure, and she carried herself with poise and dignity. She had lovely, warm brown eyes, and dark chestnut hair slightly touched with white at the temple, which I could see because her scarf was sitting way back on her head. She was simply and neatly dressed in an outfit very much like mine.

I approached her, and greeted her in Aramaic, introducing myself by the name Ambar-Anati, which I was sure would be more familiar to her than Victoria. She seemed extremely surprised and delighted. "Are you from Judea, Ambar-Anati?" she asked in a very pleasant voice.

"No, I am Phoenician," I said. A half truth, but I really could not do any better.

"It is nice to hear you speak Aramaic," she said. "My husband and I speak it at home, and taught it to the children, but most of our friends here do not know it. Won't you come in and rest, and have some refreshments? And tell me what is it that you wished to speak to me about?"

I accepted with pleasure, and we entered the living room, a simply furnished but very clean and pleasant place. She went to place her basket elsewhere, probably a separate little room devoted to cooking, thus giving me time to observe the room carefully.

This was clearly the house of a middle class family. It had many comforts and conveniences, though certainly not ostentation or overt luxury. The walls were neatly plastered and whitewashed, the floor was tiled, and the windows had a lattice structure that provided security and decoration at the same time. There were three or four niches in the walls, each containing an oil lamp. This family obviously did not go to bed with the sun, as poor people were forced to do; the lamps spoke of reading and writing and spending time with family and friends after the sun had set. A few small rugs covered the floor. The room was very adequately furnished with a large table with two benches, each with a few colorful, embroidered pillows on it, storage boxes made from beautiful dark wood, and a built-in stone pallet, with a throw and pillows providing comfortable sitting. Here and there, on the rugs, there were also large cassock-like pillows covered with beautiful fabrics. A couple of copper braziers stood by the wall, awaiting the season of winter and glowing softly. In a corner stood another large table, covered with manuscripts, including one that was currently worked on, writing implements, and inks. The whole room was scented by a big bunch of cut herbs and flowers in a clay jar that stood on the dining table.

Mary Magdalene came back with cold water, wine, cakes, dried figs, and honey.

"As you might know, the Romans decided to make a law here that women cannot drink wine when a man is not around, but we don't pay much attention to it… they don't really follow you into the privacy of your home, I must say." She poured me a glass of wine. The wine was delicious, and she pressed some of the food on me.

"I noticed that your beautiful throw on the couch is white and striped with blue," I said. "These are our colors in Phoenicia, the symbolic colors of the god Melkart."

"Well, there is little difference between our nations, and white and blue are our colors as well. I knitted this throw, thinking all the time of Judea…" said Mary

Magdalene. "Our nations are related, you know. Not only through the marriage of King Solomon and King Hiram's daughter, but even before. I like to hear Yeshua tell me, and the children, about the history of our people. And he told us that many people believe that Joshua, the one that helped Moses during the Exodus, really was a Phoenician Prince. As a matter of fact, he entered Canaan independently, from the north, and settled peacefully. He never even knew Moses, they say."

"I had no idea," I said, making a mental note that this would be a subject worth pursuing at the Akashic Library on my next visit there. "This is fascinating. I really must look into it. I like history too, you know, very much."

"You must visit us often, then, and discuss this matters with Yeshua. He will be happy to meet another enthusiast of his favorite subject."

"I would love that... I promise I will come back, if you will let me. But I might as well tell you what I came to ask you, before I go on enjoying your hospitality," I said, a little guiltily. "You may be angry with me, since I am about to rake up your husband's past."

"I am rarely angry," said Mary Magdalene. "And I don't really mind talking about the past, as long as it is with another woman. I am still afraid of men, though. I always feel we are forever in danger. I constantly warn my husband to stay out of trouble. Now that he is older, he listens better. Yeshua is a very nice, kind man, and he does listen to me when I advise him on many matters, but sometimes I wonder if he understands that we should be careful for as long as we live. He is very intelligent, and extremely well-educated, but between you and me, he has absolutely no common sense."

"I know little about your husband, only that he was falsely arrested by the Romans and you had to leave Judea."

"Indeed, that is the truth. I always knew we would get in trouble," said Mary Magdalene, her smile disappearing. "As I said before, and I mean it, Yeshua just did not have any sense whatsoever. He was a healer, and he had great success in curing many people. Unfortunately, he was also a bit of a magician, and instead of keeping his talents to himself, he would go and perform his healings and miracles in front of important people. They hated him."

"But they could not object to his healings?" I asked. "Nothing is wrong with making people feel better."

"Even healing can seem to be blasphemy, particularly if you also do magical tricks as part of your performance. There was even foolish talk about his making the dead rise – of course this was sheer nonsense. The person that 'rose' from the dead, his name was Lazarus, a relative, simply fainted and Yeshua made him feel better – but such stupid talk would cause trouble. Yeshua never even heard of the story – he was away with his friends the Essenes when it circulated, and I kept it from him when he came back; no point in giving him ideas... But his talents of healing got him a bunch of followers, disciples of sort, and they were good for nothing. All they wanted was magic and sensational tricks, and they went about saying blasphemous things about Yeshua being the Messiah. Naturally, the Sanhedrin, once they heard the word Messiah, took a dislike to him."

"They would be sensitive about it, I suppose," I said. "The Messiah is an important issue with your religion."

"Well, yes, and I must admit Yeshua was quite annoying," said Mary Magdalene, smiling somewhat indulgently at the memory. "The business of having disciples made him think himself of more importance than was good for him. He insisted on preaching, and told people he was the Son of God. Now, that was a common thing to say if you knew the Essenes, a group of desert recluses he once lived with and kept on visiting; actually he spent quite a long time with them, enough to get him to believe in much of their doctrines. They call every honest person 'Son of God.' But the authorities did not like it. Again, it sounded to them like blasphemy. The Sanhedrin members were very set in their ways, except for one man, Joseph of Arimathea. That is because Joseph was an Essene, too. No one knew it, he kept it a secret, since belonging to a sect would have spoiled his business and his reputation, but he never gave up the connection. And of course there was Nicodemus, his young protégé. He was also an Essene. Joseph and Nicodemus were real friends to us. I don't know what we would have done without Joseph, he really handled everything when the trouble began."

"And Yeshua was tried before the Sanhedrin, right?"

"Not right away. First, he was arrested and taken to an interview with the Procurator."

"Am I right that this was Pontius Pilate?" I asked. "Yes," said Mary Magdalene. "That was him. Do you know he was replaced a few years later?"

"No, I had no idea. Why was he replaced?"

"He was accused of some crimes, which of course he did not commit. He simply fell out of favor. Joseph told us on one of his visits to Massilia, since he was very much surprised when the replacement happened. The Romans are sometimes very cruel; it is possible, though we are not sure, that they forced him to commit suicide. Anyway, Pontius Pilate was not terribly interested in Yeshua... it seems he even wanted to acquit him. We know a little because his bodyguard, a Roman centurion, heard everything that was said when Pilate spoke to the representative of the Sanhedrin, and later wrote it all down. That is because he knew Yeshua, who once cured his daughter from a terrible illness. He really saved her life, and from a distance, too. Yeshua never saw the child; he was good at such things. The Roman centurion was very grateful to Yeshua, and thought it would help if he took these notes for posterity. I imagine he knew that between the Romans and the Sanhedrin, they would execute Yeshua. But there was more to it than just this interview. As I said, Pontius Pilate probably would have let Yeshua go free, because he could not care less about religious matters, which were the chief complaints of the Sanhedrin. Rather, Pilate asked him if he had any designs against Caesar, and Yeshua answered that of course not, he had no problem with Caesar at all, he knew Caesar ruled Judea legally. So Pilate asked him if he would admit to Caesar being the strongest god, which was the standard thing to ask, and that was Yeshua's downfall. I would have advised him to admit Caesar's superiority, since it was a private interview and none of his friends was there to hear it. But Yeshua could not bring himself to blaspheme against God. The fool, all he had to do was just nod his head... and what is more, he went very far in his protestations about Caesar. He told Pilate that he, Yeshua, was more powerful than Caesar because there was only one God, and he was the son of God. Again, more Essene nonsense. Naturally, after that, Pilate simply had to turn him over to the Sanhedrin, he had no choice. Someone, years later, was circulating the rumour that Pontius Pilate never forgot Yeshua. Apparently, he was quite interested in his capacity as a healer, and even intended to send him to Caesarea, to be his own healer, since he had some illnesses.

Ah, well. Sometimes, the Sanhedrin can be more cruel than the Romans."

"And what happened then?"

"A huge, famous trial took place. The high priest, Caiaphas, was after Yeshua's blood. He was a Sadducee, you know, one of the rich, higher classes. He felt that Yeshua was a threat to the usual order of rich and poor, high and low... you know, a rebel. Caiaphas was a really nasty man, eager for power. And he had power, lots of it... Our friend, Joseph of Arimathea, did a brilliant job of defending Yeshua, and it would have gone well, but for once Joseph made a horrible mistake. He questioned him, 'Do you consider yourself the Messiah?' and Yeshua denied that in the most sensible manner; after all, Yeshua never thought of himself as the Messiah! Never came into his head to imagine that! Then, Joseph asked the question that destroyed everything. He said, 'Who are you, then, Yeshua?' and Yeshua was stupid enough to say, 'I am the Son of God.' I know, I know, he should have known better, but he was very foolish at that time. That gave the Sanhedrin the excuse to send him to the crucifixion. Caiaphas practically jumped with joy when he heard Yeshua say this thing. Horrible, horrible man, Caiaphas. I will hate him as long as I live, and believe me, I am not quick to hate."

"So he really was crucified," I said, sadly.

"Yes, Yeshua was crucified. I cannot tell you how cruel, how horrible, this practice is. He suffered so much, blood all over his body. I was with his mother, and one of his disciples, but nobody else. All the other disciples ran away, they were scared to death, fearing they would be arrested by the Sanhedrin. It broke my heart that these people, who always claimed to love Yeshua so much, were not there for him as he was dying. A few people gathered around, probably just curious people, and they stood near the cross, but not very close, because the Roman soldiers did not allow them to do so. His poor mother collapsed twice in my arms."

"His mother, Mary of Nazareth… Yes, please tell me, what was Mary like?"

"Mary… I miss her so much. She was very kind, always so sweet. I loved her very much, she never said an unkind word to me. And she had every reason to be mad at me, because I broke God's law and lived with Yeshua before we were legally married, I am ashamed to say…"

"But you always meant to be married, so it does not signify," I said.

"Oh, indeed, we always meant to be married. It was just because of all these delays and troubles, and things sometimes just happen when you are young… Still, many other women would have held it against me. But not Mary. She was too kind."

"What did she look like?"

"She was incredibly beautiful," said Mary Magdalene, her eyes misty with the memory. "I have never seen anyone as beautiful as Mary. She was only fourteen when Yeshua was born, so she was still young when the trouble happened. She had very long black hair, which she always put in one long braid. Her skin was white, like the finest ivory, and she had big, clear blue eyes, rather unusual for our people. She always wore a lot of blue, she was a little vain about her eyes and about her great beauty, but not in an unpleasant way, and who could blame her… My daughter Sarah inherited these amazing eyes, every time I look at her I think of Mary…" She wiped a tear. "Do you know, Mary's hair began to gray very quickly after Yeshua's crucifixion. It only took a couple of months before it was all silvery white; it must have been the agony she went through, seeing her son undergo such pain. But even with the silver hair she looked young and beautiful. Perhaps even more beautiful. There was something so delicate, so soulful about Mary."

"So the two of you stayed by Yeshua's side. It must have been heart-breaking."

"We just stood there, crying and helpless. The men on the two crosses on Yeshua's sides fainted, off and on, like Yeshua. Then, Nicodemus came and asked the Roman soldier, who was guarding this row of crucifixes, if he can wipe the face of Yeshua, and give him something to drink from a sponge. The soldier said 'Yes, go ahead,' so Nicodemus dipped the sponge in a bucket and brought it to Yeshua's mouth. I saw him sipping from the sponge, and blood kept pouring and pouring from his hands and his feet. A few moments later, it was clear that he passed away; Mary fainted and fell to the floor. As for me, I felt this was not happening, as if it was a nightmare, and I was expecting to wake up. As if in a dream, I approached the Roman soldier and asked him if I could take Yeshua home for burial. I simply could not bear to leave him there on the cross. But he said that this was against the rules. I asked him, 'What are you going to do with his body? He is dead, after all.' The soldier told me that the law requires that all crucified people first be checked to see if they were really dead, because sometimes it takes them two or three days to die. And after that, the Romans would take them and dump them in a place reserved for crucified people and other condemned dead prisoners."

"This is disgraceful," I said

"Yes, it was very hard. But we were helpless. What could two women do against the Roman soldiers? So we left, and returned to the house, where we kept crying all of the late afternoon and evening. Suddenly the door opened, and Joseph of Arimathea came in. He looked hurried and upset. 'I have some news for you,' he said. 'I went to Pontius Pilate and I asked him for a favor. I know Pilate through business, so they let me in. I asked him if I could take Yeshua's body to be buried in my own family grave. Pilate said 'Fine, go ahead.' To tell you the truth, Ambar-Anati, I don't think Pilate cared one bit about anyone in Judea. He was so bored with us and all he wanted was to get out of this nasty job."

"So Joseph got the body? What did he do with it?" I asked.

"I can repeat the exact conversation, I remember it like yesterday," said Mary Magdalene. "Joseph said, 'this is a great secret, which you cannot tell anyone, especially Simon and Peter and the rest of the disciples.'"

"I will say nothing," I said to him. "Just tell me what you have done."

"I had to do something very quickly so no one will find his body," said Joseph. "I got Nicodemus, and we took Yeshua right away to the grave of my family, making sure everyone saw that. Then I put some of his clothes there, arranging them so that they would look as if they contained the body, but we only stayed there for a few minutes."

"Clothes? But what did you do with the body?" I asked him, perplexed.

"As soon as we were alone, Nicodemus and I transferred Yeshua to another place, which for the moment must remain secret. We rushed to do it as fast as possible, which was extremely lucky, because as soon as I came back to my family grave I saw Roman centurions marching toward it. I asked the Romans what did they come for, and one of them told me that they got an order to guard the tomb, and they must seal it first. I did not want to ask them who gave the orders, but I suspect it was some of my friends at the Sanhedrin... The Romans helped me to roll the big stone that usually sealed the grave. I felt so relieved, since I knew no one will get in anymore, and no one will ever know that Yeshua was not there."

"I don't understand anything, Joseph," I said. "Why did you have to go through all that? Why not simply bury Yeshua properly?"

"Just wait, Mary," he said. "I find it very hard to explain. I went your relative, Elizabeth, and told her what I did. She said that she would like to go and anoint the body in preparation for the burial. So I told her, 'You don't need to do that.' 'What do you mean?' she said. 'This is out tradition!' So I told her the truth. 'Yeshua is not going to be buried. He is going to be all right.' She thought I was crazy, probably you think I am crazy too."

I interrupted him, and I asked, "Are you mad? Are you trying to tell me that Yeshua is alive? How can that be? I saw him die on the cross, right after Nicodemus washed his face and let him sip some water. Did you witness a miracle? Is Yeshua really the son of God?"

"It was not a miracle, Mary, but the water were not plain water, either," he said. "I know something about herbs, from my days with the Essenes. I put a very strong herbal concoction in the water, one that creates a death-like state that would last a few hours. And with the blood that Yeshua lost, and his weakened condition, he will be like dead for at least a night, but then he will wake up."

My mother-in-law heard all that in total silence, in complete shock. She obviously could not accept the good news so soon after the horrible ordeal. But then she said, "I must go to him, right away. I have to help my child, whether he is dead or alive."

"You cannot do so, my dear," said Joseph gently. "If you don't stay at home, and receive your friends and neighbors' condolences, the Romans will suspect something. Tomorrow morning, very early, Elizabeth and Mary Magdalene will come to see him. But you must be brave and stay here and pretend that Yeshua is dead and buried. It is essential if we are to save his life."

And this is exactly what we did. We stayed all night. The next day, Mary stayed home, but Joseph came and led me to a cave, quite a distance from our village. Nicodemus was guarding the entrance, and moved to let us in. Yeshua was lying on a large stone, which was covered with some soft blankets. He was exhausted and could not talk at all, but he was alive! Joseph saved him! I immediately saw that Joseph thought of everything. There was a bowl of grapes and olives by Yeshua's side, and some flat bread, and a jar of water. And Joseph brought clean clothes for Yeshua. We treated his wounds as best we could, cleaned him, and dressed him with the fresh clothes. He felt better and could mumble a few words of thanks, but he was not entirely conscious.

"What will happen now, Joseph?" I asked.

"We are going to take Yeshua away, to the house of two fishermen I regularly do business with. They are very loyal to me, and one of them is from Tyre, which will ease our escape."

We went there, a rather long journey, Joseph and Nicodemus carrying Yeshua on a large board which they covered with the blankets. The fishermen were waiting for us. They were really very scared, but they were trustworthy and kept their word. We took Yeshua inside the house, and there were two women there, one of them a Phoenician woman who rushed to help us, and took Yeshua to a small room where he could rest. We spent a short time with him inside the room, while the two other men were guarding the house.

"Mary," said Joseph, "Yeshua must leave Judea right away. He is in grave danger here."

"That is fine," I said. "I have some money, perhaps we should hire a boat?"

"Do not concern yourself with that," said Joseph very kindly. "Everything has been taken care of. You stay right here, look after Yeshua, and I will go and talk to his mother and his brothers."

The next day Yeshua's brother James came, with his mother; the other brothers and sisters did not believe what Joseph told them. But Mary and James came, and they could not believe their eyes. James behaved rather strangely, he told Joseph, 'What kind of trick was that? This is not my brother!' So Yeshua looked at him and told him, 'Do you remember the cut I had on the upper side of my left shoulder?' I knew he had the cut. So James, said, 'Yes, let me see.' And Yeshua showed him the cut, and James fainted. Joseph told us that by tomorrow at the latest, we would go to Tyre for a few days, then get a bigger ship and go the Island of Arwad. He had friends there, business associates, dealing with the olives and olive oil business.

I went to Arwad with Yeshua, Nicodemus, and Joseph, while Mary and James went back home to Judea. Joseph told Mary that within a week, or ten days, I don't remember exactly, he would come back to Judea and take her with him to see us somewhere else. He did not tell her where we would be, just in case if she would be questioned. So Mary, James, and the other brothers and sisters stayed in Judea. We spent three days in Arwad, a beautiful small island. Many Phoenicians were there, of course speaking fluent Aramaic, so we could mingle with the crowd and nobody knew who we were. Nevertheless, we mostly stayed inside the house Joseph rented for us. We did not feel safe.

Then one afternoon, Yeshua was amusing himself doing one of his old tricks. He was trying to lift himself up in the air, attempting to fly, or float. He did manage to float a little bit. He used to do a lot of tricks like that. While we were enjoying his attempts, Joseph returned from an errand, and told us that tomorrow we were going to Cyprus, since Arwad was not really safe. Unfortunately, I started to feel extremely tired, and I suspected I was pregnant, but nobody knew; I did not want to worry either Yeshua or Joseph, particularly since we were not married yet. We were planning on getting married, as we discussed before, but so many things happened to prevent it. However, now, there was not time to lose; we had to be married before the child was born. But first, we had to get to Cyprus. So when we arrived, a few days later, the very first thing we did was to get married, and I felt so much the better for it.

Joseph again rented a house for us, and then he and Nicodemus returned to Judea. Actually, his plan was to bring Mary to us. He was uneasy about her safety there, and so were we. One month later, he indeed brought her to Cyprus, and I was so happy to see her and tell her about our marriage and the coming child.

Joseph stayed a very short time, and then returned again to Judea. He warned us to stay put and wait until we hear from him before we did anything. And so we lived quietly, and Yeshua regained his strength, but he was limping, and could not walk straight without leaning on me as he walked. I realized that his full healing will take some time, but I was very happy in Cyprus, away from the trouble in Judea. After another month, Joseph returned. I asked him, in confidence, about the disciples. He told me to forget them, never count on any of them. They were cowards. Only Peter showed some regret, and visited Joseph once in a while. The others just went on with their lives. I am sorry to say that Yeshua's brothers and sisters also avoided him, pretending they did not know he was alive. Fear would do such things to people.

Eventually I gave birth to my eldest daughter, Sarah. We stayed in Cyprus until Sarah was three years old, and in the meantime Yeshua found jobs here and there. Everybody liked him, but he lived very quietly and did not go out much. Most important, I insisted that he should not make trouble, or start preaching. No more stories or sermons. The truth is, he did not want to do so anyway. I think he had enough of sermons, disciples, and preaching. Of course, he could no longer do physical work, so there was no carpentry or handyman jobs for him, which made him a little sad because he liked physical labor. But he put to use his considerable knowledge of languages, and became a scribe.

Once every five or six months, Joseph came to see us. Life was pleasant enough, but Mary never quite recovered from the ordeal of the crucifixion. She was so delicate, and the ordeal broke her health for good. Eventually she became very ill, and even though we tried everything to cure her, she died rather suddenly. We buried her in Cyprus, but years later, Joseph took her body back to Judea for her final resting place, next to her husband, who was also called Joseph and who I have never known, to my sorrow, since he died before I met Yeshua. I still miss my dear Mary.

Following Joseph's advice, we decided to go to Gallia Narbonensis, which had a few large Jewish communities. We planned to settle in Massilia. Joseph went with us, and also an Ethiopian maid we had in Cyprus, a seventeen years old girl that Joseph brought us for help. She loved us and did not want to part from us. Later, in Massilia, she married a very nice young man, had a family, and we still visit each other. On the way, I asked Joseph why he took so much trouble to help us.

"You went beyond friendship, even beyond family requirement, Joseph," I said to him with gratitude. "Why are you so kind to us?"

Joseph was quiet for a short time, thinking, musing. "I love you like my own family," he said to me, his honest black eyes looking earnestly into mine. "But it is more than that. I have caused Yeshua, his mother, and you, all the suffering that you have undergone. I will never forgive myself, and forever I will have to atone for my sin."

"You? Caused us suffering?" I asked, incredulously.

"Don't you remember?" he said. "I was the one who asked Yeshua the fatal question during the trial. If I had not asked him who he was, they would have set him free."

I had to cry. "No, Joseph, it was not you. Certainly, the question was misjudged. But the Sanhedrin would have tried to kill Yeshua no matter what. Please, please, don't think about it anymore." We never discussed it again, but I don't think I had any luck in changing his mind, the poor, good man that he was.

Joseph, of course, knew many people in Massilia, since he had much business with them. He took us to a small shop owned by a Jewish friend, who had rented a house for us and got it ready. I loved our house from the first day, it felt like home, even the smell of the house was a little like the houses in Judea, for some reason, possibly because we always lived in fishing villages, and Massilia was a fishing town.

For the first time I felt really safe, far from everyone, Caiaphas in particular. You see, until we came here, I was always afraid Caiaphas will somehow hear about us. He had his spies everywhere. But Gallia Narbonensis was far enough from Judea, and only business people, like Joseph, would have much to do with it. Yeshua, too, began to get used to the place, and consorted with Jews only, since we thought they were the safest. He got a job as a scribe. He kept on surprising me. In Cyprus, I saw him writing Greek. I told him I never knew he spoke Greek, and he laughed and said, 'I speak all the languages.' 'I asked him, where did you learn it?' He said, 'I learned it in Qumran, from the Essenes'. So here he developed more skills. He brushed up on his Latin, and started to learn Gaelic, he was so good with languages, so now with Hebrew, Aramaic, Greek, Latin, and Gaelic, business was okay, and life became comfortable. We had two more children, a boy and a girl. The boy is called Joseph, after Yeshua's father. You can't say he is named also after Joseph of Arimathea, since we are not allowed to call babies after living people. The girl is called Rachel. And you know our eldest is Sarah. They are all good children, I am happy to say."

Mary Magdalene suddenly stopped talking, and I saw she was smiling at someone behind me. I turned my head, and saw a man entering the room.

"Ambar-Anati, this is my husband, Yeshua. Yeshua, this is a new friend, she came all the way to hear your story."

We greeted each other. It was hard to believe that I was looking, meeting, talking with Jesus Christ. This pleasant, ordinary, normal man? Could it be? He was not at all what I expected. He did not have fair long hair, he did not possess an ascetic, pale face, or an emaciated body. Instead, Yeshua had frizzy dark hair, a little curly on the back. He had dark skin, black eyes, and was strongly built, stocky, and not very tall, probably five eight or nine; you could say he was a little plump, though certainly not fat, Just comfortable looking. He wore sandals, a blue gray

244

outfit, and carried two bags. One was a leather book bag, and the other a basket full of eggs and dry fruits. Jesus Christ, shopping at market? And yet, it had to be him, Jesus of Nazareth, Jesus Christ... There could be no one else with a history so similar. I lost my head and I asked him, "Are you the One?" Fortunately, he did not understand what I meant. He smiled and said, "I am sorry, what did you say?" Stupidly, I asked him again, "Are you the Messiah?" He laughed like a child, and said, "Don't bring up old stories and memories, all this is well behind me..." Well, at least I did not kneel before him. That would have not gone too well. So I recovered myself and smiled at him, just as if he were a normal new acquaintance.

"Let me make some supper," said Mary Magdalene. "Please stay and eat with us, Ambar-Anati. You will also like to meet the children, I am sure."

"I am sorry, Mary. I really must go, I have to meet someone and go home."

"May I take you where you need to go?" Yeshua asked helpfully.

"No, really, there is no need. I am meeting them by the shore, just a few steps."

"If there is any trouble, though, and they don't arrive on time, come right back, won't you?" said Mary Magdalene.

"I will. And with your permission, I would like to visit again, and meet the children."

"I am counting on it," said Mary Magdalene. We parted cordially, and I left. I was going to the shore, where I could be hidden from sight as I planned to give the code and go back to Nibiru through my Monitor. As I was turning around the house, slowly, thinking about this wonderful experience, I was passing the window and heard Yeshua's voice. I stood for a moment, listening. I did not mean to eavesdrop, it was just that it was hard for me to part from these two wonderful people who meant so much to me, and I just lingered.

"Wait one minute, Mary, before you go to make the supper," Yeshua said. "I have something really interesting to tell you, which I want to do before the children come. I don't want them to hear it. It is downright amazing... there is a Greek man out there in the public plaza, he is doing what I used to do... but he is much smarter than me. He was preaching about God, and of all things, who do you think he was also talking about, to a dozen of people? Me! was talking about me!"

There was a short silence. Then I heard Mary Magdalene say, her voice full of anxiety, even terror. "Yeshua, did you get in trouble? Did you do something stupid?"

"No, no, I did nothing dangerous. I just asked the fishermen, 'Who is this man?' They said he was a Roman, or a Greek, and his name is Paul, or Saul, or something like that... he came from Judea. They said he personally knew a demigod, Jesus, something like that... Well, I had to talk to him, because I know the language, and Jesus is a version of my own name. I was terribly curious."

"You talked to him? He could have gotten you arrested!" cried Mary Magdalene, aghast.

"He is much more likely to be arrested himself, my dear. He is talking blasphemy, while I am just the respectable scribe everyone knows around here... I took him aside and we talked for a short time. I said to him that I think it was I he was talking about, my name is Yeshua. He looked at me, and his eyes were shifty, mean, and shrewd. I usually like people, as you know, but I did not like this man. He said, 'Maybe you are, maybe you are not, my man. I really don't care either way, because you don't count. I

246

have come with a new religion, I have brought the Messiah. Don't interfere with me – I plan to have a following all over the world.' Now, when he mentioned the word Messiah, I just had to laugh, and so I slapped him on the shoulder and left him alone to continue with his business."

"So did he go back to his preaching?" asked Mary Magdalene. Her voice, I was pleased to tell, was not so strained anymore.

"Yes, he went right back to his preaching," said Yeshua, his voice full of laughter. "I stood at a little distance and listened to him as he talked on and on. Do you know what he said? He was telling everyone that I died on the cross, and then I rose from the dead and came back to life! Even I, in my best days as a magician, could have never invented such nonsense. Rose from the dead! Can you believe it?"

*** *** ***

CHAPTER FOURTEEN
Envoy to Earth

How my daughter, Sinhar Ninlil, persuaded me to take up my new mission. How the Council sent me to negotiate with high echelon government and military personnel on earth. Roswell's legacy, Eisenhower's historic first meeting with the Grays, Dulce Base, and more information about the treaties between our governments and the Grays.

1990, Nibiru

When my daughter was born, I stayed on Nibiru for twelve years of perfect happiness. There is little to tell about a time like that, spent with family and friends, enjoying a world without strife, trouble, or poverty, knowing that while you are happy, so is everyone else. I studied, both alone and in the Academy with Sinhar Inannaschamra, concentrating on history, but also picking up other subjects. The seasons, so beautiful on Nibiru, followed each other like golden dreams, and I loved the flakes of snow, the warm rain, the blooming flowers, and the changing leaves as they came and left. I refused to make changes in my home. Most people on Nibiru allow their children to play with the décor, but I loved my garden-inspired home so much, I wanted to keep it like that for a few hundred years. Fortunately, my daughter's creativity took another turn. She became a linguist and a poet, and her greatest delight was to play with words, translate, create new combinations, and enjoy the sounds of one language after another. Besides attending her lessons at the Academy, she spent hours with Marduchk at both the home library and the Akashic Library, fleeting from cone to cone like a little butterfly, soaking knowledge.

Marduchk had finished his own mission with the ape-like beings whose image scared me so much on the night of my wedding. He succeeded perfectly. The ape-like things were saved, the diplomatic arrangements made as smooth as silk, and Marduchk became even more respected and admired on Nibiru than before. He was now considered a full Leader, there was talk about asking him to join the High Council, and in my opinion, no one deserved the honor more than my husband. Yes, there is nothing to tell about such a wonderful time.

One afternoon I was sitting in the garden under my favorite tree, relaxing and enjoying the flowers around me. It was a softly lit day of pearly mists, not sufficiently thick to be dank, just enough to filter the golden light and make it dance among the leaves. The mist floated in ribbons and sheets all around me, and I thought of nothing at all, allowing my mind to wander peacefully.

Suddenly, I received a message from my daughter. I opened the Conduit and invited her to join me in the garden, and in a few minutes I saw her slender little figure outlined against the golden mists, as usual flanked by two cats. All our cats, unless very busy with some issues of their own, followed Sinhar Ninlil wherever she went. She came and sat on the bench next to me, with her demure, elegant attitude, so typical of Anunnaki children from an extremely early age. I never failed to marvel at the maturity these children expressed, while not losing their childlike joy and endless creativity. I smiled at her, as always impressed by her great beauty. I cannot tell what her genetic lineage was, since she was born Anunnaki style, with genetic material derived only from me and activated by the Light, but somehow she resembled Sinhar

250

Inannaschamra, except for her curly chestnut hair, which looked more like Miriam's. The Anunnaki, who understand their own genetic material, were probably not at all surprised by Ninlil's looks, but to me it was a closed book. Was my genetic material somehow related to that of Sinhar Inannaschamra? I could not tell. One day, I always promise myself, I will take a greater interest in the life sciences, and find out more about my genetic relationships.

"Mother," said Ninlil, "there is something very important we need to discuss." Naturally, the conversation was telepathic, but I will translate.

"What is it?" I asked, expecting a new interest or plan on my daughter's part.

"I have come to the conclusion that you are shirking your duty on my behalf," said Ninlil, quite bluntly.

"Shirking my duty? What do you mean, my dear?" I said, mystified.

"You have been postponing your mission indefinitely in order to be with me," said the child. I stared at her, incredulous, but she did not wait for my reply.

"I asked Sinhar Inannaschamra why you are not following any mission. I never thought about it before today, but when I was at the Academy, a few of the other children discussed their parents' missions, and I stayed after class and asked her."

I must say I was deeply grateful the girl did not bring it up in front of the other children, but I did not say anything about it. Instead I asked, "And what did Sinhar Inannaschamra say?"

"She told me that you prefer to wait until I was older. That is not necessary, Mother."

"It is true," I said, rather humbly. "I know I should go, but am afraid you will feel abandoned if I go away."

"Abandoned? Why, most of my friends' parents are on various missions, on and off. Surely you don't want to deprive yourself of serving Nibiru until I am seventy-one years old?"

"I was thinking of going on my mission when you reach eighteen," I said.

"What is so special about eighteen?" asked Ninlil, intrigued. I laughed. Of course, she would not know that on earth people left home and went to college at eighteen. "Won't you miss me, Ninlil?" I asked.

"Of course I will. But it seems to me that this is how everyone lives here. Won't we talk to each other every day, if you go?"

"Yes, every single day."

"And now Father has just finished his off-planet mission, and plans to spend a few years working on the results in the Akashic Library, so he will be here for me. And my aunt, and cousins, and great-great-grandmother will all look after me, Mother. You should feel free to go. After all, I am twelve years old, and I attend the Academy regularly. I am mature enough to manage."

I laughed, hugged the darling little thing, and also cried a bit. I knew that my mission will be very, very long this time. Not so long for the full Anunnaki, but very long for me, a half Anunnaki that was not as yet fully adjusted. "Very well," I said. "I will speak to your father and to the Council. What must be done, must be done."

As usual in moments of crisis, Marduchk suddenly materialized next to us. How he always knows instantly when things happen, I can't figure out, since he never attempts to read anyone's thoughts without permission, being too ethical for that. But somehow he does know and he comes as soon as he is needed. We explained, and he said, "A few years, Victoria, that is all. Ninlil will still be a child when you come back. Remember, on Nibiru they are children until they are seventy-one. I know why it is hard for you, after you had to give up your son, but this is different. She will be with me, Victoria. And we will wait for you together." So that was that, the decision was made, and I contacted the Council.

"Well said, Sinhar Ambar Anati," said the Council. I was in the usual meeting room, presenting my new plan. "Yes, we are happy that you are ready to go on your mission. We want you to represent us on earth. Are you sure this is done entirely with Free Will? You do not feel pressured to do it?"

"I am doing it with complete Free Will," I said. I hope this was the whole truth; it was still hard to leave my daughter and Marduchk for the long years on the mission. But come to think of it, the Council would have caught the false tone with their Conduits, if I were not certain, so I suppose I meant it whole heartedly.

"Following your previous mission with the hybrids, we have been using your data and correlating it with material we knew about from the past. The problem, as you know, is the Grays' involvement with humans, which exists on many levels. We know what is on their minds, since through the Miraya, and through the rest of our apparatus, we can read their thoughts, minds, and intentions. Unfortunately, the humans cannot do so, and the Grays have kept them in ignorance about many aspects of their conduct and agenda.

To begin with, the humans believe that all the Grays come from Zeta Reticuli. That is not entirely true. Yes, Zeta Reticuli is their original planet, but they have lived on earth, mostly underwater, for thousands of years. In their minds, the Grays own the earth, and the humans are

253

interlopers. Another thing the humans don't understand is the degree of viciousness of the Grays' agenda. Therefore, they were willing to negotiate with the Grays, more than once.

We, of course, could not counter-negotiate with either species. The Grays, as we know only too well, are too treacherous to deal with anyway. They pretend to obey us, out of fear, but go on with whatever they want behind our backs, knowing we would not annihilate them. We cannot eliminate them, ethically, since they are not our creation; we can only eliminate races we have created. That is the policy. As for the humans, we would not want to negotiate with the humans like the Grays did, because since when does a creator negotiate with his creations? It is not seemly. And yet, we knew for many years that there are reasons for serious alarm. We became very concerned because the abduction of humans, mutilation of animals, and the implants in human bodies were already severely contaminating earth. We did not know how far it went until you gave us your report, after your mission with the Hybrids. But now we know that their actions could lead to the destruction of the planet."

"Even supposing earth is destroyed, how will it affect the Anunnaki?" I asked. "It is a great distance from Nibiru, after all."

"If the earth is destroyed by the Grays and their experiments, it will affect the total solar system, and consequently, have major implications on other systems, including ours. Everything is connected, as you know, through All-That-Is. The humans have a saying which applies very well: 'No man is an island.' We could paraphrase it for star systems, and be entirely correct. We wanted to postpone our return to earth for dealing with this situation, and follow the correct planetary time when

254

Nibiru is closer to earth's location, but this is no longer practical. If earth, or any planet in the Milky Way is destroyed, it will jeopardize many of our projects, and threaten our security. We needed to explore all the issues."

"I imagine there were other envoys, before me?" I asked.

"Yes, we tried, since 1947. That was the year when a spaceship crashed on earth; we will soon tell you more about the crash. But even before that, we had contacted humans of great distinction in the fields of art, literature, music, science, etc., and we guided them in their research and creations. From such people we drew a few envoys. We thought they could influence and correct the psyche and code of ethics of humanity, since we had no intention of achieving our success through the low practices of exchange of technology in return for abductions, of course. But we failed in these attempts. The humans in control could not be influenced by the goodness of our delegates, and worse, to our chagrin, many of those illustrious people were murdered. Mahatma Ghandi, to give you one example, was killed for his attempts. There were many others.

And so we think that sending you as our envoy would be the right thing. You are both a full Anunnaki by genetic makeup, and a human by upbringing. You will be our best chance to warn the humans and change their ways; perhaps you will be our last chance."

"I understand," I said, "and I will do my best. You were going to tell me about the events of 1947?"

"Yes, you must have heard of the Roswell incident," said the Council. "In 1947, a Grays' spacecraft crashed in Roswell. Two Grays died from the impact, but one survived. The Americans held him underground at Andrew Air Force Base. Strangely enough, a sort of friendship was developed between the Gray and two American civilian scientists, something that we still don't understand, but there it was."

"I agree, the Grays don't usually show any emotion," I said. "They are much like a hive mentality, insects…"

"Right, and at the same time, the Americans were only interested in acquiring advanced military weapon systems, not in a friendship with an alien. But somehow they became friends. At that time, the American military kept everything under cover and did not inform even the Congress or the President of the United States. One general actually said, 'Civilians and politicians come and go. But we, the military, that is our career. Therefore, they should not be informed and if the Congress will not be told, consequently the American public should not be told either.' That was the policy that was adopted on a regular basis ever since."

"This is frightening," I said. "The military should not control the decision."

"Indeed they should not. Look at the Miraya, Sinhar Ambar Anati. Here is one of the first conversations between the surviving Gray and the two American scientists."

On the screen, I saw an office, quite ordinary and simply furnished. Two men and a Gray sat around an empty desk. They seemed comfortable, there was no tension that you would expect in such a company. Then, the sound came from the Miraya.

One of the American scientists,[8] asked the Gray, "So where did you come from? And why are you here?"

---

[8] A note from Victoria: I cannot reveal the scientist's name, since this could endanger his family.

"We have been here for thousands of years, sir," said the Gray, in perfect English, though his voice had the usual scratchy sound of his race. "We have our bases underwater, in the Pacific, near Puerto Rico, and under Alaska's glaciers."

"Thousands of years?"

"That is so, sir. We consider ourselves the first and the legitimate inhabitants and owners of the earth. You are not. We are here because we need natural resources that exist on earth and in the oceans."

"Seems to me this is not all you need, buddy," said the other scientist, grinning and lighting a cigarette.

"This is true. We also need some live organisms, and various substances we can extract from human bodies."

"And do you get all you want?" asked the first scientist.

"Yes, by and large. We need them on a constant basis," said the Gray. "The natural resources of the earth and the water are regularly mined. The human substances are more difficult to obtain. We get them from the humans we abduct."

To my disgust, the two scientists nodded in agreement, totally unimpressed by the mention of the abductions. They really did not seem to mind.

"What bugs me," said the first scientist, "is that we tried so hard to reverse engineer your spaceship, ever since we got it after the crash in Roswell. We just can't do it. You have to help us decipher the codes on the screens we found inside the spaceship, and also the geometric and scientific symbols on the grids and measuring tapes we found scattered around the spaceship. Our team is getting impatient; they may even threaten to kill you, you know. The two of us are friendly with you, but the team is getting ugly, and the boss is mad."

257

"What is the point?" said the Gray without showing any emotion, not even fear regarding the threat. "Even if I teach you how things work, and decipher all the codes for you, you will not be able to reverse engineer our technology, because you don't have the raw materials. Look at this."

From somewhere around his body, he pulled out a piece of metal.

"This is a very light metal yet stronger than any material known on earth. Yet this sheet of metal could float in the air, and can be bent and folded like paper and then, open up on its own. Look!" He demonstrated. The metal seemed to be indestructible.

"You must understand that we are willing to reveal plenty of information," said the Gray. "But we can only do so if you will allow me to go home. I need to recharge my body, it's like a battery, you know. I will die if I stay much longer, and that will be useless to you. Let me go, and I will arrange for others to come back with me, others who know much more than I do. I am a simple pilot. I will bring you scientists. We have no intention of hiding this knowledge from you, on the contrary, we have every reason to cooperate with you and do some joint projects. And we can supply the raw materials and the knowledge of how to turn it all to your advantage."

"So since we are such good friends," said the second scientist, "tell me, where exactly is the home you speak of? Since you have lost the spaceship, obviously, we will have to take you there.'"

"If I tell you, you will not understand and you will not be able to take me there, since it involves getting through additional dimensions. Our scientists constructed our bases' entries like that, as a precaution against intruders. But if you take me back to Roswell, exactly where we crashed, I will find my own way."

"How will you do that?"

"Simple," said the Gray. "When a spacecraft lands on a particular spot, automatically it marks the spot, scans it, and sends data to our mission control for identification and location purposes. Thus, we are never lost. If I can contact my people, they will come for me."

"But if you go away, how do we communicate with you, and find out when the others are coming?"

"In the spacecraft there is a communication device. Let's go there. I am sure it is functional, because it is really indestructible. I'll teach you how to use it. We will contact my people from there and tell them about our plan. You will be there to supervise everything. Bring the boss, too, just in case."

The scientists looked at each other. They seemed rather pleased.

"Very well," said one of them. "We'll come back for you later tonight, after we talk to the boss. I am sure he will agree to our plan."

"It will be a feather in his cap," said the Gray, using an old human expression unexpectedly. The two scientists burst out laughing.

The Council stopped the record, and spoke to me.

"And that, Sinhar Ambar Anati, was indeed what happened. They took him back to Roswell, and left him there on the exact spot of the crash. They did not leave the area, though, but hid in a small canteen which was placed at some distance, to watch what was going to happen to the Gray. In a very short time, a spaceship came, landed, and he went in. The spaceship took off directly and vanished into the sky.

259

The scientists sent the piece of metal which the Gray has demonstrated with to a military laboratory, and they called one engineer from Lockheed Corporation and another one from MIT to analyse the piece. Nobody could figure out what it was made of. Still, prior to his departure, apparently the Gray did reveal many secrets of very advanced technology, that American corporations started developing right away, and began to use ten years later. Many of the highly advanced electronic gadgets American consumers used for a quarter of a century came from the Grays."

"And what happened then?"

"A few years passed. Then, a historic meeting happened. In February 1954, President Dwight Eisenhower went for a week's vacation to Palm Springs, California. This was a little strange, and many did not quite understand the timing, because he just came back from a quail shooting vacation in Georgia. Actually, it was less than a week before his trip to Palm Springs. Taking two vacations in a row was not his style, but nevertheless he did go, and arranged to stay there for a week. Now, a president, as you know, is always surrounded by other officials, not to mention body guards; he is never out of sight. But on the night of February 20, the President of the United States disappeared. The press, which somehow was alerted despite all the efforts for secrecy, spread rumors that he was ill, or that he suddenly died. The president's people were alarmed, so they called an emergency press conference, and announced that Eisenhower lost a tooth cap at his dinner, and had to be rushed to a dentist. To make it more believable, the dentist was presented to the people. He was invited to a function the next evening, and was introduced all around. This, again, was strange. Why would a dentist be invited to such an affair, and why would the

President's personnel take such care to make him visible to everyone?"

"I imagine it must have been a cover-up for the President's real business."

"It was. Eisenhower was actually taken to Muroc Airfield, which later was renamed Edwards Air Force Base. There, he met with Grays. No president had ever done so before. The delegation of the extraterrestrials consisted of eleven Grays. Six from Zeta Reticuli, and five from earth's underwater bases."

"But of course, this was not the last meeting," I said.

"Certainly not. This marked the beginning of negotiations between the government of United States and the Grays. The situation was no longer only in the hands of the military, but went much further."

"How was this meeting arranged, in the first place?" I asked, intrigued.

"It started a year before the meetings. In 1953, astronomers discovered some large objects that at first were believed to be asteroids, and later proven to be spaceships. They were very large, but since they took a high orbit around the equator, they were not visible to laymen. Two projects were installed – Project Sigma, created to interpret the Grays' radio communications, and Project Plato, created to establish diplomatic relationships with the extraterrestrials. There were talks about other races that contacted the humans at that time, arguments regarding who the treaties should be signed with, and so on. As a matter of fact, the Nordics, a benevolent race, tried to prevent the humans from accepting these evil treaties, and wanted them to dismantle their nuclear weapons and abandon their road to self destruction, but they were not listened to. The Nordics wanted the humans to go on a path of spiritual growth, but what the humans wanted was military secrets."

"Probably because they are so badly contaminated, they would not even consider a peaceful offer," I said, rather sadly.

"Precisely. And the treaty with the Grays was signed. It basically said that the Grays and the humans will not interfere with each other's affairs. The humans will keep their presence a secret, and they will be allowed to experiment on cows and on a limited number of human abductees. The abductees' names would be reported to the U.S. government for control, they were not to be harmed, and they should be returned to their homes after the memory of the events was erased."

"But, as we know, they did not keep the promise, and extended their experiments without telling the U.S. government," I said.

"True. They could not be trusted. But let's face it, the humans were treacherous as well. For example, there was the issue of the Gray that had arranged all that. He came back with the delegation of 1954, and agreed to stay on earth as a hostage of good will, on condition that he would be allowed freedom to go back and forth to recharge himself. This lasted for a year, but soon enough the Americans, having learned a little about the vicious plans of the Grays and the excessive number of abductions that was not agreed upon, turned back on their word to the hostage and locked him up for three years. As a result, he developed extreme claustrophobia that eventually killed him. They won't let him recharge himself."

"Frankly," I said, "The humans are no better than the Grays."

"There are still good humans out there, those who are not contaminated," said the Council. "But they usually don't go into government business. That is why we try to develop and keep some good, clean ones, like your son, the Senator. He will accomplish much good as the years go by. He is already attempting to do quite a lot."

"Well," I said, not wishing to discuss the permanently painful subject of my son, "I suppose I am ready. I will prepare to go in a few days."

"Farewell, Sinhar Ambar Anati," said the Council. "We shall keep close contact with you, and hear your reports regularly." They bowed, smiled, and vanished.

It was hard to leave, but I will not go into the heartbreak of the good byes, and concentrate on the positive side. I was taken to earth, and went to a hotel in New York. I had with me a special device, an ingenious thing that had on it the special telephone numbers of top members of the National Security Agency, or NSA as everyone refers to them. Only two or three people in the world have these numbers, not even the president of the United States has access to them. They are used only for matters related to extraterrestrial reverse engineering. The device makes sure the phones will be promptly answered, and when I called, I gave them data that they recognized as their own extraterrestrial material. They were shocked, but nevertheless they agree to meet with me. I suppose they realized they had no choice. Rather politely, they offered to fly me to Washington DC, where they wanted to have the meeting, but I informed them that it was not necessary. It was easy for me to simply materialize in DC, and I did not want them to know my current address, if this could be prevented. They directed me to come to the Four Seasons hotel in Georgetown, where they were to meet me at the lobby. I was instructed to say, if questioned at the hotel, that I was heading for the suite that was reserved under the name of a Middle Eastern gentleman who owned a limousine service in DC, and had often used the hotel for similar purposes.

I materialized a little distance away from the hotel, and walked there on M Street. Three members of the NSA were waiting for me, and they took me to the reserved suite, where fifteen more people were sitting around a huge table. They rose and greeted me politely, but I could clearly see the suspicion in their eyes and in their thoughts.

I noticed that the shades of all the windows were closed, and I saw no telephones. However, they all had gadgets in their hands which I recognized immediately. They were navigation devices, which at the time were known only to extraterrestrials, not to any humans. For a moment I assumed that they got it from the Grays, for communication purposes, and then noticed that quite a few of these people were really Grays who had shape-shifted to resemble humans. I can easily identify them, because even while shape-shifting, the Grays cannot turn their heads independently of their body. They have to turn the entire body if they wish to look to the sides. As they turn, their eyes cannot follow their heads quickly, like humans' eyes, but they have to refocus. All that is done rather discretely, but after living with the Hybrids and the Grays, I could not miss that. In addition, humans usually fidget, move around. The Grays never do. When seated, they sit quietly, immobile. When standing, they are straight and immobile as well. In addition to that, I had more instructions from Nibiru as to how to recognize all shape-shifters, which I cannot explain because it involves using the Conduit.

One of the Grays at the end of the table was tapping nervously on the edge of the table with something that looked like a pen, and from time to time pointed it towards me. I recognized this gadget as a scanning device, such as we use on Nibiru. It was not held by any of the humans, because this fiber/scanning device was not known to the humans' scientific community until much later, 2006 or 2007. I supposed the Grays kept it to themselves for a while.

I did my best to ignore the fact that half the people there were Grays, and proceeded as if I had no idea and was talking only to humans. I had nothing to fear, really, since I could annihilate the Grays with one thought, and I decided that discretion was the best approach. The Grays maintained their pretence throughout the meeting, and I said nothing at all. Come to think of it, I was used to the treachery of the Grays, but I have to admit I was a little distressed by the humans' duplicity and stupidity. Did they really think I won't recognize the Grays?

I explained to them who I was, telling the absolute truth, and giving my name as Ambar Anati. Naturally they did not believe me. To help persuade them, I first of all projected certain images on one of the walls. These were holographic pictures that showed them the entire sequence of the Roswell crash, where the Gray was held, and data pertaining to their research. They still were not persuaded that I was who I claimed to be, but the fact that the projections were done without any equipment made them uneasy and less sure of themselves. They were at least ready to listen.

I told them quite a lot about the Grays and their agenda. "By now," I said, "you must be aware that they do not tell the truth, that they are not to be trusted."

"Business is business," said one of them. "They have given us more than they promised, too, so we have gained additional knowledge. It's not really a big deal if they abduct a few more people."

"First of all, it is not a few people. Thousands are tortured and killed."

"What can we say?" answered another. "Sometimes harsh measures cannot be avoided." I did my best to hide my disgust about such a statement, and went on.

"Are you aware of the fact that they are trying to take over earth?"

"No, we were not informed about such intent," said another.

"And are you aware of the invisible radio plasmic belt around earth? They want to isolate earth from the universe. This belt can expand up or down, and can affect missiles, rockets, or airplanes, and blow them up. It explains what has happened to various airplanes in Vietnam, and also to human spacecrafts and space missions."

"We don't understand what you want us to do," said one of them.

"I want you to trust the Anunnaki. They intend to help you get rid of the Grays. This is really very simple. Either you go with the Anunnaki, in which case much can be done, or you stay with the Grays. If you choose to stay with the Grays, the Anunnaki will return and clean up the earth, in a way that you will not like. They are perfectly capable of annihilating the entire population if the atrocities do not stop."

"Are you threatening us?" asked one of them. The rest stared at me, impassive.

"I would not call it a threat," I said. "I would call it a fair warning. Remember, the Anunnaki are stronger than both humans and Grays. They did not have to send me, they could do what they wanted without warning. But they prefer to save as many humans as possible."

"How do we know how strong the Anunnaki really are?" said one of them. "After all, they have been away for so long. They don't seem to have much interest in us."

"Let me show you a small example of what the Anunnaki can do," I said. In a blink, I multiplied myself into thirty Victorias; we arranged ourselves around the table, behind the sitting people. They jumped off their seats, shocked.

"It's a trick," cried some of them. "Grab her!"

"Please, do grab," I said. "Touch all thirty of me, and see that this is not an idle trick. We can become billions, if we wish." Hesitantly, they touched some of the multiples. A few multiples offered to shake hands, which the humans did, trembling. They could not deny the multiple's tangible presence.

I contracted myself into one person again, and sat down. "Please," I said. "I have no desire to frighten you. Sit down and let's be reasonable."

"Truth is, Ms. Anati," said one of them, "The Grays are an immediate threat. They are right here and we cannot control them. The Anunnaki are far away. But still, we can see that you wish to help us, and it should be considered. What would you want us to do?"

"I want to start by going into some of the more important places where humans and Grays interact," I said. "I need much data to deliver to the High Council of Nibiru and receive instructions before I meet the President of the United States, among others."

"I think the best thing to do is to go to Dulce, in New Mexico. It is the most important joint laboratory of the Grays and the U.S. Government," said one of them. The others nodded in agreement. "There are bases in Nevada, Arizona, and Colorado, among others, but Dulce is the most important."

"Very well. Would you assign one of the members to come with me, act as my escort?" I asked.

"Yes, Colonel X— will go with you." The colonel rose. He seemed to be a respectable, middle-aged man. In reality, he was certainly a Gray. As before, I pretended not to notice.

"Would you like me to materialize you there?" I asked.

"No, I think it's best if we go in a more traditional way," said the colonel. "We don't want to startle the people in Dulce too much. It's best if they don't panic." I agreed and we decided to go the next day, in a military plane.

On the plane, the colonel, who had become reasonably friendly, gave me some information about Dulce. "It's all underground, you know" he said. "People know about seven layers, but in truth, there are nine I am aware of, perhaps more I don't even know about. It's really a very large compound."

"Where exactly is it?" I asked.

"It lies under Archuleta Mesa on the Jicarilla Apache Indian Reservation, near the town of Dulce. Very easy to keep it a secret, the way it is constructed," he said. "And they are very careful about security. You will see."

We finally landed at the small air field. A medium sized building, guarded and surrounded with a high wire fence, stood in the desert. We entered a normal room. I noticed the cameras in the entrance, and a woman in military uniform looked at some papers Colonel Jones presented to her, but the security was not impressive. I realized later that the deeper you went into the compound, the stricter was the security. She pressed a button, and a man came to escort us through a door that led to an escalator. From then on, it seemed we were descending into Hell.

Everything was clean, shiny, and metallic, much like I remembered from my unpleasant stay with the Hybrids. No matter where you looked, you saw a security camera. There were side doors everywhere. Apparently, many secret exits and entrances existed, and each was loaded with security features, some visible, others hidden.

On the first level we were joined by a Gray. He was polite and distant, and showed us into various offices without much comment. The offices were normal, military, and stark. Maps hung on walls, with many pushpins in various colors stuck into them. The individual colors, the Gray explained, showed sites of high activity of different subjects. Green, for example, showed sites of heavy spaceship activities, including those of extraterrestrials that were not Grays, and were considered enemies by them. Red were for areas of cattle mutilation and collection of animal blood. Blue indicated underground activities and caverns. I do not remember all the other colors and sites, but the arrangement was quite elaborate.

The offices were monitored constantly by humans, who wore military-like jumpsuits. Each carried a gun, quite visibly. All the uniforms were decorated with the symbol of the Triangle, much like the Phoenician symbol. They had various letters in each triangle, supposedly signifying rank, but I never found out if this was true. When they saw that we were accompanied by the Gray, they simply ignored us.

The second level was exactly the same, full of offices, but after the first level, which we reached by the escalator, we used only elevators. I was told that the elevators had no cables in them, and were controlled magnetically, using extraterrestrial technology. Magnetism also supplied light, which came from flat, circular objects, and there were no regular light bulbs in sight.

The third level was devoted to hospital-like environment, used for impregnation of female humans. I was not allowed into the surgical ward itself, but the Gray explained that the experimenters removed the fetus, and placed it for speeded-up growth in an incubator, creating Hybrids. In this facility, more than in the one I visited during my previous time with the hybrids, they tended to experiment with genetic manipulation during the very early time in the incubator. The results were quite monstrous sometimes. Through windows in the walls, I saw cribs, or really a sort of cages, with some of the results. Deformed humans were the norm – extra arms and legs, small or very large heads, and creatures that did not really look humans. "What do you do with these?" I asked.

"We harvest certain tissues and then kill them," said the Gray. "We learn quite a lot from them about genetics. We apply them for further research."

On level four, there were genetic labs that created half human/ half animals. Their shapes, as I saw them sitting in their cages, were so horrific, that I had to avert my eyes. Some of them had a reptilian look, some had fur, and others looked like gargoyles. "Do you harvest tissues here too?" I asked.

"Yes, we combine this research with the materials we get from the cows. The research is extremely interesting and useful," said the Gray.

The extraterrestrials had their living quarters on levels five, six, and seven. These looked much like military barracks, as we passed the corridors and peeked into the rooms, but I saw no reason to enter.

I asked the Gray if it was true that there were additional levels. This did not seem to phase him at all, and he said, in

270

his perfect English that seemed so unpleasant, coupled with his scratchy alien voice, that yes, of course. Apparently, they took advantage of the huge natural caverns under Dulce, and created additional levels. They carried even more security there, and the Gray said that if we wanted to go there, he would have to call two more Grays to accompany us, and we would need to use an eye identification system. These details were quickly accomplished, and we used a side elevator to the eighth level.

Here they experimented with manipulation of the nervous system by various means. It allowed them to cause disease and even death from a distance.

"I am afraid you cannot enter the place where the subjects are kept," said the Gray. "These subjects are mostly insane, dangerous, and very susceptible to changes in their routine. If we enter, we might destroy some of the experiments."

Level nine, where we were invited to enter, contained storage of fully grown creatures and tissues in vats, all dead. This included tanks full of embryos in various stages of development, waiting to be used. The place was kept as clean as the rest of the compound, but the smell of the chemicals was overwhelming. I simply could not stay there long, and Colonel Jones, who until that time showed no emotion, suddenly shape-shifted and appeared in his real, Gray form.

"You knew all along, Ms. Anati," he said, his voice turning scratchy. "I never thought we could trick you, and would have preferred to appear in my true form in the first place, but my group insisted."

"It does not signify," I said. "Of course I knew." The other Gray did not pay much attention to the shifting, being used to such practices.

271

Level ten, the most secret of them all, was devoted to human aura research, and other extra sensory abilities, including dreams, hypnosis, etc. The researches were able to record dreams on specialized machines; the dreams were studied as part of the major advanced study of psychic power and phenomena.

"Once we are more advanced in this research," said the Gray, "we will have total power over other races. Of course, we mean no harm to humans nor to the Anunnaki. We are merely concerned with the Reptilian races." I almost laughed. No harm to humans? Was the Gray trying to be a PR person?

When we finished our tour, we were escorted out of the complex. The plane waited for us outside. I said nothing about my disgust, horror, and disbelief to anyone. But I have seen enough, and I knew that this was just the tip of the iceberg. Such treaties must have been entered into by more than the United States government. The Grays have reached almost total control over humanity.

After materializing myself back in New York, I knew I will always be watched, but I also knew how to handle it and avoid my watchers. I needed time. First, I spent a few days just digesting what I saw. I made myself invisible, and left the hotel for hours of exploration. I walked the streets, took the subway, went on buses, visited museums, stores, offices, hospitals, senior citizens homes, schools, and more. Everywhere I went I saw Grays in shape-shifted form. Obviously, they did not only infiltrate the military, but spread out much more. They flooded the city. Some worked in offices, some in restaurants, obviously doing it as part of their agenda. They were nurses, teachers, officials, sanitation engineers. They were probably doing the same in other cities, urban areas, towns, and even other countries. For me, as I mentioned before, it is easy to recognize a shape-shifter. I was taught how to do it by the best teachers on Nibiru. But a human cannot do so very easily. Your doctor could be a Gray. The nice lady in the department store could be one. The teacher of your young child could be one. In addition, I saw many hybrids. Vicious, unfeeling, and manipulative, they flocked mostly into the entertainment industry, the financial world, and the advertising field. It seemed they liked glamour. The Grays and their slaves, the Hybrids, have invaded the world.

After a few days I got to work. Using the same device that had gotten me the telephone numbers of the NSA members, I spent my time contacting and negotiating with hundreds of people from a number of governments on earth. I also visited other laboratories, bases, and Air Force fields. Each time I negotiated, I encountered the same road blocks. Every government on earth was in terror of the Grays. The Anunnaki were feared, too, and the knowledge that they will very likely attempt to clean the earth, terrified the humans, but not enough to get them out of their fearful paralysis regarding the Grays.

But that was not the worst. Unbelievably, many individuals in power simply did not care. All they wanted was to keep their power, to control, to wage war. They wanted to make billions and keep it within a tiny group of the financial elite, while the rest of the world was permitted to go to the devil.

This was a long mission. For years I went from country to country, getting in touch with the people in power, acquiring knowledge, collecting data and transferring it, every night, to Nibiru. The High Council took it all very calmly, and when I despaired, reminded me that my services were invaluable despite the seemingly unachievable goal of converting humanity. The only bright

273

points of my day were my evening conversations with my daughter and my husband, who were always supportive and loving. I drudged on and on, until I thought that nothing more could be achieved. I stayed until late 2007, and then I made the call and requested permission to go back to Nibiru and make my final report. As always, Marduchk was there for me and I left an earth I no longer loved. I was going home.

*** *** ***

CHAPTER FIFTEEN
The Return of the Anunnaki

> I report to the Council about my years of envoyship, and I view the frightening plans for the cleansing of the earth before the return of the Anunnaki, and their plans for the complete change of the earth.

The years of envoyship have taken their toll on me. I was tired, discouraged, and worse, I began to feel old. It did not show in my appearance, which was one good thing, but I was no longer the strong young woman I used to be. This time, putting the results of my mission before the High Council, letting go of the burden and putting it on stronger shoulders, would be a relief. I was not at all nervous about meeting the Council. I knew I had done all I could, and more than that I could not do – unless the Council thought that there was more to accomplish. If they would, I would most certainly obey.

The whole Council came to the meeting. No one thought that there was anything more important to do or to attend. I bowed at them, and started giving my report. Basically, it was a simple one, signifying that the United States military authorities, which were the greatest part of my contacts, would not cooperate. I presented many reports, charts, lists, analysis, whatever I could do to validate my findings, but in the end, it boiled down to one thing. The United States government, and the military in particular, were more afraid of the Grays than of the Anunnaki. Officials and military from other countries, such as England, Russia, and China, with whom I also spoke, were no better. The fact that I had promised the officials that the Anunnaki will return, and may destroy them if they continue to associate with the Grays, frightened them a great deal. But, they argued, that no matter how you look at it, the Anunnaki had been away, physically, for thousands of years. Their contacts and connections with the humans were not numerous, and they obviously did not care much. But the Grays had been on earth for these same thousands of years, their technology was enough to annihilate the earth just as much as that of the Anunnaki, and they were more likely to act violently because their habitat, their experiments, and their hopes would be threatened. The results were that I could not persuade any government to disassociate from the Grays, or to trust me.

At the end of my report I bowed, and sat down again, rather exhausted. All I wanted was to go home, sit under my favorite tree, have a cat or two lean against me, and wait for Marduchk to come home and tell me things were not so bad. But this was not to be.

The Council members deliberated without opening their Conduit to me, which was fine with me since I felt almost dissociated from it all. But after a short time, they opened it for our conversation.

"You have done well, Sinhar Ambar Anati," they communicated telepathically. "We now know where we stand, and we made our final decision – we will go to earth and cleanse it. Humanity is so utterly contaminated, only drastic measures will apply."

"How will you do that?" I asked. Cleanse an entire planet? Just like that? It seemed like a hopeless task, even for the Anunnaki. "Please explain to me, I am not sure I understand your plan."

"Very well," said the Council. "But we will need to go back a little. The point you must understand, is why did the Anunnaki originally come to earth. You know some of the reasons, but it won't hurt to put everything in perspective for you."

"Yes, please do," I said. My fatigue passed away completely, and I was eager to hear the details.

"Well, the Anunnaki did more than just come to earth. They have created it, million of years ago. At that time, a group of Anunnaki scientists on Nibiru, including Sinhar Inanna, Sinhar Enki, Sinhar Ninlil, and others, decided to extend their experiments in creating biological, living forms. To do that, they needed a good plan and permission from the Council, so they worked it out and requested a meeting. The Council considered their suggestions, and agreed that such work would greatly increase Anunnaki knowledge and therefore would be an excellent idea to pursue. However, they had one condition. The scientists were welcome to start working – but their laboratory would have to be off-planet. The Council suspected that the introduction of new life forms, even in the isolated conditions of a laboratory, might be a threat to everyone already on Nibiru. Large and small animals, and particularly people, even if they were to be created in the image of the Anunnaki, could not be tolerated to wander freely on Nibiru.

The scientists devoted more thought to their project, and agreed that what they really needed was a planet-sized laboratory, where the creations could interact in a controlled environment without the interference of previously existing life forms. The solution, to which the Council readily agreed, was to create a planet specifically for the purpose, at considerable distance from Nibiru, just in case.

And so the scientists went to the edge of the galaxy, and caused a star to explode and create a solar system. The sun, which they named Shemesh (Sol) was surrounded by a few planets, and after a suitable amount of time (eons to humans, but nothing to the Anunnaki who can play with time as they wish) went there to decide which planet would be the most appropriate. For a short time they considered the planet humans call Mars, which at the time had plenty of water (the most important ingredient necessary for the laboratory, after oxygen) but finally settled on choosing earth.

They went to earth, started creating the life forms, fostered the evolutionary process, and managed to accumulate an enormous amount of useful knowledge, all of which they telepathically transferred to Nibiru, where it was much appreciated. Unfortunately, the knowledge leaked to the Grays at Zeta Reticuli, and they decided to use the humans, and sometimes the cattle, in their doomed experiments that were geared to save their own miserable race. While doing this, they sadly contaminated the pure genetic material the Anunnaki scientists so painstakingly created, and the humans that resulted were no longer suitable for the study. That was the reason why the Anunnaki deserted their research on earth.

"But you have never completely deserted the humans," I said.

"No, not completely. We kept our connection. But the Grays really dug in, made their bases, lived underwater, and we had to keep away. And the Grays' DNA have created greed, violence, and unbelievable cruelty within human nature. Such characteristics were not part of the original DNA we used to create the humans. We had intended to create the humans in our image. Right now, we will assume, based on your research, that humanity is divided into three groups, regarding their level of contamination."

278

"Yes," I said, musing. "I have noticed the same thing. There are levels of contamination that make for various behaviour patterns. Actually, I have a lot of charts about it."

"Indeed," said the Council. "And excellent charts they are, and they gave us the structure. The first group is those who exhibit heavy Grays' DNA contamination. They include:

- Those who torture or support torture by others, *for any purpose whatsoever*
- Murderes (unless in self defense, which sometimes occurs in situations such as domestic abuse by a contaminated spouse)
- Rapists
- Child molesters
- Child abusers
- Senior abusers
- Spouse abusers
- Those who commit violent robberies
- Illicit drug manufacturers, distributors and pushers
- Those who engage in enslaving women, girls and young boys in prostitution rings
- Criminals who use their form of religion as an excuse for their heinous crimes; this include all religious fanatics, such as suicide bombers
- Those who destroy lives by depriving them of ways to support themselves, for their own greed. This include the top echelon of corporate executives, who have lost any sense of humanity in their treatment of thousands of people and feel that this is "strictly business"

- Elected officials who have sold out for power and greed, and who are willing to destroy their own countries to aggrandize themselves
- Elected officials who are willingly participating in destroying the ecology of the planet because of their close association with the oil and other forms of commercial energies producing countries and their corrupt rulers
- Any politician, military personnel, or anyone else who is engaging in trade with the Grays, allowing them to continue the atrocities in exchange for technical and military knowledge
- Lawyers and judges who play games at the legal system for their own gain, sending child molesters, murderers, and other violent offenders back into society, ready to prey again on the innocent, all in the name of "reasonable doubt"
- Those who destroy lives and reputations by "identity theft"
- Those who torment animals. These include not only people who hurt and mutilate animals for their own sick pleasure, but also those who support dog fights, cockfights and bullfights, those who beat their horses, donkeys, or dogs, those who "legally" mutilate cats by removing their claws or hurting their vocal cords, owners of puppy mills who force female dogs to reproduce by "animal rape," and those who abandon their animals, or chain them indefinitely, sometimes allowing them to die by such neglect."

"Extremely dangerous people," I said. "I don't believe there is much chance of reforming them."

"None whatsoever," said the Council. "People who engage in such practices are doomed, as far as we are concerned. They are pure evil. Anyway, here comes the second group, people who exhibit a medium level of Grays' DNA contamination. These would include:

- People who believe that discipline requires physical punishment (in children or adults)
- Middle echelon executives who "only take orders" from their superiors as their corporations are destroying the economy of their own countries to save their own skin
- Those, who in the name of fashion and beauty, have hurt countless young girls who have succumbed to eating disorders, some of whom have actually died, while the owners and designers made a fortune for themselves
- Irresponsible parents who allow their children to grow up with Grays' values rather than human and Anunnaki values
- Hunters of animals who kill only for food but do not feel a joy in killing and do not mutilate or torment the animals
- Owners of "factory farms" whose animals are not deliberately tormented, but live a miserable life
- People who eat any form of meat, since we believe in strict vegetarian diet, supplemented by milk and eggs from animals that are treated humanely and allowed to live out their life comfortably and die naturally"

"They may have some chance, I suppose" I said.

"Not much. Still, we hope they will try to work on their own redemption. We offer no guarantee, of course. Then, there is the third group, people who exhibit light Grays' DNA contamination, and they include:

- People who are willing to advertise products that may be harmful, for gain

281

- People who are willing to import products that may be harmful, for gain
- People who object to social reform that may help the greater number of others, such as health care or better equalization of income, for gain
- People who are engaged in the fur trade
- People who are willing to influence others through brainwash-style advertising, such as the cosmetic industry, for gain
- Racists, sexists, and ageists, who are willing to allow their prejudices to influence their behaviour to others
- People who are willing to spend millions of dollars on frivolous pursuits, such as diamond studded collars for dogs, who really don't care about anything but love and food, or a $200,000 wedding cake, while millions around them are starving
- People actively engaged in aggressive corporate take-overs, thus destroying the livelihood of many
- Anyone deliberately sending a computer virus for "fun and games" and thus destroying other people's livelihood and property

"I assume," I said, "that this is just a partial list. I can understand that. But what are your plans? What will you do with the people? With the animals?"

"We will plan a cataclysmic event, the likes of which can hardly be imagined by humans. As we told you, we had done it before, many times. Other races had destroyed some of our experiments, and sometimes only a drastic cleansing would help. We will show you one soon, a cleansing that happened a few hundred years ago on a humanoid civilization much like the humans, but first, let us explain what will happen.

We will bring a bubble of a special substance, resembling anti-matter but not destructive, and cause it to touch the earth's atmosphere. The bubble will be exactly the size of earth. As soon as the two globes touch, all the humans that have been lucky enough not to be contaminated by Grays' DNA, and all the animals, plants, and those inanimate material which the Anunnaki wish to preserve (such as beautiful and historic monuments, art-filled museums, and great libraries, in addition to the homes of those saved) will be stripped from earth and absorbed into the bubble. The fish, and other animals who need water, will be taken to an artificial ocean within the bubble. The birds will have plenty of places to perch on. Nothing will be hurt or damaged – the humans and animals will feel nothing – they will be secure and comfortable within the bubble. It is unlikely that they will even retain a clear memory of the event, because we would not wish them to be traumatized.

Then, the earth will be cleaned of all the pollution. For lack of better description, try to imagine a huge vacuum cleaner removing all the landfills, eliminating all the plastics, all the dirt, all the smog from the air, and all the filth from the ocean. In a few short minutes, the earth will be sparkling clean, a pristine planet, the way it was when we had first created it. Disposing of the garbage involves a very high technology which humans simply do not as yet understand. The beautiful clean planet will be ready to be repopulated, and in an instant, the humans, animals, plants, and inanimate objects that were saved in the bubble, would be returned to earth. Anunnaki guides will be there for the humans, who would naturally need quite a bit of help to adjust to the new life."

"But those are only the uncontaminated ones," I said. "What about the others? How will they meet their fate?"

"Those who were heavily contaminated, and who were engaging in cruelty, greed, and violence for their own gain, will have no chance at all. They will simply be destroyed, and there is no need to even think about them any further. What is left are those who are the medium-level of contamination, and the lighter level.

These groups will receive a warning to mend their lives, now, fourteen years before the event of 2022. When the event occurs, some of the people of light level contamination would have completely cleaned themselves through their efforts, and therefore would have been transferred, as clean beings, into the bubble. Others would have remained lightly contaminated. Those of medium level contamination, who obviously require more work, would be divided into those who had succeeded in the cleaning, and had brought themselves into a light level contamination. Those who remain medium level, who did not do the work of cleaning properly, will be destroyed with the heavily contaminated ones.

All that will remain now would be the group of light contamination level, and if they wish to save themselves, they must go through Ba'abs, or Star Gates, into other dimensions, so that they could be evaluated by the Anunnaki. If they can be cleaned, they go back to earth. If not, they will live out their lives in another dimension, where conditions are much like earth before the cleaning. They will lead a normal life, but will not be able to reproduce, so eventually they will die out.

As for those who would succeed passing through the Ba'abs, the procedure is extremely difficult. Ba'abs exist everywhere. There are huge, magnificent Ba'abs that are used regularly by the Anunnaki to cross from one dimension to another. But there are also small ones, located in the street, in a tree, in an apartment building, in private homes, everywhere. They will become visible when the bubble clashes with the earth, and those who were not taken into the bubble, or were not destroyed, must find their way into a Ba'ab. All Ba'abs look the same – they are a circle of shifting light of rainbow colors, very clearly defined. People wishing to enter a Ba'ab must hurl themselves against it, and it will open and absorb any number of travelers.

As soon as you enter the Ba'ab, you are already in another dimension. It is extremely frightening, a deep blackness illuminated by explosions, thunderbolts, and streaking comets. There is a very high level of a stormy, whoosh-like sound – the noise can be deafening – and the traveler is swept with violent speed forward, unable to resist or help the move, and constantly twirled and twisted in one direction, and then the other. The traveler will feel dizzy, disoriented, and scared, and this will last for an indefinite amount of time. When this part is over, the traveler is thrown by a huge gust of wind into a tunnel, which is so brightly lit by orange, yellow, and white light, it is impossible to keep one's eyes open for more than a few seconds at a time. The traveler hears horrible shrieks, screams, and howling of wind, and when the eyes are open, he or she sees bizarre faces, weird creatures, and unknown vehicles which always seem almost on the verge of colliding with the traveler, but somehow never do. After a while, the traveler is thrown out of the tunnel into solid ground, which may be quite painful but not permanently harmful. The light becomes normal and the sounds stop."

"Does that mean they have arrived safely?"

"Yes, at that point, the travelers have reached their destination. It looks much like earth, but it is empty of people or animals, and plants and houses look very dim, as if the travelers found themselves in virtual reality. Then, the traveler begins to see people materialize against the cardboard-like background. This takes time, the images of people float as if from thin air, but then, all of a sudden, reality shifts and the travelers find themselves in a real world. The animals, incidentally, will never materialize. All of them have been returned to earth, to their proper places, as mentioned before. They are not needed here, since no animal labor or the eating of animals is permitted by the Anunnaki, who abhor such practices. From then on, the travelers will only eat vegetarian diet. In this dimension, the travelers will meet a few Anunnaki, who will direct them to their evaluation and possible cleaning. Only those who make it would be returned to earth. Those who cannot be cleaned will be sent, through a Ba'ab, to the dimension we have mentioned before, where they will live out their lives, but will not be able reproduce. The Anunnaki do not wish to kill them, since they are not inherently evil like the heavily contaminated ones. But they cannot let them reproduce the bad DNA; the Anunnaki do not indulge in sentimental pity, and are fully aware that any form of evil should not be allowed to exist."

"The treatment of the humans is extreme," I said calmly, "but not unjust. They have brought it upon themselves since they would not listen to the warning."

"Well said, Sinhar Ambar Anati," said the Council. "Spoken like a true Anunnaki."

"You said you would show me how this is done," I said. "I do wonder how the earth would be cleansed."

"Yes," said the Council. "Look at the Miraya." Naturally, there was a huge Miraya on one of the walls, and

I waited while the Council made preparations for the visions to appear.

"It will be emotionally harrowing to watch that, Sinhar Ambar Anati," said one of the Council. "Are you sure you want to see it?"

"Yes," I said. "I think I should. Perhaps there is still something I can do."

"I think there is," said the Council, and at this point a small light appeared in the Miraya. The light grew, and I suddenly saw a bubble, looking much like a simple soap bubble, on the screen. It started to travel, and in a very short time I saw it approach the unmistakable shape and color of a planet with atmosphere. The two globes touched, and I saw streams of light emanating from the planet and disappearing into the bubble.

"In these streams of light, all the clean people, all the animals, and all the inanimate objects we have chosen are transferred to the bubble for safe keeping," said the Council. "Also, the Ba'abs are opening for those who might try to escape. We will now zoom closer and show you the cleansing itself."

The Miraya showed a growing image, and after a few minutes I saw a terrain which I did not recognize, but it seemed earth-like. The people were ape-like humanoids, but obviously they bore a very close resemblance to humanity. They even wore similar clothes. The area looked devastated – after all, the houses the people lived in, any animal they may have had, all the plants, and many buildings, have already disappeared into the bubble. So the environment was totally alien and frightening to these people. They looked disoriented, staring at the sky, running around, searching for missing people. The whole scene was one of terrible confusion.

The sun seemed to undergo an eclipse, but it was not a natural one. A massive ceiling of metal shapes of machinery, gadgets, wheels, and shifting lights covered the sky. They were ominously silent, as if waiting. I imagined that looking at them from below was immensely frightening. The people seemed to lose their heads, they were running around in circles, some stampeded and trampled each other. I saw people running into churches and heard the bells toll. Naturally, some religious leaders were already saved, or gone through the Ba'abs, but others, the false ones, still tried to call their congregations, hoping for some miracle. Everywhere I saw Ba'abs, those colorful circles, and people smashing themselves against them in the attempt to escape. Some went through. Others were thrown away. The Ba'abs could determine the level of the contamination and only allow the right ones to pass through, hurling the others to some distance.

"Total chaos," I said.

"It's even worse than you can imagine," said the Council. "In various cities, people tried to reach their governments, without much success. The only officials that have stayed on their posts issued orders to avoid any interference with the extraterrestrials, since it would make everything even more dangerous and no one on the planet we are showing you has the technology to match. The officials' orders were ignored, particularly by those in rural areas, who were used to self sufficiency. These people confronted the Anunnaki, started shooting at them with their guns. As in other areas, which of course have had many good people living in them, only the violent ones have remained, since the others have already escaped. Acting so stupidly, they annoyed the Anunnaki with their inept shooting until the Anunnaki decided to paralyze them with special beams of light, for a limited time. When the beams' effects wore off, some resumed their doomed attempts to fight, and at this point the Anunnaki started the final stage."

"Let me see the final stage," I said.

From the bottom of the spaceships, a special substance was diffused, and it landed in huge, swirling streams. It was a black liquid, mixed with light and electricity, and some strange sparkling particles, which I was sure was a form of energy or radiation.

"It smells like fire and brimstone, but strangely, it is cold to the touch. Yet, it burns everything that touches it. This is a tool of annihilation, a tool that no one can fight," said the Council. I looked on, without comment.

The substance slithered inexorably over the ground, the buildings, and the stranded cars like icy cold lava waves. It swept away many people, killing them instantly. Once it covered a large area, it began to coagulate, and as it did so, it expanded and rose up, foot by foot, until it reached the height of eight storied buildings. Slowly, it seemed to harden, solidifying itself into steel-like state. Huge stacks of smoke rose up into the sky, cars melted, buildings collapsed, and fires started everywhere, seemingly not only by the touch of the substance, but spontaneously, when the wind carries the particles of energy into flammable materials. The combination of images and sounds was that of chaos, pain, confusion, and death. I imagined that the fire and brimstone smell had now mixed with that of burning flesh and of melting metal, plastic and rubber.

Then, all of a sudden, the substance stopped growing, and assumed the appearance of craggy mountains, with sharp edges and canyons. The very few who had survived, but had nowhere to go to, tried to climb on the substance, since the earth itself was buried in it. This was futile, since the substance was too slippery for the climb. They started to fall and slip, and were instantly killed.

"These conditions will continue over the entire world for two days; no one will be left alive on the scorched earth," said the Council. I remained silent. "Let us move the scene into the fourth day," said the Council. "You see, at that point, which must have been the third day, all the spaceships left, and in twenty-four hours, the substance and all it consumed turned to dust. The earth became ready for the vast cleaning."

Other spaceships appear on the screen, of completely different appearance. The new ones were not be circular like the others, but crescent shaped, and of pleasant colors, nothing frightening about them. They activated the huge vacuum system, and an enormous cloud of black dust came up in swirling, filthy streams. It did not take long; in a few minutes the whole cloud was sucked into the machines, and the planet was ready for a new life.

With so much death and destruction, a small part of me wanted to pray for the souls of the ones who were killed. Something in my head wanted to turn to God. Then I laughed. If our kind of paternal God had existed, He would have not allowed humans to be so cruel, so horrible, as to cause a need for such massive cleansing. I was beginning to grasp the nature of All-That-Is, the concept of a creative God that encompassed everything and learned from it voraciously. He, she or it would not have mercy on our souls. I bowed my head, and then raised it and looked at the Council.

"I see the need," I said. "I would like to request one more trip, one more attempt to convince the officials about this cleansing, let them warn the earth. If I fail, my blessing goes with your cleansing. The evil must be removed."

"We are proud of you, Sinhar Ambar Anati," said Sinhar Inannaschamra verbally. "High Council, I have told you that, years ago. She is a true Anunnaki."

"Indeed she is, Sinhar Inannaschamra. Indeed she is, and she has our permission to go for the final attempt," said the Council. "We shall have a plan soon." Then they bowed and left.

As usual, Sinhar Inannaschamra stayed with me, and we walked home together.

"So the earth will be cleaned," I said. "The contaminated DNA will be removed. So far so good. But what is going to happen after? I imagine the world will be considerably changed."

"You won't recognize it," said Sinhar Inannaschamra. "It will be vastly improved, believe me. The first thing to disappear is the root of all evil – money."

"Really? Money will no longer exist?"

"Think about it, Victoria. Would the Anunnaki support any of humanity greed-infested systems? The most profound change will be the abolition of money and every system that is attached to money. People will work in their chosen professions, or a new profession that they will adopt, and produce or serve as usual."

"But how will they survive? How will they get food, lodgings, clothes? In other words, if they don't have money, how will they be paid?"

"They will not be paid, but they will have everything that they need, just like we do on Nibiru. Everyone will have a comfortable home, designed to his or her taste. Good food for them and for their pets, beautiful clothes, nice jewelry, cosmetics, diapers for the babies, toys, hobby supplies, etc. will always be available in huge cooperatives that will look like excellent supermarkets, open day and night so that no one will ever lack. What

291

everyone considers luxury items will also be available – the Anunnaki have no desire to have the humans live in austerity. Humans will always have books, TV, radio, home films, etc. They can go to the theater, the ballet, the symphony orchestra, chamber music performances, movies – always for free. The only thing the Anunnaki will deprive the humans of is *excess*. There will be no need for hoarding, since everything will always be available, but no one will be able to be richer than their neighbors. Equality will be established, and appreciated by those who are not contaminated by the greed and meanness of the Grays."

"So what about places like Fort Knox?"

"No need for such places. Ford Knox is going to be destroyed, and the gold used for ornamental purposes. That is the only reason people will value gold now – its beauty. A good artist can create some pretty good pieces from such lovely substance, which will be widely available after the great change. The same will happen, incidentally, with diamonds, and other gems. Their intrinsic value will disappear, so jewelry will only be appreciated for its intricate and elegant design, not for how many carats a stone weighs. Because of that, there will be no need for the IRS, the Social Security system, and other such organizations. The elimination of the money system will cause many professions to disappear, such as accountants, bankers, tax preparers, security guards, and IRS employees."

"Any other changes?"

"Of course. Money will not be the only 'victim.' In a society that consists of good people, people who have no need or desire to commit any crime whatsoever, there will be no need for the legal system. All organizations pertaining to the law will disappear, including the Supreme Court. And of course, no prisons. This will eliminate many professions as well, such as Lawyers, judges, court clerks, and prison officials and guards."

"You know, Sinhar Inannaschamra, this sounds like a lovely place to live in."

"Built in the image of Nibiru, of course. All governments will be abolished. No elected officials, no presidents, no kings. People who are good do not need anyone telling them how to live, they do it instinctively. This will eliminate thousands of positions, such as presidents, kings, governors, mayors, all government employees, social workers, and child protection agencies. And don't forget that since the Anunnaki technology is going to keep humans healthy, there will be no need for hospitals or clinics, other than those devoted to childbirth, and much of the work there will be done without the need for people. In addition, there will not be any incidents of mental health. This will eliminate the positions of most doctors and nurses, and of additional employees such as hospital administration, hospital billing, psychiatrists, psychologists, and hospital janitors, to name a few."

"So no one will be sick, what a world," I said. "I can imagine that humans will no longer have the need for cars and airplanes, right?"

"Indeed. There will be advanced technology that will allow for much more efficient forms of transportation and the use of clean and efficient energy, and in the process, we will eliminate the need for any fossil fuels. This will remove more professions from the list, such as gas stations, agencies supplying us with electricity and gas, car manufacturers, airplane manufacturers, and highway builders."

"It will be hard to adjust to such living."

"I am not sure about that. Remember, the only people remaining are not contaminated. They don't need or want wealth, really preferring to be happy, creative, comfortable and spiritually fulfilled. There will be even more changes. Some miscellaneous professions will not remain, since they will no longer be appreciated or needed. For example, the fashion industry, with its cruel attempts to make women into slaves of someone else's ideas of beauty, will entirely disappear. Beautiful clothing will be created by individual designers or by anyone who likes to indulge in it as a creative hobby. Advertising, of course, will vanish as well. So no one will need runway models, beauty contest organizers, manicurists, cosmetologists, or advertising commercials actors and voice over artists."

"So what will happen to the clean people who worked in these professions?" I asked, envisioning a mass of unemployed, confused people.

"Nothing to be alarmed about. Those who will lose their professions will be trained for another profession, always entirely of their choice, that will give them pleasure and pride to pursue. Even those who have not lost their profession, but who feel the need for a change, will be encouraged to pursue a career change. As a matter of fact, since the life expectancy of each and every person will be greatly increased, it is expected that many people will have numerous career changes as time goes by. Life- long study is always encouraged by the Anunnaki, who consider the acquisition of knowledge the most enjoyable thing a person can do."

"From what you say, many professions that are very well respected today, mostly because they are highly paid, will disappear. I wonder if such individuals will be able to adjust."

"They usually do. Remember, many professions will change in the way they are perceived. For example, the teaching profession, for both children and adults, will become the most highly respected profession in the world. Librarians will be very highly regarded. Gardeners will be of great importance. Historians and writers will be greatly valued. But of course, in a world that judges a person by what he or she is, not by how much money is accumulated, every profession will be appreciated for its usefulness to the entire community. So I think the great majority of people will be pleased with our changes."

"Only the survivors..."

"True," said Sinhar Inannaschamra casually. "The population will be greatly decreases, of course." We entered my home in silence, and I materialized some coffee and fruit for us in a state of half dream. I found it hard to believe that I, of all people, had contributed one of the major reasons why the end of the world was about to occur. I always used to think it will be accomplished by fanatics or by governments that supported nuclear explosions. Well, one lives and learns.

*** *** ***

CHAPTER SIXTEEN
Final Clash

How I went to earth to make one final attempt to convince the humans to give up their affiliations with the Grays. How the humans tried to betray my trust, and the explosive results that would bring not only extreme danger to myself, but the return of the Anunnaki in 2022.

One last time, I said to myself. This is their only chance. If they agree to accept the final option of changing their ways, good. If not, I would not stand in the way of the Council's plan of cleansing the earth. It would hurt me a great deal to think of the millions that were about to die. But there will be no more opposition on my part. I would obey the Council, no matter how badly I will feel.

With the weariness of an act that was performed hundreds of times over the past seventeen years, I contacted the highest level military personnel in an important air base which I will call North X, since of course, I cannot reveal the real name. As always, they had no choice but to meet me. At this time, anyway, after all these years of negotiations with everyone, including some presidents of the United States and Europe, I was pretty well known – and highly disliked. Perhaps I was even a little feared.

The individual I spoke to was very agreeable, and proceeded to arrange the details for the meeting with me. "By the way," I said, after all was decided upon. "If a single shape-shifting Gray will be at the meeting, I will leave immediately. And believe me, I always recognize a shape-shifter. You see, this is the last meeting I plan to have with any human, and the presence of a Gray will defeat the purpose of it."

"There will be no Grays at the meeting, Ms. Anati," said my contact. "I can promise you that. My colleagues and I have already discussed the issue before you and I came to arrange the meeting. They feel the same way as you do." Well, that was a good sign, I thought. We shall see.

Arriving at the air base, I was immediately taken to a small, ordinary conference room. A few people rose from their seats at the conference table as I came in. There were two generals in military uniform, one retired admiral, who worked for the NSA as a consultant and was a co-proprietor of a major civilian jet propulsion company, a colonel who worked as test pilot for Douglas and Boeing companies, and a person that I guessed represented the White House. As always, they were extremely polite, and indeed, none of them was a Gray. Perhaps by that time they finally believed that I could recognize a shape-shifter, or perhaps they had their own agenda. I think, in light of what took place later, that the second option was the correct one. They wanted to hide the meeting from the Grays.

We sat around the table, and they turned to me, ready to hear my offer. They thought that I still was ready to negotiate. Of course, the time for negotiations was over, but they did not realize that.

"Allow me to summarize the current situation for you, gentlemen, I said. "Whether you take action now or later, you will be facing an extraterrestrial threat. The threat you have now comes from the Grays who are controlling your science and space program, and dominating a major part of the earth. The Grays know that you have tried, for many years, to find a weapon system to counter attack them. And they know very well that you have started this

298

program when President Reagan took office. They also know that you failed to develop such a weapon system on your own. That means that you are defenseless. You know it, and they are aware of it. This is why you allow the Grays to go on with the atrocities and the abductions of human beings. It makes you feel safer with them. However, what you don't understand is that the Grays will not be satisfied by only kidnapping people and going on with their abominable experiments. All their experiments were aimed toward saving their own doomed race, which is dying slowly from an epidemic of Progeria which they cannot control. By and large, they failed. So now they want permanent visible bases on the surface of the earth, and much more scope for further experiments on a larger scale."

"They have never mentioned this plan to us," said the White House representative.

"Of course not. This is top secret. They know you will feel like cornered rats and fight back."

"So what will happen when they take over?" asked the Admiral.

"They will kill many humans. The rest will be put in concentration camps, to be available for use whenever needed. In other words, you will be taken over, and this, to all intents and purposes, will be the end of the human race."

"I see," answered the Admiral, in a low voice. He was clearly thoughtful.

"What is the later threat you have mentioned?" asked one of the generals.

"It will come from the Anunnaki. You don't feel it now, not quite yet, but it is just as real. However, it is very different from the threat of the Grays. The Anunnaki are not interested in establishing any bases on the surface of the earth or in the oceans, nor do they wish to experiment on you. They want, quite simply, the complete destruction of your military systems, submarines, carriers, and satellites. They will throw an electro-plasmic shield over the earth, which will prevent airplanes from taking off. This will apply to every airplane, no matter how big or small, military, commercial, or private. Gravity will become twelve hundred times greater than the way it is now, preventing everything on earth from moving, including human beings. Then, a kind of artificial lava will finish off the biosystem of the earth. You will not be able to fight it, for the simple reason that you don't know what it is made off. In addition, the Anunnaki will bring on huge tsunamis. However, the worst part will be the issue of magnetism. Positive and negative magnetism will be distorted, and this will alter the laws of physics on earth. This scenario may sound like science fiction, but you know better than that. It will start around the end of 2021. You will suddenly be confronted by confusion, when all clocks and watches will stop, and ships in the sea will collide with each other without knowing the reason, among other results of the changed polar magnetism."

"We would consider severing all relations with the Grays," said the representative of the White House. "That is, on one condition."

"I don't think the Anunnaki will be willing to negotiate conditions," I said, "but do tell me anyway. Perhaps something can be done."

"If the Anunnaki will send an official military delegation from Nibiru right away, bringing with them scientists to develop a system like the plasmic belt and the Star Wars program, and guarantee to us that the United States can have complete military control over the earth, we will be willing to cooperate with them. Also, we want a system that will allow us to cause major ecological catastrophes to North Korea, Iran, China, Afghanistan, and parts of Russia. Naturally, it should look like a natural catastrophe, not anything man-made," said the White House representative.

"The Anunnaki will not give you such programs," I said resolutely. "It is not at all within their plans."

"So you are refusing to protect us! If you don't protect us, why should we break our agreement with the Grays? After all, how do we know you are really coming back, or even if you are telling the truth about the Grays' plans? And quite frankly, why such a sudden interest in human affairs on the part of the Anunnaki, and in Americans in particular?"

"Nonsense," I said. "They are not particularly interested in the Americans, you are not more important than anyone else on earth. The only reason for contacting you in particular is the fact that the Grays have their bases in America. All the star gates, the genetic laboratory facilities and installations are either underground in America or in the American military bases. In short, the Grays are contaminating the human DNA from right here."

I could see that they believed me. But they were still naïve enough to believe that the Grays will eventually help them develop the Star Weapon system they have promised but failed to deliver. The Americans still wanted to buy some time, and they were not really sure how to do that. I could feel their confusion.

"Ms. Anati," said the Admiral. "We would like a little time to confer before giving you our final answer. If you don't mind, allow me to escort you to one of our private guest lounges. They are quite comfortable, I'll arrange for coffee and some refreshments, and we will come back for you in an hour to finalize our plan. Would that be all right?"

It would have been just fine, had this been the real plan. Very natural and appropriate. But my Conduit was open all along, and I read their thoughts freely. I knew what they meant to do to me, and it did not include coffee or refreshments, nor did it take place in a guest lounge. But I decided to play their game, and went quietly with the Admiral, who chatted pleasantly while escorting me to an elevator.

The ride on the elevator was long. Very long. We went down, obviously into some underground facility. I said nothing about it and pretended all was well. Eventually, the elevator stopped, the door opened, and at the door, three or four soldiers waited for me. I was grabbed unceremoniously, while the Admiral went back into the elevator, not even giving me a glance. I was shoved into a cell, they locked the door behind me, and I was left alone in their underground prison.

As I said, I knew this was coming, but having my resources, I had no reason to fear these people. I could, of course, dematerialize myself and get out any time I wanted. So I sat on the narrow bed, directed my Conduit, and listened to their conversation. I must admit that I experienced a slight feeling of claustrophobia. I have come so close to being an extraterrestrial that it was inevitable. But I suppressed it, reminded myself that I could leave any time I wanted, and listened carefully to the conversation in the conference room.

"It won't take long, they are all terribly claustrophobic," said the Admiral. "Her energy will drain away, like a battery, very soon."

"Will she die?" asked the White House representative anxiously. "I am not sure this is a good strategy, we may be held accountable for any issues that may arise from her arrest."

"She won't die so quickly. She will go insane first," said the Admiral.

"Well, so what do we do now?" asked the retired pilot.

"We have all sort of options, but what is clear to me is that we must confuse the Anunnaki and get them off our trail," said one of the generals.

"But she may contact the Anunnaki first," said the other general.

"This will be a good thing," said the Admiral. "At the same time she contacts them, we will send signals that will confuse them. They won't be able to decide where to go to get her. In the meantime, she will go mad."

"Are you sure they drain away like the Grays?" asked the first general.

"Oh, yes, they are all the same, these filthy aliens," said the Admiral. "Let her rot here, and we will have the Anunnaki and the Grays so confused, they will fight each other, and that will take care of all our problems."

At this moment, something happened in my own mind. I realized that I no longer wanted to save these people. They were pure evil, and the Anunnaki do not tolerate evil. I felt, to my own amazement, that I no longer cared about how many contaminated humans would die in the cleansing. I knew the Anunnaki will save the clean ones. Let the others go. I grinned. Yes, I finally started thinking like a full Anunnaki. What's more, I felt that I was quite capable of killing them myself.

I remembered how shocked I was when my dear, kind, loving husband killed without batting an eyelash. I was even more shocked when my beloved sister-in-law told me that she had killed too, on various missions she had undertaken. Now I understood.

I was not angry with these treacherous creatures. A cold, determined feeling went through my mind instead. It was all so simple. They were evil, and so they had to die.

Calmly, I created a plasmic shield around me. Nothing in the known universe could penetrate it. Wearing it, I could pass through an exploding star and survive. Then, I made some calculations, figuring out how much energy was needed to blow up the entire building, killing everyone inside it in an instant. The plasmic shield was invisible and I could hear perfectly well through it until I chose to switch the audio off.

I materialized myself back into the conference room. The look on their faces when they saw me was so priceless, I had to laugh.

"Well, gentlemen," I said quite politely, "this is the end. I could have exploded the building, or even the airbase, from anywhere on the face of the earth, but I wanted to give you the news personally."

They must have communicated quickly with some of the personnel, because about fifteen soldiers, well-armed with all sorts of paraphernalia, burst into the room and rushed to grab me. The plasmic shield made them fly backwards, and some hit the wall. One or two fainted from the blow.

"I would not bother, if I were you, gentlemen," I said. "Believe me, there is absolutely nothing you can do. Well, it's time to blow up the building, and so good bye."

"Please, Ms. Anati, we will do what the Anunnaki ask us!" cried the White House representative. "Yes, yes, tell the Anunnaki we have no conditions! We will obey them implicitly!" said the Admiral. The others just stood there, terrorized.

A few years ago, perhaps I would have taken pity on them. I would have thought of their wives, children, pets... by now I knew this was stupid sentimentality that made me less than an Anunnaki. That was over now.

"Too late, gentlemen," I said. "Good bye." I turned down the audio, and activated the explosion.

It looked like a small uclear bomb. It sounded like one, even through the plasmic shield. And it worked like one, too. Nothing was left of building; I was now standing alone in a huge, black, gaping hole in the ground. From other buildings, people came out, screaming, running wildly. I ignored them, nodded with satisfaction at the cleanliness of the job, turned away, and proceeded to materialize myself in another continent. I did not want the CIA agents hunting and bothering me like flies and gnats. Of course, I could kill them. But what is the point of doing the Anunnaki cleansing job for them all by myself?

Well, it was time to leave earth. If I ever came back to it, after it was cleansed, I would no longer be the same woman. I have changed, and my place now was on Nibiru. However, I could not just call on Marduchk and ask him to pick me up as usual. Ahead of me was another task, the most important task of all. This task will be dangerous, tremendously risky, but unavoidable, and I will have to do it alone. Somehow or other, I will have to leave everything of me that was human right here on earth. Only then will I be able to place my mind into the clean, perfect Anunnaki body that was prepared for me some years ago. I will have to do that with no traces of humanity, or of any possible contamination. For that, I would have to shed my old body like the skin of a snake, leave it on earth, and go home not in a space ship, but rather, send my mind through a multidimensional ba'ab. Which meant, in human terms, that I simply had to die.

***   ***   ***

305

EPILOGE
Farewell to Victoria

> The most amazing revelations we have heard so far, and time to say goodbye to our dear friend whom we have grown to love.

It was a gray early afternoon, and it looked as if a storm was gathering. We[9] were at the office, working on various projects. It was a couple of weeks since the last time we talked to Victoria, but generally she called in the early evening, so we did not expect to hear from her quite yet. Suddenly the phone rang, and there she was, to our surprise.

From the first moment, we knew that this telephone call was not one of our usual sessions. Victoria just did not sound the same. As our readers probably know by now, she is usually calm, pleasant, and can say the most amazing, even harrowing things with the most matter-of-fact simplicity to which, by now, we have become quite accustomed. But this time her voice was strained, and she seemed to be in a hurry.

"What is it, Victoria? What is wrong?" we asked.

"My friends, I have come to say goodbye. This is the last time I will be able to talk to you."

"What happened? Are you in need of help? Can we do anything?"

"I am a hunted woman, to tell the truth," said Victoria. "I exploded a contaminated building in an air

---

[9] Authors of this book

307

base, killed many contaminated people. I tried to warn them, one last time, but instead of listening, they decided to lock me up until I died of claustrophobia. It's time for me to leave."

"So why don't you get in touch with Nibiru, and have Sinhar Marduchk come and get you in his space ship?" we asked.

"Because saving me and taking me to Nibiru will not be enough to make me survive," said Victoria.

"Are you wounded?"

"No, that would be nothing. I can heal wounds on my own, like all Anunnaki."

"So is there anything else wrong? Do you need medical attention? We can get a doctor and say nothing about who you are."

"No, I am quite well," said Victoria. "I am not sure how to explain this... well, the point is, the time has come and I must die, right here on earth."

We both jumped to our feet. "Die? Why must you die? Surely with your superior powers you can best any humans who want to harass you?"

"It's not that... You see, after what happened, I cannot stay on earth, and with this body, I cannot live on Nibiru and still achieve the long life I have been promised if I become a full Anunnaki. And to become a full Anunnaki, I must die. But there is more to this than just the practical aspect. By living here for so long, by associating with the Grays, Hybrids, and contaminated humans, I am contaminated myself. I have to get rid of all this filth. If Marduchk just takes me to Nibiru, and I change into the new body, I will still carry some of the contamination to Nibiru."

308

We were confused. If she wishes to live a long life, how can she die? We did not even know what to ask, and waited for her to continue.

"My body will die. But my mind, loaded with the imprint of my DNA, will not die. It will rush to a place we call the Ba'ab. This word in Ankh means gate, and I believe it was adopted by various language on earth. The Ba'ab is something like, but not exactly, a white wormhole. Things can pass from one universe to another, or traverse huge distances, through the Ba'ab, in a blink of an eye."

"And what happens to your mind when it passes through the Ba'ab?" we asked.

"Everything has to be fully coordinated," said Victoria, "or else, the mind can be lost in the universe. They will wait for me on Nibiru, with a body-copy they have already prepared years ago. This body, incidentally, is full Anunnaki, without any human characteristics, as I committed myself to many years ago when I married Marduchk. My mind, which on earth you will probably refer to as my soul, must hit the Ba'ab at the absolute right moment, pass through it, and in a split second enter the body-copy. Otherwise, I will be lost. They may look for me, and perhaps even find me, but the odds are against it; the universe is just too vast. Therefore, I must hit the Ba'ab properly. It would have been easier if I were transferring from my body into a copy on Nibiru, with Sinhar Inannaschamra to direct me, since she is an expert on such things. But I have no choice, since my earth body must remain here. In other words, I simply must die. Unfortunately, I am not experienced with navigating the Ba'abs. But I must take the chance. I must risk it."

By that time we were crying. "So why not stay here, in hiding? At least live out your life before you chance it all?"

Victoria sighed. "I am sixty years old," she said, "and while sixty is not old by any means, I have lived a very intense life for the last thirty years. My body is worn out, and I am very tired. I am willing to take the risk."

"And what about your son?"

"I finally have to realize that I must give him up, let him live his own life, stop worrying about him. He will be fine, he is young, he will do his work for which he was conceived, and later prepared from birth and on. There are a couple of options for him. I believe the Anunnaki will destroy the earth in 2022, and only the uncontaminated will survive. Of course, in this case, he will be saved. If there is a postponement of the destruction, another option exists. By the time he is relatively old, and his work done, we will come for him, since he is really one hundred percent Anunnaki, and he deserves some reward after a life in service of humanity. Not too many Anunnaki are so inclined..."

"Why is that so?"

"The Anunnaki still love you, deep down, since you are their creations. But they are very strongly disappointed in humanity. The cruelty which humanity expresses is more like the Grays' than the Anunnaki's, who revere all life. You torture, you kill, you abuse the children and the elderly, and you eat animal bodies. The greed and disloyalty that you express would have been easier to bear, for the Anunnaki, they would have been willing to teach you how to overcome it, but not the viciousness. And yet, they still help, occasionally intervene, and wait until the right time to return. Once the earth is cleaned, the Anunnaki will return and bring long life, health, and joy. But not before."

"But won't you miss your son?"

"Of course I will, but I have learned that it is essential not to be too strongly tied to anything on earth. There have been Anunnaki who got attached to things of the flesh, or to personal associations, to such an extent that they have lost their Anunnaki spirit and are still wandering earth, thousands of years later, unable to reconnect with their true home."

"But Victoria, how will we know that you have reached the Ba'ab and entered your body-copy? We would not be able to bear not knowing. The thought that your beautiful soul might be lost is too much."

"If I succeed, if I am not lost, I will give you a sign. Let's agree on a very clear one. Let's see... I know! Do you have houseplants in the office?"

"Yes, many, on a large and sunny windowsill."

"Then when I reach home, every single one of your houseplants will burst into bloom, even those that normally have no flowers. And the lights will flicker three times, off and on." She laughed, and we laughed with her, with tears in our eyes.

"How will you die, Victoria? You won't be in pain, will you?"

"Oh, no. I was told to go to a place that has water, trees, and flowers. I will sit under a tree, close my eyes, and my mind will separate from my body, quite peacefully. They taught me how to do it and promised me that it will be entirely painless."

"It is rainy and dark here. Are you somewhere warm and sunny? Will you get wet and uncomfortable?"

"No, I am far away from you. It's sunny and pleasant here. The tree I am going to sit under is a big, beautiful willow."

"Will you sleep? Will you feel anything?"

"Oh, no, I have to be fully aware of the circumstances to be able to do the job. I will be completely alert, and in an instant use my Conduit to enter the Ba'ab, if all goes well."

"Will your body be found by anyone?"

"I have no idea, it really does not matter in any way, it's just a body; perhaps it will disintegrate, who knows."

"May we ask where it is going to happen? Perhaps we could go there afterwards, just to feel that we have been with you?"

"You are so kind, my friends, but no, I can't tell you, I am not permitted. You see, in the very distance past, humans thought that the Anunnaki were gods. You know some of their names – Inanna, Enlil, Ninlil, El... of course they were not gods, they were Anunnakis, and as a matter of fact, they are alive and well on Nibiru, engaged in their new missions. One name I daresay you already recognize from my story, but we will not dwell on it, or she may be angry with me. At any rate, if my place of death is discovered, how are we to be sure that it won't some day become a place of worship, when humanity is just a little more attuned to the Anunnaki again? We can't risk that. But please don't be upset with me about it. After all, I won't be there. I will be flying to my destiny in Nibiru through the Ba'ab."

"It's so hard to part from you, Victoria. Will you ever be in touch again?"

"Who knows? If I survive, I might see you in 2022."

"Are you sure we will be alive then?"

"Oh, yes. I have already taken care to extend your lives. This will happen to all the surviving humans when the Anunnaki come back. You will experience a much, much longer lifespan."

312

"How wonderful and kind of you. And it is so strange to think about a very long lifespan…"

"The universe is so full of strange things, strange phenomena," said Victoria. "I will always love you and think kindly of you, no matter what happens."

"But you will be a full Anunnaki. Won't you lose your human interests?"

"I have always been almost a full Anunnaki, to tell the truth. My DNA was ninety percent Anunnaki. From the time I enter my new body, I will be a hundred percent Anunnaki. They will probably start calling me by my Anunnaki name, Sinhar Ambar-Anati. I hope Marduchk doesn't and goes on calling me Victoria… it will feel so strange to have him call me by a new name. Incidentally, the only reason I was human in my views is because I was raised by humans. But think about it, I never cared about so many things humans care about, such as money, or sex, or possessions. That did not stop my friendship with you and my caring about all things human. One way or anther, we shall meet again. You know by now that death really does not exist, even if you can't fully grasp it. Someday you shall. So we have time."

"When will your trip begin, Victoria?"

"In a few minutes, I expect. I am now sitting under the willow, talking on my cell phone. Incidentally, I have a gift for you, which I have already mailed you a couple of days ago and you should receive shortly. It is something you will like very much, and it was sent with the blessings and approval of my husband. A surprise!"

"Goodbye, Victoria," we said, crying. "Good bye and a safe, good trip. We are watching with you." But she was no longer on the phone.

We sat in silence. Will she make it to the gate? Would the Ba'ab open for her? Would our dear friend make it to her new body and be warmly welcomed by her family, or would she forever wander the universe, alone, homeless? We waited for the sign, breathlessly. We had no idea how long it would take. Suddenly the doorbell rang, and the mailman came with a package. We knew what it was. It had to be Victoria's last gift. What could it be?

We opened the package carefully, and inside were two notebooks and a letter. "Dear friends," said the letter. "This is the facsimile of the notes of my husband, containing much information about the upcoming cleansing of the earth in 2022 and the creation of a new human race that will follow. It should be very useful for you in your future work, and you are allowed to reveal anything you wish from it to humanity, with Sinhar Marduchk's fond wishes that it may help at least some people overcome their contamination and grow in the right direction. The small book is a dictionary. We know that Ankh is a difficult language, and the dictionary may help. Enjoy both! With love, Victoria."

We looked at the books with reverence, trying to decipher the words. The large notebook had a title, which we understood to be "Sinhar Marduchk's notes for 2022." The small book was titled something like "Lexicon of the Ankh Language." Understanding the books should take some time, naturally, but what a treasure. Naturally, thought, we could not concentrate. It was already about fifteen minutes after our conversation with Victoria. Surely, by now she would either have succeeded – or she has failed... The tension was too much to bear, and yet, there was nothing we could do but wait. She said, a few minutes... it was much later than that. We were losing our hope. It became dark in the office, the clouds were driven by the wind and became a heavy layer. We turned on the light and just sat there, waiting.

Suddenly, the light flickered. We looked up, hoping against hope. Could it just be the brewing storm? It flickered again. The thunder rolled, and the rain started falling down in sheets. And then it flickered for the third time. There was no question, it had to be her sign – and at this instant, without warning, the room filled with intense floral scent. We ran to the window sill. Every single plant was covered with immense flowers – yellow, white, rose, red – flowers that were never seen on earth, flowers that had to come straight from paradise – or from Nibiru. Victoria has made it home.

*** *** ***

INDEX

319

320

325

Made in the USA
Las Vegas, NV
27 July 2022